Fighting Sail

SWEDEN

Copenhagen

DENMARK

BATTLE OF
COPENHAGEN (1801)

BALTIC SEA

Hamburg

PRUSSIA

Dresden

Prague

Austerlitz

Vienna

AUSTRIA

RUSSIA

THE ALPS

ITALY

BLACK SEA

Mt. Vesuvius

Naples

Capri

KINGDOM
OF THE
TWO SICILIES

Corfu

GREECE

TURKEY

Mt. Etna

SICILY

Syracuse

Rhodes

Malta

Valletta

GULF
OF KORONI

Crete

MEDITERRANEAN SEA

BATTLE OF
THE NILE (1798)

ABUKIR BAY

Marabut

Rosetta

Alexandria

Sinai Desert

Cairo

River Nile

EGYPT

The Seafarers FIGHTING SAIL

TIME LIFE BOOKS

The Cover: At the height of the Battle of Trafalgar on October 21, 1805, Horatio Nelson's H.M.S. *Victory* (*left*) and another British ship, the *Temeraire* (*right*), are shown in the process of reducing the French *Redoutable* to a splintered hulk in this reconstruction by the contemporary Paris master Louis-Philippe Crépin.

The Title Page: In heavily gilded bronze, this two-inch commemorative medal shows the twin squadrons of Nelson's fleet at Trafalgar as they bear down on the combined French and Spanish line.

The Seafarers

FIGHTING SAIL

by A. B. C. Whipple
AND THE EDITORS OF TIME-LIFE BOOKS

TIME-LIFE BOOKS, AMSTERDAM

The Seafarers

Editorial Staff for *Fighting Sail*:
Editor: George G. Daniels
Designer: Herbert H. Quarmby
Text Editors: Anne Horan, Sterling Seagrave
Staff Writers: William C. Banks, Susan Bryan,
Gus Hedberg, Henry Woodhead
Chief Researcher: Martha T. Goolrick
Researchers: Patti Cass, W. Mark Hamilton,
Barbara Levitt, Katie Hooper McGregor, Nancy Toff
Art Assistant: Santi José Acosta
Editorial Assistant: Feroline Burrage

Correspondents: Elisabeth Kraemer (Bonn); Margot
Hapgood, Dorothy Bacon (London); Susan Jonas, Lucy
T. Voulgaris (New York); Maria Vincenza Aloisi,
Josephine du Brusle (Paris); Ann Natanson (Rome).
Valuable assistance was also provided by: Penny
Newman (London); Bill Lyon (Madrid); Carolyn T.
Chubert, Miriam Hsia (New York).

The editors are indebted to Barbara Hicks, Elizabeth D.
Meyer, Wendy Buehr Murphy and Jean I. Tennant for
their help in the preparation of this book.

The Author:
A. B. C. Whipple is descended from sturdy
seafaring New England stock; among his
ancestors was William Whipple of New
Hampshire, one of the founders of the Continental Navy. Himself an inveterate sail-
or in Long Island Sound and the Bahamas,
Whipple has written extensively on sailors
and the sea; his books range from the general history *Tall Ships and Great Captains*
to *Yankee Whalers in the South Seas*. He
is a former Assistant Managing Editor of
Time-Life Books.

The Consultants:
John Horace Parry, Gardiner Professor of
Oceanic History and Affairs at Harvard
University, took his Ph.D. at Cambridge
University. During World War II he rose to
the rank of commander in the Royal Navy.
Among Parry's numerous and illustrious
historical studies are *The Discovery of the
Sea*, *Trade and Dominion* and *The Spanish
Seaborne Empire*.

Christopher Lloyd, former Professor of History and Lecturer at the Royal Naval College, Greenwich, has published notable
seafaring studies, including *The British
Seaman* and *The Nation and the Navy*.

Edward Hunter Holmes Archibald is curator of oil paintings at the National Maritime
Museum at Greenwich, England. He is the
author of the definitive *The Wooden Fighting Ship in the Royal Navy, 1779–1860*.

Lieutenant Commander Peter Whitlock,
R.N., is commanding officer of the restored
H.M.S. *Victory* at her berth at Portsmouth.
He has written with particular authority on
the Royal Navy during the Napoleonic era.

Antony Preston, who was for some years on
the research staff at the National Maritime
Museum, is editor of the journal *Navy International* and author of many expert books
and articles on warship design and other
technical aspects of naval history.

Contents

Chapter 1

The mighty ship of the line

Looming fortress-like in this painting by J.M.W. Turner, a 100-gun British man-of-war takes on supplies before sallying forth to battle the French.

hatham, England, 1771. A raw March wind blew white-caps across the harbor and splashed the piers with spray. Sails flogged and tavern signs creaked. An officer of the Royal Navy was walking along the waterfront when a youngster approached him. The boy was neat despite his plain clothes, and he projected an air of quiet self-assurance. He did not ask for money, as the officer had expected him to. He had a sea bag over his shoulder, and he wanted directions. Where could he find the *Raisonnable*? And how could he get out to her?

His Majesty's ship of the line *Raisonnable* lay in the Medway River estuary, along with other warships that had recently been recommissioned. The youngster confided that he not only knew the name of the *Raisonnable*'s commander, Captain Maurice Suckling, but he was, in fact, Suckling's nephew. He was reporting for duty as a midshipman.

The Naval officer was acquainted with Captain Suckling. He escorted the lad to his own lodgings, gave him some food and hot tea, and then arranged for a boat to take him out to the *Raisonnable*. No doubt he forgot the incident, as well as the boy's name. He would remember it later, though, when this slender child became the most famous fighting admiral in the Royal Navy—or the entire world, for that matter.

Horatio Nelson was 12 years old when he became a midshipman. He was the son of a genteel but impecunious upcountry pastor who had been left a widower with eight children to care for. What had stimulated the enlistment of young Horace, as the family called him, was an account in the local newspaper to the effect that the ship of the line *Raisonnable* was being readied for combat in view of a likely war with Spain. Her captain would be Maurice Suckling. The youth had persuaded his father to write to Uncle Maurice, who had replied: "What has poor Horace done, who is so weak, that he above all the rest should be sent to rough it out at sea? But let him come; and the first time we go into action, a cannon-ball may knock off his head, and provide for him at once."

The *Raisonnable* had been captured from the French after a fierce battle 12 years earlier, during the Seven Years' War. The Royal Navy had followed the usual proud custom of retaining the ship's French name; it was good for morale to keep everyone mindful of ships captured from the enemy, and unlucky to change the name in any case. The Seven Years' War had ended in 1763, and the Admiralty had decommissioned the *Raisonnable*, along with many other vessels. Officers were placed on half pay and the crew dispersed. Now in 1770 came a new threat of war—and from a most unlikely corner of the globe: the barren Falkland Islands, some 200 miles out in the Atlantic off the tip of South America.

Spain claimed the islands. So did Great Britain, which for a number of years had maintained a marine detachment and a settlers' outpost in the Falklands to secure its claim. Suddenly in June of 1770 a large Spanish force sent from Buenos Aires descended on the handful of British colonists at Port Egmont, the British Falklands settlement, and attacked and occupied the place. It was four months before anyone in England learned about this little flurry in the South Atlantic; then the news triggered a wave of national indignation. England had been the world's dominant power ever since the Treaty of Paris in 1763 had ended the Seven Years' War. For the first time it could be said that the sun never set on the British Empire, an empire that owed its existence largely to Britain's mastery of the seas. The very thought of a Spanish landing party humbling His Majesty's subjects was more than Britons could bear.

To make matters infinitely worse, after the news reached Britain, the Spaniards behaved in an astonishing manner. Confronted by demands for restitution, Spain's King Charles III equivocated, meanwhile turning to Britain's old enemy, France, for an alliance. Charles' behavior triggered an outburst of war fever in England. Ships of the line were recommissioned; officers were recalled to duty; crews were rounded up.

As it happened, the Falkland Islands dispute evaporated after a few months. France's King Louis XV had no appetite for another war with England so soon, and Spain, left on its own, quickly capitulated, yielding the Falklands to Britain in 1771. England's war fever cooled as swiftly as it had risen. Young Midshipman Nelson had spent barely five months aboard the *Raisonnable* before she was decommissioned.

Nelson's uncle managed to find him a job as apprentice to the captain of a merchantman sailing to the West Indies. That experience almost cost England its admiral-to-be.

Merchant seamen detested the Royal Navy—for its forced recruiting, for its brutal discipline, for its miserable food and quarters, above all for its risks of danger, disfigurement and death. Young and impressionable, Horatio listened with mounting anger and apprehension to his shipmates' horror stories about the Navy and its callous officers. After a year aboard the merchantman, Nelson related afterward, he returned home with a hatred for the Royal Navy.

It took many long talks and all of Uncle Maurice' persuasive powers to restore the 14-year-old Nelson's faith in Naval service. But at last he agreed to resume his midshipman's training, and in July 1772, Suckling arranged for a berth aboard the 74-gun *Triumph*, stationed as a guard ship at the Nore, the sandbank at the mouth of the Thames.

It was fortuitous that Uncle Maurice salvaged his nephew for the Navy. Although few Englishmen realized it at the time, the Falkland Islands incident signaled a crucial turning point for England, and particularly for the Royal Navy. It was the beginning of the greatest challenge to Britain's command of the seas since the Spanish Armada almost two centuries before. The challenge would continue and grow in intensity for the better part of four decades. Within a few years, an infuriating, but relatively minor, threat would come during the American Revolutionary War; but the major crisis would occur in European waters as France and Spain joined forces during the Napoleonic Wars in an attempt to destroy the Royal Navy. At the height of the challenge, England would be threatened with invasion, defeat and occupation by the looming power of Napoleon Bonaparte.

And who, in this time of terrible ordeal, would turn out to be Britain's chief protector, indeed, its savior? The little midshipman of 1771, the sensitive youth who at first had quailed at the harshness of Navy life, the reluctant boy now learning the ropes aboard a patrol ship rocking back and forth along a coastal sandbank.

A boyhood to mark the man

Like so many other Royal Navy officers, Horatio Nelson came from a proper and solid, if not aristocratic, family. Nelson's father, Edmund, was a country parson of modest means. His mother, Catherine, was a great-niece of Sir Robert Walpole, the illustrious prime minister. Thus when Catherine bore her sixth child on September 29, 1758, it was only fitting that he be given a Walpole family name, Horatio.

Even as a toddler, Horatio, or Horace, as people called him, demonstrated a remarkable force of character—at least, so legend says. Out bird-nesting, according to the story, the tot wandered off into the forest and was missing for several hours. When he was finally found again, his grandmother wondered aloud if the poor dear had not been paralyzed by fear. Piped Horace, "I never saw fear. What is it?"

When Horace was only nine, his mother died, having borne 11 children. The Reverend Nelson never remarried, but he managed to rear his eight surviving children and provide them with what he regarded as the essentials for proper upbringing, "Air, Exercise, Warmth and Cleanliness."

In spite of his small size, Horace proved a natural leader at boarding school, to which he was sent at the age of 11. One day he found his classmates gazing hungrily at the ripe fruit on the headmaster's pear tree, but none would pinch even a single piece—the headmaster was known as a "keen flogger." That night Horace climbed down from his dormitory window on a knotted sheet and returned with an armful of pears—all of which he gave away. "I only took them," he recalled, "because every other boy was afraid."

The Nelson family enjoys a sunny day at Burnham Thorpe rectory in Norfolk—Horatio's birthplace. Though the Reverend Nelson loved the "charming open lawns and fields" of his isolated parish in the country, he confessed that "Variety, the Great Idoll, has no shrine here."

These portraits of Edmund and Catherine Nelson reflect the dignified sobriety of their lives at Burnham Thorpe. Nelson's mother's side of the family boasted a long tradition of government service, and she grew up hating the French.

On a 1773 Arctic expedition, coxswain Nelson swings his empty musket at an enraged polar bear. He had sneaked off to hunt the bear, "that I might carry its skin to my father." The musket misfired, but a timely shot from the ship's cannon frightened the animal away.

In those desperate days, England's ultimate defense was the Royal Navy—"the wooden-walls of England," as it was so proudly called. And it was the confrontation between the Royal Navy and the burgeoning fleets of France and Spain that precipitated the greatest and most awesome Age of Fighting Sail. Though scarcely 35 years in duration, from the first impudent challenge in the Falkland Islands to the climactic Battle of Trafalgar in 1805, it was a period of titanic clashes, of death and destruction at sea, of boundlessly brave sailors and brilliant, though sometimes foolhardy, tacticians and strategists. If Horatio Nelson's name was to become the most conspicuous in the international pantheon of naval heroes, there were others almost as lustrous: Rodney, Jervis, Troubridge and Collingwood, Brueys, Villeneuve, Gravina and John Paul Jones—not to mention a landbound genius named John Clerk, who devised, as an exercise on paper, the revolutionary naval maneuvers that ultimately secured victory for England.

Those few years of fierce struggle saw as well the perfection of the sailing warship, bristling with scores of cannon and billowing with acres of canvas. From the time of Alfred the Great every English monarch could muster a fleet of ships. Yet not until the reign of King Henry VIII could these collections of vessels be called a permanent fighting navy. In earlier days, ships were used mainly to ferry armies, and when battles were fought at sea, the soldiers boarded the enemy and fought on his decks. It was Henry VIII's 1,000-ton *Great Harry,* with her massive bronze guns, that first symbolized England's sea power. The vessel was the greatest of the Tudor monarch's "great shyppes" and had the distinction of being the prototype of the modern, as opposed to the medieval, man-of-war. But only during the 18th Century were sailing ships truly perfected as weapons in themselves. The ship's wheel, which activated pulleys to move the rudder, replaced the clumsy deck-wide sweep of the old-fashioned tiller, and provided greater maneuverability in battle. Copper-sheathed hulls were developed to retard the marine growth that had fouled and slowed the older wooden vessels. The first use of copper sheathing on the hull was nearly disastrous because of the corroding action that caused the iron hull fastenings to fall out. In short order, copper bolts were substituted for the iron ones.

As the state of the art progressed, the high fore-and-aft castles of yesteryear were eliminated; with a lower center of gravity, vessels could raise more sail for greater speed. Moreover, the sails themselves were vastly improved; triangular fore-and-aft jibs at the bow and staysails between the masts helped warships sail closer to the wind than had been possible with nothing but square sails. Even the motive power of the square sails was enhanced by the addition of studding sails (pronounced and often spelled "stuns'les"), which could be extended from the yardarm of the traditional sail. Under full sail a large warship might mount as many as 36 sails and surge through the water at a speed of 10 knots.

The most telling refinement in the 18th Century warship could be found belowdecks: row upon row of deadly cannon. A 200-foot-long ship of the line, mounting over 100 guns in three tiers of its massive hull, could fire half a ton of devastation, each cannon ball as big as a man's head, in a single broadside. It could also let loose clouds of grapeshot the

Specially designed to destroy sails, spars and rigging, these small iron missiles were a devastating addition to the standard cannon balls in a man-of-war armament. This chain shot (top), multiple bar shot (center) and elongating shot all expanded in flight, the better to mangle the enemy on impact.

size of musket balls, screaming tangles of chain, rockets, red-hot cannon balls and howling storms of nails and assorted razor-edged junk. Nothing then known to man could match the murderous firepower of a fully armed, well-fought ship of the line.

These engines of destruction were made even more formidable by their method of fighting, as signified by their name: "ships of the line." They were warships powerful enough to fight in the great line of battle in major fleet actions. The ultimate weapon at sea, at least from the Royal Navy's viewpoint, was the battle formation of these ships of the line, perhaps a dozen of them sailing single file, bowsprit to sternpost, all bearing down past the enemy, firing as they came and concentrating all their withering impact on their targets. On the Royal Navy's six-stage rating scale for warships *(page 14)*, only first-, second- and third-rated vessels mounting between 120 and 64 guns in their main armament qualified as ships of the line.

In their dramatic and unprecedented battles, these mighty war machines were employed as part of an elaborate orchestration to outwit, outmaneuver and overcome the enemy fleet. In the early days of naval warfare, individual captains tended to command their ships in battle more or less as they saw fit. As fleets grew larger, this method resulted in great thundering melees that no commander could begin to control. In 1653 the British Admiralty issued a set of *Fighting Instructions*, designed to bring order out of this confusion and thereby to greatly increase the fleet's efficiency. These *Fighting Instructions* decreed a "line of battle" in which each vessel followed a cable's length (200 yards) behind the other, all acting on the commanding admiral's signaled orders. Under no circumstances could a captain strike off to fight on his own. These stringently enforced tactics had won the Royal Navy some notable victories against Spain and France during the incessant wars of the early and mid-18th Century.

But now times were changing and the Royal Navy found itself forced to adopt radical new methods in order to meet the challenge of the enemy's improved ships and firepower. And providentially, a new system of communication—a signaling method using a reformed set of flags—was developed during the height of the challenge. The result was a series of sea battles, fought in the West Indies and off the North American coast, in the Mediterranean and off England's own shores, of an intensity and devastation never seen before.

The 18th Century ship of the line, ponderous and powerful yet seemingly light and graceful as it moved, all sails set to the lift of the wind and sea, was among man's most splendid creations. The classic example of the ship of the line was the *Victory (pages 17-19)*, fifth in a succession of ships named *Victory* starting in the 16th Century with Sir John Hawkins' flagship in the battle against the Spanish Armada. The fifth *Victory* was laid down in 1759 and launched in 1765, but peacetime economies delayed her commissioning for another 13 years. She was lying idle at her mooring at Chatham on the March day in 1771 when young Horatio Nelson reported for duty aboard the *Raisonnable* nearby, and from her deck he could study the ship that would one day wear his flag.

The fighting fleet, from flagship to sloop

"Beelzebub's grand arsenal" was how one chronicler described the warships of the 18th Century, and it was easy to imagine that these fearsome weapons were the devil's own creation. Such was their destructive power that the biggest of them could bombard one another with 30 tons of shot in an hour's time, and such was their ability to withstand punishment that engagements frequently lasted hours on end.

In the Royal Navy, major vessels were rated on a six-point scale according to their combat capability. Only first-, second- and third-rated vessels, mounting at least 64 heavy cannon, were designated as ships of the line. Their sole function was to sail in the Navy's line of battle and fight in great fleet engagements.

Smaller vessels—fourth-, fifth- and sixth-raters—served a wide variety of other purposes: they were guard ships in the colonies, convoy escorts, commerce raiders, troop carriers, hospital ships and storeships. Included in this group were frigates, which in major actions were the fast and far-ranging scouts sent to search out and shadow the enemy. In combat they remained unengaged, ready to relay messages, to rescue survivors and to take in tow any stricken ship of the line.

FIRST-RATER

Crewed by 875 men and measuring up to 206 feet on the lower gun deck, this flagship of the fleet mounted 100 or more cannon ranging from 12-pounders to huge 32-pounders. Because they cost as much as £100,000 each, fewer than a dozen of these craft were in service at one time.

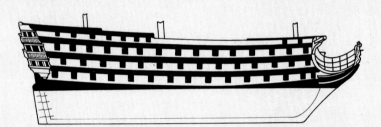

SECOND-RATER

Only slightly less imposing than the first-rater, this 195-footer carried 90 to 98 cannon in her three gun decks. One of her flaws—shared generally by ships of the line—was that her lower gunports could not be opened in heavy weather.

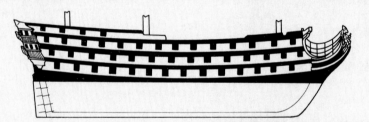

THIRD-RATER

This ship of the line came in several sizes, from 80-gun three-deckers to 64-gun two-deckers, with crews ranging in number from 720 to 490 men. Of the Royal Navy's 175 capital ships in 1805 at the time of Trafalgar, 147 were third-raters.

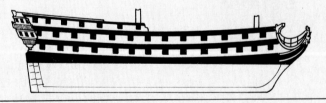

FOURTH-RATER

Mounting between 50 and 56 guns, this two-decker was about 150 feet long and was inexpensive to build (at £26,000) and maintain (350 in her crew). Her role was flagship of cruiser squadrons overseas.

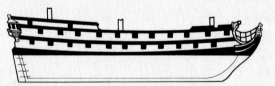

FIFTH-RATER

The commerce raider supreme, this 130- to 150-foot frigate generally carried a crew of 250 eager volunteers—because of the promise of prize money.

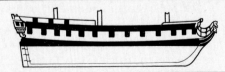

SIXTH-RATER

This nimble 125-foot sloop was favored by the Royal Navy as a courier and an escort. She could be built for only £10,000 and crewed by as few as 195 men.

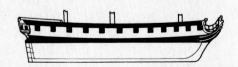

A FIRST RATE MAN of WAR,
taken from the DOCKYARD PLYMOUTH.

In his admiral's working uniform, Sir William Young seems pleased with himself in this 1809 cartoon, which labels him "A first-rate man of war." Yet as commander of the Royal Navy dockyard at Plymouth, he was notorious among the admirals for his bureaucratic delays on ship repairs; he was composed, one commander said, "of paper and packthread, stay tape and buckram."

English shipbuilders followed more or less traditional construction procedures, and the *Victory* resembled most of the other first-rate ships of the line. The major difference was that she was somewhat bigger than her sisters, and her superior sailing qualities were the result of better design and the fact that she could sail closer to the wind than most other three-deckers. These attributes made her a favorite with admirals entitled to have flagships.

To anyone approaching by boat, the *Victory* loomed out of the water like a huge wooden building, and indeed her ornate stern with its three rows of gilt-edged windows gave her the appearance of a floating palace.

The quarter-deck occupied nearly half the uppermost deck of the vessel, from the mainmast aft. This deck was the province of the ship's 49 officers—as was the *Victory*'s entire stern. In the sharply stratified society of an 18th Century warship, no ordinary seaman was permitted on the quarter-deck—or anywhere else aft—unless summoned there or required to perform some specific duty. The province of the ordinary crewman was the top gun deck, the forecastle (or fo'c's'le, as it was called) and the gun decks below. As crowded as a London slum and often as evil-smelling, this area offered none of the amenities enjoyed by the officers. The men endured it because they had to—and because life aboard a man-of-war was in some ways better than the brutal existence to which the poor were universally condemned during the 18th Century.

The men slept, ate and, if they were gunners, spent virtually every waking moment beside the monster 24- and 32-pounder cannon on the two lower gun decks. At night the men not standing watch unrolled their hammocks, hung them from hooks attached to the overhead beams and slept swinging over the guns. By day they ate from wooden boards slung from the beams, leaning their backs against the cannon. The decks were cramped and confined, the overhead beams less than six feet from the decking, and the only windows through which natural light and fresh air could enter were the gunports.

The manger at the forward end of the lower gun deck served both as a bulwark against the seas that leaked in through the anchor hawseholes at the bow and as a cage for the live animals shipped aboard to provide fresh meat for the admiral and his officers. The larger animals—cows, goats and sheep—were securely penned. But chickens, ducks and an occasional pig often managed to escape from the manger and roam through the deck, fouling it like a barnyard. Being but a few feet above the water line, the lower gun deck was a noisome place on a stormy day at sea, with the gunports closed, water sloshing through the manger forward, livestock littering the deck and nearly 600 wet and dirty men crowded together in the stinking dark.

A crewman's life was just as harsh and hazardous as his quarters were cramped, airless and uncomfortable. The man-of-war's day at sea commenced at dawn. With the shriek of the boatswain's pipe and the cry "All hands!" the boatswain's mates went through the lower gun deck, flicking knotted ropes at the hard outlines in the hammocks. Those seamen who did not tumble out at once were dumped onto the deck. In short order, spurred on by more stings of the knotted ropes—this encouragement was called "starting"—the men dressed, then lashed their hammocks and headed topside. There was a way of lashing the hammocks and looping the ropes seven times around the heavy canvas, and the boatswain's mates made sure each man did it correctly. The hammocks were then stowed in special nettings along the upper deck's bulwarks, where, in battle, they provided extra protection against small shot and could also be used as life preservers if anyone fell overboard; a well-lashed hammock could float for several hours.

Once on deck, the men were immediately put to work washing down the decks and scraping them smooth of splinters with holystones, so named because the smaller of these sandstone scrapers were the size of a prayer book. The deck was sprinkled with sand: the sand helped scour the surface, but it also cut into the bare knees of the men, who had rolled up their trousers to conserve the precious clothing.

At 6 a.m. the boatswain's pipe shrilled again and the men took their first meal of the day, usually "burgoo," a gruel of water and oatmeal, washed down with Scotch coffee, a bitter concoction made of burned biscuit dissolved in hot water.

Food on an 18th Century man-of-war was usually adequate in quantity, but miserably short on quality. The main meal of the day came at noon and often consisted of salt pork or beef, biscuits, a pease pudding, beer and occasionally, butter and cheese. Hearty and not wholly unappetizing—until the later stages of a patrol when the salt beef became so hard that it could be carved into mahogany-colored trinkets and the cheese was filled with long red worms. As for the biscuits, they were not so bad when infested with maggots; this was only the first stage of decay. The maggots did not deter a hungry man. In fact, they were regarded with a certain relish. As one midshipman described them, they were "very cold when you eat them, like calf's foot jelly." But later, when the weevils took over, the biscuits crumbled into powder and lost all their nourishment. At this point, the men would eat the ship's rats—if they could catch them. The rats were wryly known as "millers" because of the white coats the animals got from spending much of their time in the flour; a large, neatly skinned rat was a much-appreciated item to a hungry tar.

It was this noon meal that, perhaps more than anything else, pointed up the double standard of the Royal Navy. While the men at their swinging tables on the lower gun deck were eating—and sometimes gagging over—their humble fare, the officers in their wardroom, and the captain and admiral in their dining cabins, were served, as available, roast beef or lamb freshly butchered and fine wines.

The men, however, would not have preferred the officers' wine to the beverage that followed dinner and made their day: grog. The fifer struck up a jolly tune and a selected man from each mess took a tub up on deck that a mate filled with a ration of rum and water; some men gave it an extra little zip by mixing in the lemon juice they were issued for its scurvy-preventing Vitamin C. Each sailor's grog portion was strong enough, and copious enough, to bring the drinker to the edge at least of happy inebriation.

After grog the men not on watch were permitted to nap and loaf around the gun decks and the forecastle. The men on watch had to stick

H.M.S. "Victory": a fearsome engine of war

Commissioned in 1778, H.M.S. *Victory* bordered on old age, with almost 30 years' hard service under her keel, at the time of Trafalgar. Yet she remained a fearsome fighting machine.

As a first-rater, she commanded the power of 102 cast-iron cannon ranging from 12- to 32-pounders lining three gun decks, plus two short-range carronades that could fire an immense 68-pound ball. In a single devastating broadside, she could let loose half a ton of iron shot propelled for more than a mile by 400 pounds of gunpowder. Even at that extreme range, the round shot from a 32-pounder could smash through two feet of solid oak.

The great hull that cradled this terrible arsenal displaced 3,500 tons and measured 226 feet from figurehead to sternpost, with a beam of 51 feet. Aside from her keel, which was constructed of elm because it could be obtained in the large sizes required, the *Victory*'s hull was built almost entirely of oak. It took 2,500 prime trees—equivalent to 60 acres of century-old forest—to fashion her massive ribs, some two feet thick, and her heavy double planking.

Her rudder, an oak blade six feet wide at the base and 38 feet tall, was controlled from the double wheel on the quarter-deck by ropes and pulleys connected to a 29-foot tiller on the

lower gun deck. Both the rudder and the hull below the water line were sheathed in copper as a guard against borers and speed-retarding barnacles.

The tallest of the *Victory*'s three masts towered 205 feet above the water line. The masts were made of fir, for its flexibility, and were constructed in three sections for ease in maintaining and because no trees were tall enough by themselves. These spires, up to three feet thick at the base, were secured to the *Victory*'s hull by five miles of standing rigging; from their yards could be hung 36 sails—four acres of canvas all told when she was under full sail. With everything ship-

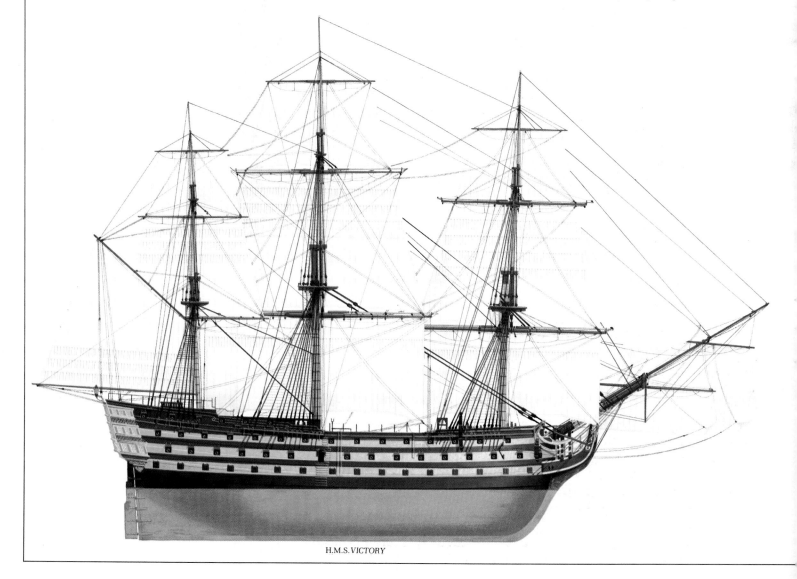

H.M.S. VICTORY

shape the *Victory* could plow along at 10 knots in a stiff breeze—though six knots was more usual.

Except for two spacious suites for Captain Hardy and Admiral Nelson, the *Victory* provided scant comfort for her 850 officers and men. Officers slept in closet-like cabins in the wardroom. The midshipmen, numbering about 20, were packed into one 10-by-18-foot room on the orlop deck and into another small space on the lower gun deck. The rest of the crew slept on the gun decks in hammocks slung above the cannon. For toilet facilities the seamen used open boxes debouching into the sea at the bow. This was the location also of the marines' catwalk, a lookout post where guards were stationed while in port, with orders to shoot anyone attempting to slip down the side of the ship.

Hot meals were prepared in the galley on the middle gun deck. The huge stove, fueled by coal and charcoal, could roast a whole pig on its six-foot spit and turn out 80 pounds of ship's biscuit in one batch. On its hood was a copper condenser that produced about six quarts of distilled water a day for the ship's surgeon.

To get under way, the anchors, each of which weighed nearly five tons and hung on rope cables two feet thick, were drawn up to the catheads on the bow by the double-barreled capstan amidships. The strength of as many as 260 men could be applied to the ash bars attached like spokes to the capstan's drumhead. A fiddler, perched in the middle of the drumhead, would play a shanty to coordinate the effort.

Weighing anchor was onerous duty, but no less so than manning the main pumps. In heavy seas 150 men would labor around the clock in relays to rid the bilge of 120 tons of water an hour.

Fair weather or foul, the *Victory* was a mobile fortress-city, stocked with 35 tons of powder and 120 tons of shot, and capable of staying at sea for several months at a time.

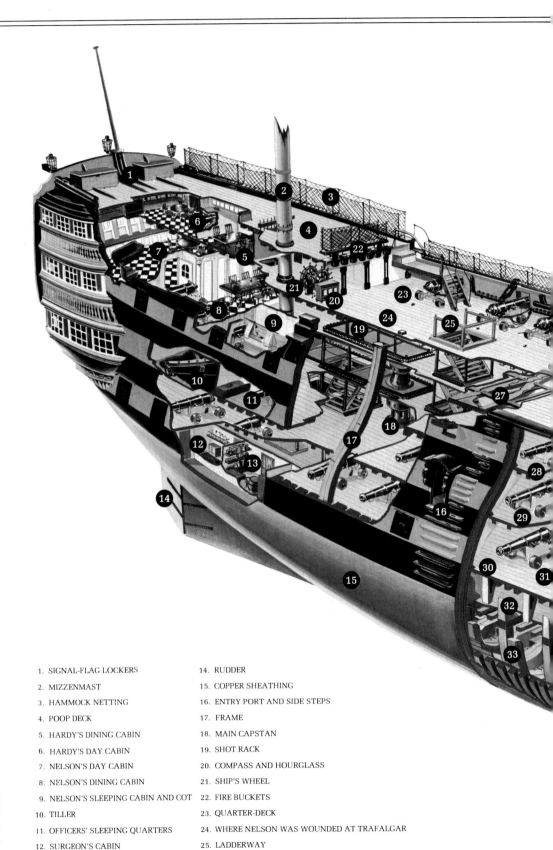

1. SIGNAL-FLAG LOCKERS
2. MIZZENMAST
3. HAMMOCK NETTING
4. POOP DECK
5. HARDY'S DINING CABIN
6. HARDY'S DAY CABIN
7. NELSON'S DAY CABIN
8. NELSON'S DINING CABIN
9. NELSON'S SLEEPING CABIN AND COT
10. TILLER
11. OFFICERS' SLEEPING QUARTERS
12. SURGEON'S CABIN
13. ADMIRAL'S STORES
14. RUDDER
15. COPPER SHEATHING
16. ENTRY PORT AND SIDE STEPS
17. FRAME
18. MAIN CAPSTAN
19. SHOT RACK
20. COMPASS AND HOURGLASS
21. SHIP'S WHEEL
22. FIRE BUCKETS
23. QUARTER-DECK
24. WHERE NELSON WAS WOUNDED AT TRAFALGAR
25. LADDERWAY
26. MAINMAST

27. DECK BEAMS
28. 12-POUNDER GUN
29. 24-POUNDER GUN
30. LOWER GUN DECK
31. 32-POUNDER GUN
32. ORLOP DECK
33. INNER PLANKING
34. BASE OF MAINMAST
35. LOWER END OF MAIN PUMPS
36. KEEL
37. GUN TOOLS
38. GUNPORT AND LIFTING TACKLES
39. SHOT LOCKER

40. MAIN PUMPS
41. MIDDLE GUN DECK
42. MAIN HATCHWAY
43. UPPER GUN DECK
44. FORWARD CAPSTAN
45. SHIP'S BOATS
46. CARPENTER'S CABIN
47. STORES IN HOLD
48. OUTER PLANKING
49. CARPENTER'S SHOP
50. CREW'S MESS TABLE
51. MOORING BITTS
52. GALLEY AND STOVE

53. FORECASTLE BULKHEAD
54. BELFRY
55. FORECASTLE
56. 68-POUNDER CARRONADE
57. FOREMAST
58. MANGER
59. STEM
60. CREW'S "HEAD"
61. MARINES' CATWALK
62. CATHEAD
63. ANCHOR
64. BOWSPRIT
65. FIGUREHEAD

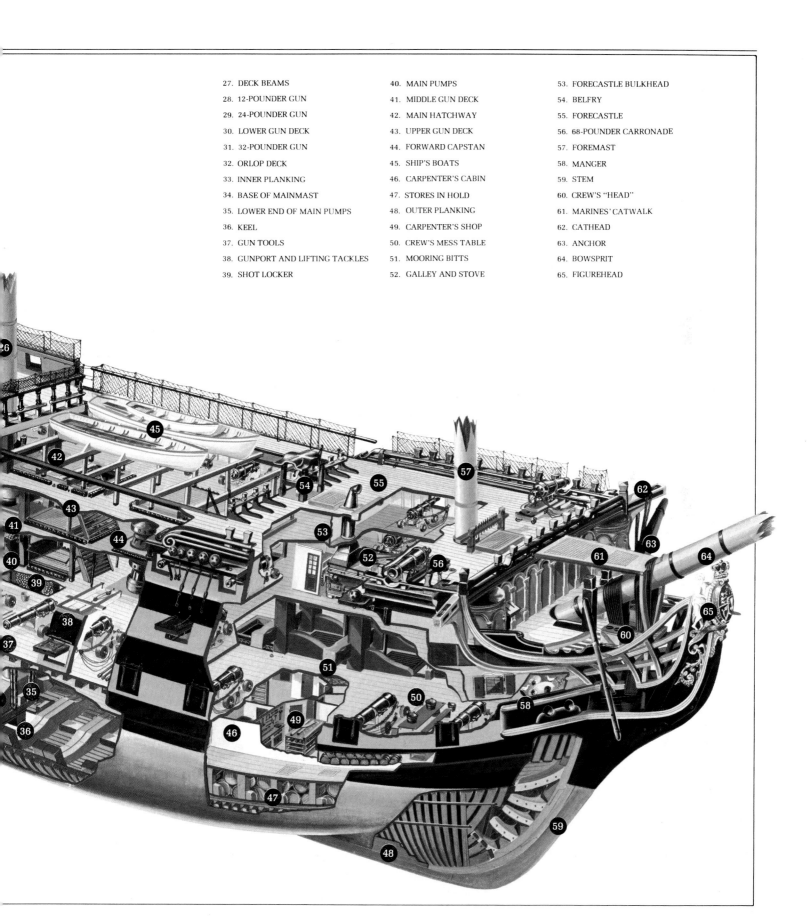

to their posts and keep their wits about them; any slight sign of drunkenness could result in a severe flogging for dereliction of duty.

The night watches were the hardest, especially when the ship was in cold, stormy seas. These watches ran four hours—8 p.m. to midnight, midnight to 4 a.m., and so on—and they could be torture for men dressed as inadequately as the average seaman was. Their clothes were usually of canvas and cotton, and there were no snug peacoats or greatcoats: the Royal Navy did not issue uniforms until the mid-19th Century.

The most brutal part of an 18th Century seaman's life was the punishment that was inflicted for even the smallest breach of the Navy's many regulations. For a minor crime such as excessive swearing a man was put in the leg irons on the exposed top gun deck. He was kept in a sitting position, with his hands secured behind him, and remained so until the captain released him.

The floggings were far worse. Punishment hour was traditionally 11 a.m. The shriek of the boatswain's pipe and a roll of drums summoned all hands to the top gun deck to see the edifying spectacle. On the quarter-deck stood the officers, in formal dress and wearing their swords. Before them stood the master-at-arms, several sturdy boatswain's mates and, guarded by a pair of quartermasters, the manacled sailor who was to be punished. The captain asked the malefactor if he had anything to say for himself. He usually did not. "Strip," the captain ordered. The man removed his shirt. "Seize him up," the captain commanded. The quartermasters tied the man's hands to a pair of gratings. "Seized up, sir," they reported. The captain then read the appropriate

The uniforms and even a bit of the spirit of the Royal Navy's officers and seamen are captured in this 1799 series of aquatints by the famed illustrator and caricaturist Thomas Rowlandson. While Rowlandson put a flattering face on most of the crewmen, he could not resist mocking "Old Nipcheese," the parsimonious purser.

CAPTAIN

MIDSHIPMAN

PURSER

passage in the Articles of War, as all those present respectfully removed their hats. He then turned to the boatswain's mate: "Do your duty."

At that, the mate pulled out the knotted cord cat-o'-nine-tails, drew back and laid on the first stroke with all his strength, grunting from the effort. The first lash left a pattern of livid red welts along the man's back. The next few lashes cut more deeply, and a dozen lashes turned the flesh into a pulpy, dripping mass. Now, between each stroke, the mate ran the cat's tails between his fingers to clear away the blood, flicking it onto the deck. A powerful boatswain's mate liked to brag that he could lay on the second dozen lashes as heavily as the first, but often a second mate was substituted just to make sure. A veteran seaman also boasted about how many lashes he could endure without screaming. Some sadistic captains ordered 100 lashes or more. No man could remain stoic in the face of that torture; not many men even survived the ordeal.

Understandably, life aboard a Royal Navy man-of-war did not attract very many volunteers. A few boys were lured to sea by dreams of glory, and some veteran seamen were attracted by recruiting posters that appealed to "True-Blue Hearts of Oak" to serve king and country amid "Old Shipmates and their Jolly Friends." And bounties were paid to sailors who had special skills.

The most effective recruiting, however, was done by force. Press gangs of half a dozen tough sailors commanded by a junior officer went through port towns dragging off almost any nautical-looking man they saw and "pressing" him into involuntary service. It was an early, and

CARPENTER

COOK

SAILOR

rough-and-ready, form of conscription into a harsh and dangerous world that few would enter willingly.

Once aboard their new ship, the pressed men were washed, deloused and divided into four groups. First were the able seamen, experienced sailors who could work aloft on the yardarms. They were paid a handsome sum for the era: 33 shillings a month. Second came the ordinary seamen, paid 23 shillings, sixpence, who knew enough to haul a line on deck. Next were the landsmen, who, at 17 shillings, sixpence a month, could do other jobs on the ship such as maintain the lower rigging or serve as the officers' servants. A special group was known as "idlers"— so called because they did not have to stand watch—who had the skill to do carpentry, make sails or serve as surgeon's mates; these men were paid about the same as able seamen.

Once at sea, the officers began molding this haphazard collection of men into an effective crew. The able seamen tuned the rigging, tightening and slackening it until the ship was properly trimmed. The carpenter and his mates made everything shipshape, plugging leaks and making the wooden patches they would use to repair shot holes during battle. The head gunner and his mates ladled powder into the bags called cartridges. The seaman who was euphemistically named the "captain of the head" made sure the officers' toilets in their stern quarters were maintained in a proper and sanitary condition.

On the three gun decks the gunners took particular care with the lashings to make sure that no gun would break loose. Except for actual combat, nothing could be more dangerous than a three-ton mass of iron on wheels breaking loose and careering wildly to and fro with each roll of the ship. Loose cannon had been known to smash clear through the side of a ship and to maim horribly gun crews that got in the way.

When ships were headed for war, the captains drilled their crews ruthlessly in the routine of preparing the vessel for battle (pages 34-43). The speed at which its gunners could fire was a matter of great pride in the Royal Navy. One captain, Cuthbert Collingwood, who would be among Nelson's devoted "Band of Brothers" at the Battle of the Nile, drilled his gunners until the best of them could fire their cannon at the astonishing rate of three rounds every two minutes.

In June 1778, the great ship *Victory*, 19 years in preparation, was finally ready to proceed to sea. It was fortunate for England that this powerful vessel was at last complete, for by 1778 the challenge to the Navy and to Great Britain was mounting. The danger came not so much from the American rebels, whose navy was correctly perceived as more of a nuisance than a threat. The true menace came from Britain's neighbors across the Channel. The Admiralty well knew that France could be expected to aid the Americans—not because of any great affinity for the colonial revolutionaries but in order to strike at England. In fact, a treaty between France and the Americans was signed in February 1778.

The French had made good use of the time since the Seven Years' War. Their navy, which had been virtually annihilated during that conflict, now included 74 major ships of the line. England at this stage had 69 ships of the line, but it was in for greater jeopardy than the numbers

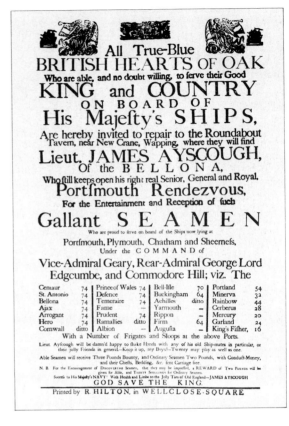

A 1780 Royal Navy recruiting poster promises enlistees jolly comradeship and cash bounties. In Nelson's era, bonuses for enlistment varied from 30 shillings to more than 25 guineas. Other rewards were available, as the fine print at the bottom explains, for "Discovering Seamen, that they may be impressed"— that is, for reporting to the authorities men who could be forced into service.

indicated. Eleven ships were in American waters, and of the rest only 35 were ready for sea. Most of the French warships were better designed and more heavily armed. Smarting from France's defeats in earlier naval wars, Louis XVI had lavished huge funds on the Navy, which was designated, for a time at least, "the first service of the realm." New academies of naval architecture were opened, a network of new dockyards was built, reserves of the finest timber were set aside. The sailing qualities of new French ships showed the result; they were generally faster and more maneuverable than their British counterparts, and more carefully constructed. Some of the French shipwright manuals and writings on design were translated into English, but complacent British shipwrights paid them little heed. They continued to build ships by what they called the "rule of King's thumb," which meant in the traditional way without constant refinement.

The scent of war was in the air when on March 12, 1778, the *Victory*'s first captain was rowed out to where she was moored off Gillingham, near Chatham. He was Sir John Lindsay, a hero of the Seven Years' War who was to hold this command only briefly: his assignment was to take the *Victory* down to Portsmouth, where she was to become the flagship of Vice Admiral Augustus Keppel. But now Lindsay was piped aboard the *Victory*. He read his commission to the assembled officers. His pennant was hoisted. And the *Victory* was finally commissioned.

There followed two months of hectic preparation. Ballast was sent ashore, to be replaced with supplies: 45 tons of biscuit, 25 tons of pork, 10 tons of flour, 50 tons of beer—and the 35 tons of powder and 120 tons of shot that were the reason for the *Victory*'s existence. The master, who was in charge of sailing and navigation, the boatswain and the carpenter scurried about fitting out the ship for sea. The purser supervised the loading of stores, and the gunner, the stowage of ammunition and the positioning of the guns.

The *Victory*'s marines—a captain, a sergeant, a corporal and 55 privates—came smartly aboard on April 11. The vessel was nearly ready for sea now, and spruced up for a special royal visit. On April 25, as the warship's cannon fired their first 21-gun salute, King George III came alongside in the yacht *Royal Charlotte*. On Monday, April 27, His Majesty spent three hours aboard, inspecting the ship and her crew. Then, nearly 20 years from the day her keel was laid down, the *Victory* dropped her mooring to proceed down harbor to the sea.

En route around the southeastern tip of England the crew shook down. The able seamen became used to the vessel's rigging, her gun crews were formed, and some semblance of order was brought to the ship.

On May 14, the day after her arrival, Admiral Keppel was piped aboard for inspection. One of Britain's most illustrious admirals, Keppel was 53, a young age for the Royal Navy. As a 15-year-old midshipman in 1740, he had sailed under Commodore George Anson on a historic circumnavigation of the globe, and had won promotion to lieutenant for his excellent service. His progress through the ranks was swift. At 34 he had commanded the 74-gun ship of the line *Torbay* at the victorious Battle of Quiberon Bay during the Seven Years' War; later in that war, he led a

His face alight with anticipation, a lad signs on with the Royal Navy in this 1794 engraving after Henry Singleton. Such boys, aged 12 to 17, were taken aboard as servants and apprentices. Despite their abysmally humble station, they were in a way the Royal Navy's secret weapon as they matured into highly skilled seamen.

brilliant assault to capture the heavily fortified Belle-Île-en-Mer in the Bay of Biscay. He had won his rear admiral's flag in 1762, after playing a leading role in the capture of Havana from France's Spanish ally.

Keppel had been a vice admiral for eight years and now had been placed in command of a fleet forming up as England's line of defense in the Channel. Not only was France joining in the American war, but there were reports that she was also planning an invasion of England. To forestall such an attack, Keppel was given 21 ships of the line and four frigates. According to the fourth Earl of Sandwich, First Lord of the Admiralty, it was "a noble fleet." Regarding his command more objectively, Keppel noted that some of the ships were not in a satisfactory state when "looked at with a seaman's eye." He had chosen the best of them, the *Victory*, as his flagship. Next day, he transferred his flag from the *Prince George*, a 90-gun first-rater, on which he had been waiting. By custom, commanding admirals also brought their own favored captains

Mustering a crew by hook or by crook

CHARLES REECE PEMBERTON

While strolling along the Liverpool wharves with a chum one day in 1807, 17-year-old Charles Reece Pemberton became aware that two pig-tailed fellows in clean white trousers and neat blue jackets were following close behind. Pemberton, shown above in his middle years as a well-known Welsh actor, recalled afterward that the men "were our constant companions; walking where we walked, and stopping as we stopped." Finally one of the men ventured to ask, "Are you looking for a ship, boys?"

The lads were. They had romantic notions of running away to sea—and that was all the two men needed to hear. " 'Well, come along with us,' said first pigtail's duplicate," Pemberton remembered, " 'our ship is a gallows deal finer than any you've seen yet.' " Making liberal use of nautical terms calculated to impress the boys, the sailor went on about the ship's "jolly good Captain" who "splices the main brace every week. Aye, and he'll order the pusser's steward to choke your luff with figgy-dowdy."

"What splicing the main brace and figgy-dowdy meant, I could not guess for the life of me," Pemberton wrote, "but as they were illustrations of the 'jolly captain's' good qualities, there was a spell in the unintelligible jargon. And so," Pemberton went on, "we stepped lightly along." The next thing he knew, he and his friend had been led aboard a Royal Navy man-of-war from which there was no escape until Pemberton was released from service six years later—with little time spent splicing the main brace (celebrating with an extra ration of rum) or choking his luff on figgy-dowdy (feasting on steamed fruit pudding).

Pemberton and his companion were compliant victims of impressment—the Royal Navy's franchise to man His Majesty's ships by any means necessary in wartime. They were pressed the easy way; less gullible men not taken in by such spellbinding sailor's double-talk were simply seized by the scruff of the neck, as in the cartoon at right. In 1805, the year of the Battle of Trafalgar, no less than one third of the fleet was mustered in this fashion.

No one liked the press. Owners of merchant ships, who saw their crews pressed in wholesale lots, complained bitterly about it. Horatio Nelson declared that he was embarrassed by it: "Something should be attempted to make our seamen, at the din of war, fly to our navy, instead of flying from it."

But nobody had an alternative. In a celebrated case brought in 1776 by the Crown against a boatman who had resisted impressment, the Lord Chief Justice handed down the opinion that the press was inescapable, and that "private mischief had better be submitted to, than that public detriment and inconvenience should ensue."

aboard their flagships. Keppel's choice was Captain Jonathan Faulknor of the *Prince George.* Aboard the *Victory,* Captain Lindsay signed the ship's log over to Faulknor and then went to replace him as commander of the *Prince George.*

Responding to his admiral's wishes, one of Faulknor's first actions was to order the name *Victory* removed from the flagship's stern. Keppel believed that in battle a ship's name was of no use to anyone save the enemy; the gilt letters were removed as well from the other ships in the fleet.

Nearly a month passed before Keppel's force was ready. At last, on June 13, 1778, the *Victory* led the flotilla out past Spithead and into the Atlantic. Keppel sent his smaller, faster frigates on ahead; the frigates were known as the eyes of the fleet, and their vital task was to scout for enemy ships. For the next four days the *Victory*'s crewmen, along with those of the rest of the fleet, were ordered into intensive practice for the battles that would come.

Swinging swords and cudgels, members of a Royal Navy press gang seize idlers off a London street in this 1780 cartoon satirizing impressment.

On the fifth day Keppel's reconnoitering frigates came racing back to report. The signal flags snapping from the yardarms spelled action: the enemy was coming out of the harbor of Brest. France had committed herself to another naval war with England.

The first skirmish gave precious little foretaste of what was to become a titanic clash of sea power. The enemy so eagerly announced by Keppel's frigates turned out to be nothing more than a light French scouting squadron consisting of two frigates, a corvette and a small lugger. The French frigate *Belle Poule* opened the war by slamming a 20-gun broadside into the British frigate *Arethusa*, and after four hours of fighting, the *Belle Poule* fled into a rocky bay on the Brittany coast. The corvette and lugger likewise beat a rapid retreat. But the second French frigate, the

Some salty additions to the King's English

When wars ended and the ships were paid off, thousands of Royal Navy seamen returned home spouting a blustery new language all their own. Although at first incomprehensible to their landbound countrymen, the romantic seafaring jargon soon proved irresistible, and was quickly imitated and modified in common usage, as this sampling of salty slang suggests.

AFOUL: Most frequently used in connection with an entangled or jammed line or anchor, but also used to denote all manner of woes from a barnacle-covered hull to a captain's wrath.

ALOOF: To sail or point as close into the wind as possible, an antiquated term from the Dutch *te loef*. Thus "to stand aloof" was to keep above, or to windward, of another vessel.

BEAR DOWN: To sail toward another ship rapidly and purposefully from an upwind position, later in general use as a synonym for applying pressure. To "bear up" was to steer a vessel away from a difficult windward course, accepting an easier course to leeward; a midshipman who had botched his lieutenant's exam and had accepted his failure was said to be "bearing up."

BILGE: The lowest level of a ship's hull, down inside the ribs by the keel, where all manner of watery refuse collected, thus in the layman's lexicon any stale or worthless remark or idea.

CUT AND RUN: To leave in a hurry by cutting the anchor cable and running before the wind.

GROG: The eagerly awaited ration of rum issued twice daily to Royal Navy crews, so named—in no special honor—for the grogram cloak worn by Admiral Edward Vernon, who in 1740 devised the formula of three parts water to one part rum. By saving up his rations, a determined sailor could render himself blissfully "groggy."

HOOKER: An old and clumsy ship, from the Dutch *hoeker*, a fishing boat; also an affectionate, but disparaging, sailor's term for old prostitutes.

JAUNTY: The master-at-arms, from the French word *gendarme*, who supervised floggings and other disciplinary actions; a man apt to swagger about with studied nonchalance.

JUNK: Worn-out rope, or old salt meat that tasted like it. Junk rigging was sold by the mate to a "junkman."

LETTING THE CAT OUT OF THE BAG: The grim ceremony of removing the rope or rawhide cat-o'-nine-tails from its red baize carrying bag preparatory to flogging a thief; later applied to any untimely, if less serious, revelation.

POOPED: What happened to any unfortunate seaman caught standing on the aft, or poop, deck when a giant wave from a following sea crashed down.

SCUTTLEBUTT: The cask, or butt, that contained the ship's daily water ration, built with a square hole, or scuttle, in the side at the half-full mark to ensure that only half a butt would be available for use each day. Sailors often tarried during water breaks to swap rumors—or "scuttlebutt."

SKEDADDLE: To sneak away from a working party.

SLOPS: Clothing sold to seamen by the ship's purser, overpriced and usually ill-fitting, thus "sloppy."

SLUSH FUND: A small, usually illegal fund raised on ships from the misappropriation and sale of grease, rope ends and such, and used to pay for small, hard-to-explain expenses, like those incurred for an extra rum ration.

SON OF A GUN: A male child conceived on a man-of-war's gun deck in an era when wives, lovers and ladies of pleasure were permitted on board to entertain the men while in port. Strict semanticists insist that the term applied only to lads actually born on the gun deck, a considerably less frequent but not unheard-of occurrence.

STRANDED: Drifted or run aground on a strand, or beach.

Licorne, tarried a trifle too long and was soon captured. She was brought as a prize under the looming stern of the *Victory.* And it was then that Admiral Keppel received the first of a number of nasty surprises.

From papers aboard the *Licorne,* he learned that the French had no fewer than 32 great ships of the line in the harbor at Brest. And this mighty fleet, mounting close to 3,000 guns, would soon come out to challenge the British. Keppel was among the most courageous of Royal Navy admirals. But he was no fool. He knew that his 21 ships, only a few of them 100-gun first-raters, were no match for the French at this stage. He dared not jeopardize Britain's only defense, its ramparts of wood. Ordering a defensive maneuver, he cracked on sail for a dash to Portsmouth, anchored at Spithead on June 27, reported his news and pleaded with the Lords of the Admiralty for reinforcements.

There followed 12 days of frantic activity in the Portsmouth dockyards. Three more ships of the line were made ready for sea. Another six were promised from the escort of an incoming West Indies convoy, which was expected momentarily. On July 9, Keppel in the *Victory* made sail and led the Grand Fleet out to sea once again. Two days later, in mid-Channel, the promised reinforcements arrived. The admiral now had 30 powerful ships of the line, only two fewer than the French; the odds had narrowed more to his liking.

Keppel set course to cruise south of Brest. The Admiralty had given him two assignments. One was to interpose himself in a blocking position between the French fleet and the fleet of France's Spanish ally at Cadiz. It was a measure of rising English confidence—or conceit—that no one regarded this as positioning Keppel squarely between the jaws of a trap. Keppel's second mission was to watch for two more richly laden British convoys due to arrive shortly—from the East Indies this time, carrying Chinese tea, porcelain and silk. Spies on the Continent had reported that the French were also aware that these convoys were soon expected; their loss would be a devastating psychological blow to England at the very start of the war. What Keppel did not know was that on July 8, a day before he had hauled up his anchors at Spithead, all 32 French ships of the line, under the Comte d'Orvilliers, one of France's premier admirals, had sailed out of Brest to intercept the East Indian convoys. It seems incredible that this armada could slip from its base and reach the open Atlantic without being spotted by one of the British frigates patrolling off the coast of France. But the nature of naval warfare in the 18th Century—with huge expanses of water, relatively slow, small ships and every imaginable weather condition—was such that hundreds of vessels could sail around for weeks groping for one another.

For a fortnight the two fleets patrolled back and forth in the open Atlantic south of England and west of France, two vast armadas stretching as much as a mile or more across the sea, each unaware of the other's position. On the afternoon of July 23, 1778, they found each other.

The British fleet was 100 miles off the French coast, due west of Ushant, when the first lookouts high in the swaying tops called down that they had sighted sails on the horizon. Then there were more sails, and more and more until the entire French fleet was arrayed before the British. If Keppel was surprised at encountering his enemy on the open

ocean, he was also pleased; he had the weather gauge in the southwester-
ly wind—that is, the British fleet had the wind behind it, which gave it
many more options and much greater maneuverability than the French.
As dusk fell, Keppel held to his course to be ready for battle in the
morning. Meanwhile, in case the French should attempt a surprise attack during the night, he ordered all ships cleared for action.

The first light of July 24 brought another surprise for Keppel. The French
fleet was not where he expected it to be. D'Orvilliers had outsmarted
him. Under cover of darkness the French admiral, in a brilliant feat of
seamanship, and making the most of his faster, superior ships, had
worked almost his entire fleet upwind of the British. Now he, not Keppel, had the weather gauge and the choice to force or refuse battle.

There was one consolation: the new position placed the British fleet
between d'Orvilliers and the coast of France. D'Orvilliers could no longer make a run for home without affording the British a crack at him.
Nevertheless, d'Orvilliers enjoyed a decided tactical advantage—so
long as he could hold his upwind position.

Studying the enemy's disposition, Keppel spotted what he thought might be a small flaw, something that might give him a chance to engage the French after all. Two of the French vessels, it appeared, had not quite achieved the weather gauge, and were still struggling into the wind. Some of the British ships at the rear of the formation remained upwind of them. Keppel ordered a signal to the *Victory*'s masthead, and two British men-of-war peeled off to engage the French stragglers.

Keppel now focused on d'Orvilliers's flagship, the 110-gun *Bretagne*, hoping that the French admiral would come about and hurry to the rescue of his endangered vessels. But d'Orvilliers did not take the lure; instead of swooping down to protect his two ships, he left them to their own devices. The swift French vessels promptly turned tail and fled for home, soon leaving their British pursuers astern. Keppel signaled his ships to return. At least he had evened the odds: now there were 30 French ships of the line to oppose his 30.

But d'Orvilliers refused to bring his fleet downwind to meet the British. For three days he carefully maintained his weather gauge while Keppel, with mounting anger and frustration, followed in dogged pur-

Happily "out of discipline" while anchored in home port, the crew of a British man-of-war relaxes belowdecks in this 1782 drawing by satirist Thomas Rowlandson. Most captains forbade shore leave to forestall desertion, and instead ferried the entertainment out to the sailors. Wrote one ship's chaplain: "Nothing can possibly be more awkwardly situated than a clergyman in a ship of war."

suit. Westward into the Atlantic the two fleets sailed, every ship stripped and ready for action.

Suddenly, at 10 a.m. on the third day, a black squall came racing across the water from the west. It burst on the British fleet almost before sails could be furled, gunports closed and the big guns lashed down. Sheets of rain sluiced across the decks. Lines slatted and sails boomed. On the *Victory*'s lower gun decks the men held fast to the restraining gear as the massive cannon surged against the storm. In the howling wind and smashing seas, Keppel lost sight of the other ships. For more than an hour, as the gale buffeted the big flagship, visibility was virtually nil. Then, as quickly as it had come, the rain raced off to the east.

Keppel and the men aboard the *Victory* watched the edge of the squall swirling away across the ocean, revealing ship after ship as it departed. And with the return of visibility, Keppel had yet another surprise: the entire French fleet was sailing straight for him!

The wily French admiral had seen the squall coming and, knowing that he could take advantage of the change in the weather, had turned his fleet around and headed in the opposite direction, eastward toward France. But d'Orvilliers was not maneuvering for a face-to-face fight to the death: that had proved catastrophic to the French in the Seven Years' War. Instead, he was about to employ a new naval tactic of hit-and-run, of raking the enemy, particularly in the vulnerable sails and rigging, and then racing away, either to maneuver for another swift strike or to flee for home if that seemed the better alternative.

Being on opposite tacks perfectly suited d'Orvilliers's purpose. At a closing speed of perhaps 12 knots, the engagement promised to be a short one, as such things went. But now the winds took a role in events. The lingering gusts of the squall died to light breezes, and the two fleets began to move past each other at a much slower pace.

The delighted Keppel did not even have time to raise the preparatory signal. He immediately ordered the standard flags for battle: "Line Ahead" and "Engage." His ships had spread out during the three-day chase, and the squall had driven some of them out of the line of battle. But there was no time to reform.

Belowdecks aboard the *Victory* and all the other ships of the Grand Fleet, gun crews snatched away the heavy restraining gear that had been secured during the storm. With the swiftness and sureness that came from constant drill, the gunports were opened, the wooden plugs pulled from the cannon muzzles, powder and shot rammed home, and the long iron snouts run out the ports. Unlike the French gunners, who preferred to fire high, the British went for the enemy's hull, on the principle that the way to win a battle was to hole ships and kill men. The *Victory*'s gunners, taking a length of burning fuse and blowing on the end until it glowed, waited for the beginning of the downward roll. Then the gun captain yelled "Fire!"—and each gunner touched off his cannon, sending a ball roaring across the water at 1,200 feet per second.

There was no time to see what damage the ball had caused. The moment the cannon reached the end of its violent recoil, the gun crew leaped forward to clean it and load it for the next shot. By now even the slowest of the *Victory*'s gun crews could clean, load, aim and fire a

French Admiral Louis Guillouet Comte d'Orvilliers had explicit orders to avoid a fight with the British fleet. Nevertheless, he wrote prophetically as he left the port of Brest, "if the enemy really seeks to force it, it will be very hard to shun."

cannon in less than two minutes. And on this particular morning in the cold Atlantic it was well that they could.

Despite the light airs, the two fleets were passing each other at a combined speed of six knots. Keppel shortened sail to slow down, but no ship was opposite another for more than two or three minutes. Still, that meant that in running along the line each French ship and each English ship was fired on, and that the two fleets would take about an hour in all to pass each other.

The heavy cannon balls from the British ships were not doing as much damage to the French hulls as they would have if Keppel had closed the range between the two lines. Meanwhile, the French gunners were cutting up the British rigging with their high-flying chain and bar shot. The *Victory*, in the center of the British line, had already suffered considerable damage when d'Orvilliers's flagship, the *Bretagne*, came down opposite her. As the two flagships rolled past each other, the *Victory*'s gunners scored their best shot of the day; in one thundering broadside they blew open three of the *Bretagne*'s gunports, making a wide gap in her side and killing many of her crewmen. But the French gunners responded by chopping up so much of the *Victory*'s rigging that her masts began to sway perilously.

By 2 p.m. the two fleets were out of range and the firing had died. The *Victory*'s masts were threatening to topple. Smoke swirled through her gun decks, and wounded men lay on the improvised litters in the cockpit waiting for the surgeon to remove splinters of wood or cut away smashed limbs. Gunners mopped sweat from their bare chests and stuffed wads into their ears, which were bleeding from the concussion of the cannon.

On the quarter-deck Keppel began to assess the damage to his fleet. Those in the rear seemed to be hurt worst. And as Keppel watched, d'Orvilliers appeared to be rounding up as if ready for another engagement. Keppel decided to oblige him and signaled to the fleet to form line ahead on the other tack.

At the head of the British line Vice Admiral Sir Robert Harland, commander of the "van," or front squadron, was already coming about. But the *Victory*, sorely damaged, had to be brought about gently before the wind, nursing her tattered rigging. By 3 p.m. Keppel had his van and center ready; but the ships of his rear had not joined the line. The commander of the rear was Vice Admiral Sir Hugh Palliser. His ship, the *Formidable,* had been damaged more heavily than Keppel realized from a distance. Her foremast had been shot away and she was scarcely under way; since Admiralty regulations required all the vessels in a squadron to remain with the leader, the 90-gun *Ocean* and the 74-gun *Elizabeth* could not abandon the *Formidable* and hurry to join Keppel.

Keppel might have done without the rear and ordered Harland up to the front for an immediate attack. However, he doggedly refused to risk further action until he had his entire fleet in a straight line-ahead formation. He waited impatiently for Palliser in the crippled *Formidable* to bring up the ships of the rear. Three hours passed, and Keppel sent a frigate racing back, ordering them to join the line. Still Palliser delayed while he made emergency repairs. It was dusk before the three vessels of the rear formation joined the rest of the fleet.

British Admiral Augustus Keppel, stalemated by d'Orvilliers at the Battle of Ushant, criticized the French for their "paltry game of fighting at a distance."

Keppel's second-in-command, Sir Hugh Palliser, a Tory, blamed his chief, a Whig, for allowing the French to escape, thereby touching off a bitter political row.

Keppel could see that the French had retained—and tightened—their line of battle. Though they had suffered many casualties and considerable damage, their sails and rigging were in better shape than those of the British. Consequently, they could maneuver more effectively. Keppel judged that they were ready to renew the battle. But he decided, with darkness approaching, that it was too late for another engagement. He ordered the fleet to keep in formation until dawn, to stay alert for a possible French attack. Through the night he led his fleet upwind, in hopes of regaining the weather gauge. And through the night the *Victory*'s crew stood to general quarters, trying to keep awake after the exhausting day. Across the water they could see three lanterns, which they took to be the lights of the French fleet still waiting for them.

With the dawn Keppel ruefully discovered that the crafty d'Orvilliers had outsmarted him yet again. Only three French ships, the ones that had shown the lights, were anywhere near him. While they had served as decoys, d'Orvilliers had coolly sailed off with the bulk of his fleet, and the three remaining ships were now crowding on sail to rejoin the main body of its escape eastward toward France.

With widespread damage to their rigging, the British ships had no hope of overhauling the enemy. On July 28 Keppel decided that his fleet was in such disorder aloft that it was unwise even to remain off a hostile coast. He made for home.

Aboard the British fleet 506 men had been killed or wounded, 35 of them on the *Victory*. No ships had been lost, but on July 31 when the Grand Fleet reached Spithead, it sailed into a storm of criticism and recrimination. Keppel blamed Palliser for disobeying orders. Both demanded a formal court-martial, and both were exonerated.

The controversy exposed an unpleasant—and exceedingly dangerous—situation within the Royal Navy: it had become politicized. Palliser was an outspoken conservative Tory and Keppel an ardent liberal Whig. Emotions ran high at the trials. Jubilant Whigs wore light-blue ribbons in their hats with KEPPEL in gold letters; Whig ladies of fashion had made and distributed the hats. As Keppel departed from the court, a band marched before him playing *He Comes, He Comes, The Hero Comes*. So controversial did the issue become that Keppel refused to serve under the ruling Tory Government. He bitterly hauled down his flag, left the *Victory* and retired to await the downfall of the Tories.

As for Admiral d'Orvilliers, in late July he made it safely back to Brest, and a hero's welcome. He had been at sea challenging British rule for the better part of a month, and though he had lost 674 men through death or wounds, not a French ship had been sunk. In the sense that he had outmaneuvered the British and then fought them to a standoff, the Battle of Ushant was the first French success in more than a decade—since the Seven Years' War.

Ushant proved a vastly important point about the changing nature of naval warfare. By refusing to attack the enemy in anything but the traditional, sacrosanct line-ahead formation, Keppel had assured d'Orvilliers's escape. The lesson, however, was utterly lost on the hidebound British Admiralty; in fact, one of the criticisms of Keppel's tactics was that he had come into battle in the first instance without reassembling

"The merest boy of a captain I ever beheld" is how one amazed midshipman described 24-year-old Horatio Nelson, captain of the frigate Albemarle, in 1782. This portrait by John Rigaud was begun when Nelson was 18 and a second lieutenant; it was set aside unfinished when the young officer shipped out to the West Indies in 1777. Upon his return to London four years later, the portrait was completed—now with a captain's proud insignia on the uniform sleeve.

his disordered line. But how he could have accomplished this with the French line already plowing past him the Admiralty did not say.

The clear message of the Battle of Ushant was that the old textbook tactics were no longer good enough. French ships were much improved. And the French hit-and-run tactics—crippling the enemy rigging and running away—could not be countered by the powerful but inflexible line of battle that had served the Royal Navy so well up to now. But the Admiralty had not recognized the message. And now England was plunged into a naval war in which only a major change of tactics could save her from disaster.

Fortunately for England, the Royal Navy, seemingly so tradition-minded, would come up with the new tactics needed to meet and defeat the French in the long series of great engagements that would stretch almost 30 years into the future, from Ushant in 1778 to Trafalgar in 1805.

A chief designer of the new tactics would be the same Horatio Nelson who had arrived, age 12, at the docks of Chatham in 1771. At the time of the Battle of Ushant, Nelson was serving with the West Indies station, the small fleet in the Caribbean that was trying to deal with the privateers of France and of the rebellious American colonies, which were preying on British shipping. Now 20 and a lieutenant, Nelson was rising fast in the service. His boldness and initiative had been recognized by Captain William Locker, master of the *Lowestoffe*, on which Nelson was serving. Locker soon recommended the young Nelson to Sir Peter Parker, newly assigned to command the West Indies station. Parker, equally impressed with the young officer, gave Nelson his first command in the winter of 1778, the brig *Badger*. But it was the advice given to him by Captain Locker that Nelson would never forget: "Always lay a Frenchman close and you will beat him." Bold, aggressive, close-in fighting would become Nelson's trademark—and the essence of the new tactics that would make the Royal Navy once again supreme. But it would still be a while before the Royal Navy was prepared to break with its traditional ways, and in the meantime it was fated to suffer further embarrassment.

Battle at sea, from "all hands" to first broadside

Before joining in battle on the high seas, a British fleet might maneuver around the enemy for hours or even days. During this stalking period, crews went on with their usual routine. But when the time came to sound general quarters, captains prided themselves on the speed and efficiency with which their tars could clear for action. In as little as 20 minutes, a Royal Navy crew could transform a 74-gun ship of the line—the backbone of the fleet—from a simple sailing vessel into a complex and deadly engine of destruction.

At an order from the captain, the boatswain bellowed, "All hands!" and the marine drummer boy (below) rapped out a drum roll calling all 600 men aboard to battle stations. With a speed and agility to astound landlubbers, topmen swarmed into the rigging, climbing 120 feet into the upper shrouds in two minutes to bring in all but the ship's combat-necessary sails, and furling clouds of canvas on the lower yards to lessen the risk of fire aloft. Below, hundreds of other men sprinted to their posts as part of what a sailor of the time, Samuel Leech, called "human machinery."

"Each task has its man, and each man his place," Leech wrote. "Every man is a wheel, a band or a crank, all moving with wonderful regularity and precision to the *will* of its machinist—the all-powerful Captain." It was this perfectly orchestrated performance—this prowess of crew—that proved to be a cardinal factor in the ultimate nation-saving supremacy of the Royal Navy.

Galvanized by the urgent beat of the drummer boy (left), topmen quickly furl the great sail of the mainmast (right); marines with muskets and grenades take position and pass a swivel gun through the lubber's hole to mount by the topmast shrouds. Firing down clouds of grapeshot, the half-pounder could cut a murderous swath through enemy ranks on the decks below, while musketeers sought to pick off opposing topmen and easily identifiable officers. In the distance the British lee squadron hurries to join the ships already in position.

Preceded by a figurehead bearing Britain's royal orb and scepter, the 74-gun ship closes into firing range. Below, a midshipman in the shrouds studies the enemy, and crewmen run out the starboard 32-pound short-range carronade. Larboard, a carronade crew rams home a ball before turning this cannon seaward.

Fleet-footed boys called "powder monkeys" emerge from the forward hatch bearing powder cartridges for the carronade being loaded. Beyond the foremast, stacked with boarding pikes, sailors strain at a block and tackle to lower a longboat, to be used for carrying messages to other ships of the line in battle.

On command from a marine lieutenant (foreground), marines amidships prepare to snipe at the enemy from behind barricades of tightly rolled hammocks. Beside the belfry (center), the boatswain pipes orders aloft as several sailors unfurl a boarding net and hurl the livestock overboard for safekeeping.

Beneath beams where the ship's boats usually are stowed, gun crews load 12-pounders from rows of shot racks framing the ship's hatches. On the quarter-deck, sailors haul on lines lowering the longboat as two powder monkeys race by crewmen carrying the captain's furniture to safety in boats already lowered.

*As the captain paces the quarter-deck with his clerk, a hat-doffing
midshipman serving as signal officer arrives with a message.
Standing on a hatch, the first lieutenant shouts orders into
his speaking trumpet to the topmen, while gangs of sailors haul up
boarding nets. To the rear, the portly shipmaster looks on as four
mates man the helm; above them swings a line of fire buckets.*

Legs splayed in terror, a goat plummets overboard, where the boatswain's mates are hauling sheep into a boat already filled with chicken coops and officers' furniture. Towed behind the man-of-war, the small boats were safe from all but random shot. Afterward, some of the hapless livestock would provide a feast for all who survived the human carnage.

While gun crewmen clear the tackle of a 12-pounder in the captain's cabin, carpenters strike the wooden bulkheads and remove furniture to make way for other guns. The greatest cause of casualties was flying splinters, so temporary bulkheads were not merely hinged out of the way but were carried below. The floor is covered with checkered canvas.

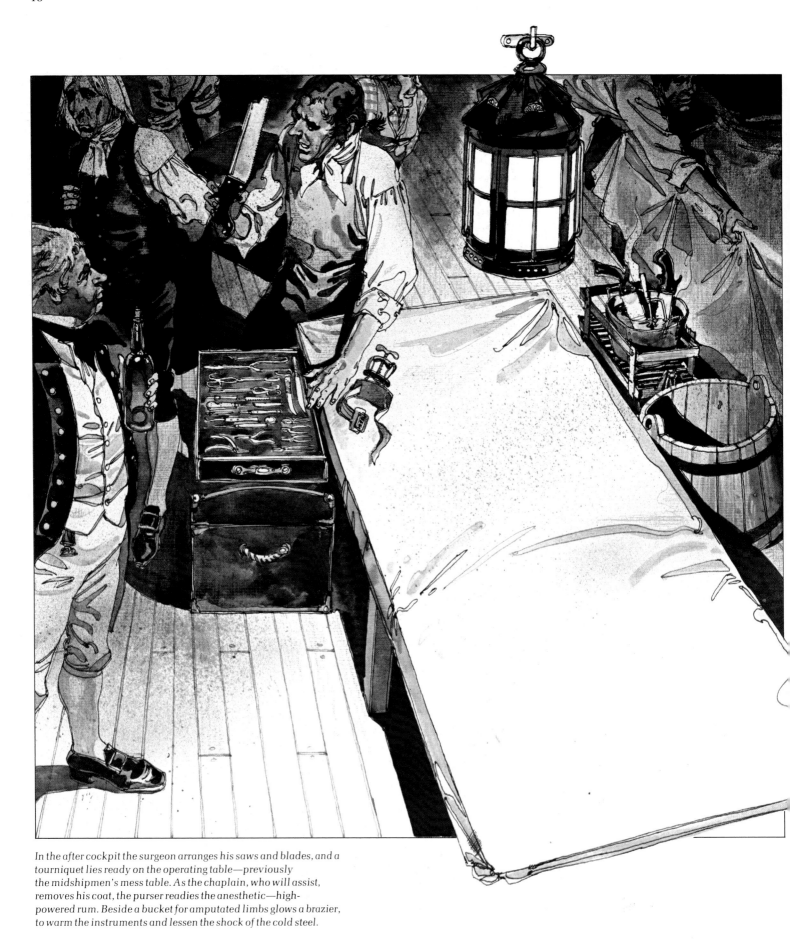

In the after cockpit the surgeon arranges his saws and blades, and a
tourniquet lies ready on the operating table—previously
the midshipmen's mess table. As the chaplain, who will assist,
removes his coat, the purser readies the anesthetic—high-
powered rum. Beside a bucket for amputated limbs glows a brazier,
to warm the instruments and lessen the shock of the cold steel.

In the forward magazine (right) the gunner's mate passes flannel-covered powder cartridges to a helper who serves them to powder monkeys through safety curtains of wet blankets. Both men wear felt slippers to avoid sparks from static electricity. In the background a lantern glows behind a heavy glass window to provide light without risk of fire. Outside the magazine (below) powder monkeys place each cartridge inside a wood or leather "salt box" and sprint up the ladder to their guns. A marine stands guard to prevent anyone from fleeing below.

In an infernal scene of smoke and belching fire, a second lieutenant shouts orders to the crews of the 24-pounders on the lower gun deck, while a midshipman waits to carry messages. After an opening broadside, the guns are now being fired as soon as they are ready. The men are barefoot for better traction.

A gun crew (directly below) wields handspikes to sight their 24-pounder, while to the right another crew holds the tackle of a recoiling cannon just touched off by the gun captain yanking the lanyard. By a tub of hand weapons (bottom) a gunner picks a round shot from a rack, behind which lie wads of felt.

Preparing to run their gun out as soon as loading is completed, members of a gun crew, among them a Jamaican, one of a number in the Royal Navy, plant their feet and take up the slack on the side tackles. At the gun's muzzle, a crewman pushes a charge into the bore, while another gets ready to ram it home.

At the 24-pounder's breech the gun captain starts to jab a stiff wire down the vent to pierce the flannel cartridge preparatory to priming and firing. Buckets (foreground) hold slow matches to discharge the cannon if the flintlocks misfire. Most of the men wear rags around their heads to keep the sweat from their eyes.

Roy Andersen

Chapter 2

A new day for His Majesty's admirals

othing equals the beautiful order of the English at sea. Never was a line drawn straighter than that formed by their ships; thus they bring all their fire to bear upon those who draw near them."

This admiring comment on the Royal Navy's battle formation was made by a French admiral in 1666. It was an accurate description of the tactics that made England supreme on the seas for 100 years—and then failed her utterly at the Battle of Ushant and most importantly at a critical juncture during the American Revolution.

As Keppel had demonstrated so unhappily off Ushant, the essential tactic was the line ahead. The French admiral had described it most accurately: the formation consisted of a perfectly straight line of sailing warships presenting a moving wall of fire against the enemy. In the constantly changing circumstances of naval battle, the line ahead had many advantages. It concentrated the fleet's firepower in one direction. It prevented such accidents as ships of the same fleet firing on one another or firing past or through an enemy ship at a friendly vessel. Most of all, it gave each captain clear and simple directions: he was to hold his place in line and focus his fire on the enemy ship opposite his own.

The first *Fighting Instructions* had been issued in 1653 under Oliver Cromwell, who was an early and ardent advocate of a powerful navy. The rules were revised and expanded in 1703, but the basic tactics remained the same. And of the orders laid down in the *Fighting Instructions*, the most sacrosanct decreed: "All the ships of every squadron shall endeavour to keep in line with the chief." Moreover, the penalty for not holding such a line was "severe punishment"—which could mean anything for a captain from a public reprimand to death, depending on the circumstances. The *Fighting Instructions* reiterated, "None of the ships of the fleet shall pursue any small number of the enemy's ships till the main body be disabled or run."

So the Royal Navy concentrated on its single majestic and overpowering line ahead. Even after the frustrating standoff against the French at Ushant, the Admiralty remained certain that traditional methods would be more than enough to win the naval engagements of the American Revolutionary War. For one thing the American navy was scarcely worthy of the name. As an organization, it had been bungled from the start. Shipbuilding contracts were let for political reasons and construction was delayed. The first American captains were no match for their Royal Navy counterparts. The statistics tell the sad story of America's first navy. Of the 50 warships built and bought for the Continental Navy during the war, all but one were lost to enemy action—having been either sunk, captured or scuttled. Meanwhile, the Americans took only five small ships of the Royal Navy.

The only significant damage done to the British by the Americans at sea was accomplished by the more than 1,600 privateers that were commissioned and sent out to harass British shipping. They captured something like 1,000 British merchantmen and caused an astronomical rise in shipping insurance rates. But they were little more than a nuisance to the Royal Navy, which destroyed even more American shipping. One officer in the Continental Navy managed in 1779 to bring the war into England's

At a time in the 1780s when British admirals were shackled to a set of strict Fighting Instructions, Admiral George Bridges Rodney daringly broke with convention and won a resounding victory at the Battle of the Saints in the Caribbean. Every inch the aristocrat as portrayed here in 1790, Rodney treated his officers like lackeys and coldly reminded them that "the painful task of thinking" was his and his alone.

home waters *(pages 48-49)*. But sensational as was John Paul Jones's victory in the *Bonhomme Richard* over the *Serapis*, it amounted to little more than a psychological blow to the Royal Navy. The real challenge, once again, came from across the Channel.

The belligerency of France in 1778 turned the American Revolution from a shifting series of land battles into a truly maritime war. The armies—British, Hessian, American and French—fought on from the Canadian border to South Carolina. But the ultimate outcome was decided by the Navies of Great Britain and France.

The Battle of Ushant not only demonstrated that the line-ahead formation was outdated, it also showed that the French Navy of 1778 was superior in a number of respects.

This dramatic change could be accounted for in London as well as in Paris. During the 12 years of peace between the Seven Years' War and the American Revolution, the Royal Navy had been victimized by false economies at the Admiralty and profiteering by the Navy's suppliers. Meanwhile, King Louis XV's powerful adviser, the Duc de Choiseul, rallied Frenchmen in a campaign to rebuild their navy. Fund drives supplemented the royal treasury with money to construct new ships. They were named after the groups and towns that contributed, the most impressive being the 104-gun *Ville de Paris*. It was Choiseul who inaugurated the academies of marine architecture that were responsible for the better designed, faster sailing French men-of-war. Under Choiseul's direction, a corps of 10,000 Naval gunners was organized and rigorously drilled in the art of accurate naval fire. By 1770, when Choiseul left office, France had 64 ships of the line and 50 frigates. By 1778, when France entered the war on America's side, she had 80 ships of the line. In the following year, Spain honored the Bourbon family compact with France by declaring war on England, adding 60 ships of the line to the combined force confronting England. The Royal Navy had about 150 major ships to counter these 140, but not all were fit for sea.

Moreover, French gunners were by then more accurate than the British and were at their best at long range. That was important because of the new French strategy of avoiding pitched battle with any enemy force that was not clearly inferior in numbers. The Royal Navy was about to meet its match, but the Admiralty did not yet realize the situation.

Up until now, the Royal Navy had not yet actually lost a battle at sea. The new French tactics of hit-and-run had so far thwarted every British attempt to force a line-to-line slugging match. In one battle after another the British admiral would stubbornly form his line ahead; the French would cut up his rigging and sail away to fight again. In strictly naval terms the situation might be called a standoff. The effects were felt on the battlefields of North America, since the French Navy was increasingly able to deliver reinforcements to the Americans and to the French soldiers who had joined them.

One of those who could see the advantage of the new French naval strategy was General George Washington. For the first four years of the war, with nothing but the ineffectual Continental Navy for support, the American war had gone badly. Now the French Navy was helping to turn the tide. In the summer of 1781, Washington thought he could see the makings of a devastating combined American-French operation. A large French fleet was in the West Indies endeavoring to take advantage of Britain's preoccupation with the colonies and to recapture some of the islands France had lost in the Seven Years' War, 18 years before. If that force, or part of it, could come north to support a campaign that Washington and the French general, the Marquis Gilbert du Motier de Lafayette, were planning, the colonists might win one of the most important victories of the war.

Major General Earl Cornwallis, with more than 7,000 of Britain's finest troops, was encamped in Yorktown, on the Virginia shore of Chesapeake Bay. If a French fleet could block the narrow entrance to the Bay, thereby cutting off Cornwallis' supply line, the Americans and French could launch a pincers attack and wipe out Britain's best army in the colonies. Washington wrote a letter to the French minister to the colonies, the Chevalier de la Luzerne, stressing what the American general saw as the "essential importance" of naval superiority in the war, and pleading for the French fleet to come north.

The commander of the French fleet in the West Indies was Rear Admiral Comte François Joseph Paul de Grasse, an aristocrat born in a feudal castle in the Alpes-Maritimes, now 59 years old and quite an imposing quarter-deck figure at six feet two inches tall—"six feet six inches on days of battle," one admirer claimed. De Grasse responded to the call from the colonies with his entire fleet. En route north he lost two of his ships to the same bizarre type of accident: a sailor doling out the ration of *tafia*, the brandy that was the French equivalent of grog, knocked over a candle and set the ship afire. First the 74-gun *Intrepide* and then the 40-gun *Inconstante* were destroyed this way, and de Grasse ordered that thereafter a responsible officer must preside over every issue of *tafia*.

Still, de Grasse had 28 ships of the line to take north. Crowded aboard the men-of-war were three regiments of French infantry, 100 dragoons and 350 artillerymen—2,500 soldiers in all to reinforce Lafayette's troops. Their equipment and artillery were carried aboard 15 merchantmen that de Grasse chartered with money from his personal fortune. To avoid detection by British frigates in the Atlantic, de Grasse led his fleet through the treacherous, shoal-dotted Bahama Channel between Cuba and the Bahamas. By mid-August of 1781 the entire armada was riding north in the Gulf Stream off Florida, and on the evening of August 29, the fleet dropped anchor inside the entrance to Chesapeake Bay, picking off in the process a few British frigates that had not been quick enough to slip out of the Bay.

It happened that de Grasse's serpentine approach to the colonies had served him in a way he did not know. His departure from the West Indies had been discovered by the British, and Rear Admiral Sir Samuel Hood left Antigua on August 10 with 14 ships of the line to search for him. By sailing a straight-line course instead of cutting between Cuba and the Bahamas, Hood was off the American coast ahead of de Grasse. On August 25, four days before the French fleet arrived, Hood looked into Chesapeake Bay, found that all was clear and sailed on to New York.

The commander of the British fleet in New York, Rear Admiral Thom-

The Yankee "pirate" who humbled the Royal Navy

JOHN PAUL JONES ON BOARD THE *RICHARD*

Though His Majesty's Navy had to admit a certain grudging respect for the American privateers who preyed on British merchant shipping during the Revolutionary War, it had nothing but contempt for the Continental Navy. The American rebels could mount only a haphazard collection of weak and ancient vessels, so poorly crewed that one colonial legislator disgustedly termed them an aggregation of "Tinkers, Shoemakers and Horse Jockeys." Yet there was one American captain who delivered as stinging a slap as the proud Royal Navy had ever received. What is more, he gave it in Britain's sacred home waters—in a classic ship-to-ship action that was witnessed by a huge crowd of Englishmen who watched from the chalk cliffs of Flamborough Head on the Yorkshire coast.

The American's name was John Paul Jones. The son of a Scots gardener, he had shipped out to the West Indies in 1761 at the age of 13. After a short career as a slaver and a trader among the islands, he had slain a murderous seaman in self-defense, decided he would not receive a fair trial on the island of Tobago and fled to Virginia. In 1775 he volunteered as a lieutenant in the new American navy and quickly proved himself as a naval officer. In command of the Continental Navy's 18-gun sloop-of-war *Ranger*, he seized several merchant ships in English waters, raided a coastal town and captured the Royal Navy's 20-gun sloop *Drake*. So exasperating did he become that he was known to the British as the Yankee "pirate."

But all that was only prologue. On the afternoon of September 23, 1779, in the *Bonhomme Richard*, an ancient French merchantman that had been hastily converted to a warship, Jones sighted 41 ships off Flamborough Head. They formed a British convoy under the protection of the Royal Navy two-decker *Serapis*, a copper-bottomed frigate—newer, nimbler and more powerful than the *Richard*.

Captain Richard Pearson of the *Serapis* had been warned by a boatload of local citizens of the *Richard's* approach. As the distance between the two ships narrowed, Pearson could see that he had a clear advantage—50 guns to the *Richard's* 40. And they were bigger guns—twenty 18-pounders to the *Richard's* six. However, Jones had the weather gauge—the advantage of whatever wind there was on this calm day—and he brought the *Richard* slowly down on the *Serapis*. By early evening, flying a British flag as a ruse, he was within pistol shot of the British warship. At this distance the two commanders could talk to each other.

Pearson was the first. "What ship is that?"

Jones whispered to his sailing master, who called back: "The *Princess Royal*."

Pearson tried again. "Where from?" Pause. Pearson continued: "Answer immediately, or I shall be under the necessity of firing into you."

At that, Jones gave an order. A red-white-and-blue ensign replaced the British colors, and the *Richard* cut loose a devastating broadside.

The *Serapis* answered almost simultaneously—and as the heavy balls tore through the oak planking, there was a shuddering explosion from the *Richard's* gun deck. Several powder charges had gone off, killing many of the gunners and putting most of the 18-pounders out of action.

With the *Richard's* heaviest guns gone, that should have been the end of it. But Jones now performed a brilliant maneuver. Backing his fore- and main-topsails, he slowed the *Richard* and turned her across the *Serapis'* stern. He thus put himself in a raking position, in which all the guns along a ship's side can fire the length of the enemy. After a brisk exchange of broadsides, Jones realized that his only chance lay in grappling and boarding the English ship. But Pearson's marines slaughtered Jones's boarders as they struggled to climb onto the *Serapis'* decks.

In the close quarters, Pearson called out to Jones. "Has your ship struck?"

Jones was astonished. He shouted back: "I have not yet begun to fight!"

A full moon had risen over the water, and the crowd watched in awe as Jones sent the *Richard* quickly forward and across the *Serapis'* bow to rake her once again. This maneuver was not successful, but Jones soon got his wish to grapple with his enemy. Just as the *Richard* was passing the *Serapis'* bow, her rigging caught the *Serapis'* bowsprit; the breeze pivoted her around until she came alongside the *Serapis*, bow to stern. Jones called for grappling hooks, and the two ships lay locked together, their guns booming, marksmen sweeping each deck and clouds of smoke swirling from dozens of fires on both vessels.

The murderous pounding went on and on, and the *Serapis'* heavier cannon were doing terrible damage. The *Richard's* hull was riddled; her decks were held up by only a few stanchions. But Jones's sharpshooters were causing carnage on the *Serapis'* decks and clearing the British from the tops as well. Now some of the *Richard's* men climbed out on the yardarms to lob grenades down onto the enemy. Incredibly, one of them, William Hamilton, scrambled clear across onto the *Serapis'* yardarms with a basket of grenades. And from there, taking dead aim, he dropped a grenade neatly through a hatch onto a pile of powder cartridges.

The explosion seemed to lift the *Serapis'* deck. It killed 20 men at the guns, horribly burned many others and knocked out half of the *Serapis'* cannon.

Nevertheless, the *Richard* seemed finished. She was settling in the water. The *Richard's* chief gunner, Henry Gardner, could stand it no longer. He screamed at the *Serapis*, "Quarter, quarter, for God's sake!" Jones grabbed a pistol and flung it, knocking Gardner down. But Pearson heard the cry and called across to Jones.

"Sir, do you ask for quarter?"

Jones replied, "No, sir, I haven't as yet *thought* of it, but I'm determined to make *you* strike." Pearson turned back to his ship and ordered: "Boarders away!" The *Serapis'* surviving marines surged toward the *Richard's* deck, but confronted by the *Richard's* pike-armed defenders, they quickly fell into retreat.

Now Jones dashed to one of the 9-pounders, whose crew had been badly wounded. With superhuman effort, he singlehandedly trained the gun on the mainmast of the *Serapis*, loaded it with double shot and fired, loaded and fired it again and again.

On the *Serapis*, Pearson looked about his decks littered with dead and at the fires burning in a dozen places. At last, he stepped around the bodies to the staff where the red ensign was nailed—and ripped it down.

One of Jones's officers escorted the English captain over to the *Richard's* splintered quarter-deck. Pearson handed his sword to Jones. As he did so, the *Serapis'* mainmast cracked and crashed over the side. Both captains watched the mast and its tangled gear splash into the sea. Then Jones returned Pearson's sword and invited the defeated officer to his smoky, shattered cabin for a glass of wine.

In a fiery three-and-a-half-hour dance of death, John Paul Jones, the American "pirate," had outmaneuvered and outfought one of the Royal Navy's best captains in one of its finest ships. The Admiralty held a court-martial when Pearson was soon after returned to England in an exchange of prisoners. But the court could find no fault with the *Serapis'* captain; he had fought well, and he had, after all, protected the merchant ships from Jones's attack. In the end, Pearson was not only absolved of blame, he was knighted for gallantry. When John Paul Jones heard the news, he exclaimed: "Should I have the good fortune to fall in with him again, I'll make him a lord."

Lashed together, the flaming Serapis (left) and the shattered Richard (behind the Serapis) relentlessly pound away at one another. Victory finally went to the Americans, Jones testified later, because of his "will of a most unalterable resolution."

as Graves, had no news of de Grasse. He was more concerned at the report that another French force, a squadron of eight warships under Commodore Comte de Barras, was transporting a shipment of siege artillery from Newport, Rhode Island, to the French and Americans surrounding Cornwallis at Yorktown. Graves and Hood agreed to join forces and, with 19 ships of the line, to sail for Chesapeake Bay to head off de Barras. While they were about it, they took along supplies and 2,000 troops to reinforce Cornwallis.

New Yorkers thereupon were given a firsthand example of Britain's press gangs at work as the Royal Navy rounded up 400 colonists to help man British ships. A press-gang officer recorded that the procedure "furnished us with droll yet distressing scenes—taking the husband from the arms of his wife in bed, the searching for them when hid beneath the warm clothes, and, the better to prevent delay taking them naked, while the frantic partner of his bed, forgetting the delicacy of her sex, pursued us to the doors with shrieks and imprecations, and exposing their naked persons to the rude view of an unfeeling press gang."

Early on the morning of September 5, as the British fleet approached the mouth of Chesapeake Bay, one of Graves's lookouts announced that there were some masts just inside the entrance. It looked as if de Barras and his squadron had already arrived; the eight French ships would be easy victims for Graves's 19. But as the British fleet drew closer to the mouth of the Bay, the lookouts reported a veritable forest of masts.

Graves did not know it at the time—and it would provide an even nastier shock in due course—but the Comte de Barras's eight-ship squadron was not among the vessels he was studying. De Barras was still en route from Newport laying a circuitous course south as far as the Carolinas to avoid detection by the British. These ships, as Graves would discover, were those of Admiral François de Grasse. There were 24 of them, four vessels having been sent on other missions, and as Graves would also discover, de Grasse was a brilliant tactician.

But for the moment, all the advantage—surprise, position, wind, tide, everything save numbers—lay with the British. De Grasse's fleet was anchored in Lynnhaven Roads along the southern shore and inside Cape Henry. As the British drew near enough to be identified, the French exploded into frantic activity, unfurling sails, slipping anchor cables and leaving them tied to buoys in the harbor. In utter confusion, they scrambled to clear the Bay for the Atlantic, where they could employ their tactics of firing at the British tops and running out to sea.

Graves was thereby presented with an even greater opportunity than he had anticipated on leaving New York. Here was a numerically superior French fleet virtually at his mercy. The wind was northeast, blowing into the Bay; the French were thus up against a lee shore, with an incoming tide against them as well. Nor could they maneuver into any fighting formation because of a shoal, called the Middle Ground, in the center of the Bay's entrance; the ship channel at this period was only three miles wide. All Graves had to do was send his 19 men-of-war down onto this scattered flock of 24 Frenchmen and pick them off one after another.

In fact, the French were in an even more parlous state than they appeared. Nearly 1,300 of de Grasse's officers and crewmen—close to half

Admiral Thomas Graves, who allowed the French to slip through his grasp at the Battle of Chesapeake Bay, was no stranger to errors in judgment. Twenty-five years earlier he had narrowly escaped being cashiered when he mistook a French merchantman for a man-of-war and refused to give battle. In both instances, Graves continued his career. He retired a hero following a wound in 1794.

Comte François Joseph Paul de Grasse, who boldly outmaneuvered Graves at the Chesapeake, was also noted as a supremely tenacious fighter when the occasion demanded. At the Battle of the Saints in 1782 his aides implored him to surrender because they were out of ammunition. Though he eventually had to strike, it was not before he ordered, "Melt my silver plate and have it made into bullets."

of the total—were ashore ferrying the troops and artillery they had brought from the West Indies. De Grasse's flagship, the *Ville de Paris*, was short 200 men. The 74-gun *Citoyen* did not have enough sailors to man her upper-deck guns. De Grasse had ordered the recall signal hoisted, but the boats were too far up the Bay and he had sailed without them.

At the moment, the situation looked hopeless for de Grasse. But soon he could cry out with delight at what Graves was doing—or rather not doing. Instead of sending a spreading net of ships to close the exit to the harbor, the British Admiral was leisurely keeping to the classic formation of the *Fighting Instructions*.

The Union Jack flew at the mizzen peak of Graves's flagship, the *London*, signaling "Line Ahead" as the stately procession moved down on the entrance to the Bay. By the time Graves, maintaining perfect formation, finally reached the Middle Ground at the mouth of the Bay, the fleeing French had largely cleared the entrance, and were in the process of forming a line of their own. Whereupon, still in precise formation, Graves laboriously maneuvered his entire fleet around in the same orderly line, heading back to sea. As if at a formal review, the British fleet sailed into and out of the entrance to Chesapeake Bay.

Each ship kept her place in the formation, without a break in the line. It was an impressive spectacle, precise, orchestrated, beautiful—and utterly worthless. What is more, by reversing his line, Graves had compounded the error: now his weakest ships, which had been in the rear, were in the van and would have to lead the attack, if there was one. He himself was the 10th ship in the line; the new leader was Captain Mark Robinson in the 74-gun *Shrewsbury*.

Following the *Fighting Instructions*, Graves intended to sail along the French line and bombard it to splinters—that is, once the French formed a line. But at this point the French had no line—and with no enemy line to oppose, Graves's single line was helpless.

It was now midafternoon. Rounding Cape Henry, the French ships finally fell into a rough line as they hurried out into the ocean. This gave Graves his chance—but he lost it. Heading for the straggling French line, he kept his "Line Ahead" signal. So his straight, unwavering column brought the British up against the French at an angle, in a V instead of in parallel lines, with the result that only the British van, the lead ships of the line, came close enough to engage the French. Graves then used a combination of signals that was argued about for years thereafter. He hoisted a white pendant with a blue-and-white checkered flag beneath it, signaling: "Bear Down and Engage More Closely." But he also kept his "Line Ahead" signal flying.

"Bear Down" meant every captain could turn toward the enemy and attack the nearest French ship. But this would no longer be a line ahead. And most of Graves's captains, especially Hood, commanding the rear in the *Barfleur*, knew what the *Fighting Instructions* said about that: "Line Ahead" always superseded other signals. So Hood and the others in the center and rear stuck by the book. They kept their straight line.

Graves was thus attacking a superior force with only a part of his inferior force, and de Grasse's gunners shortly proved their mettle. As the converging fleets met at the point of the V, the leading *Shrewsbury* shook under the fire of the leading French ship *Pluton*. One shower of cannon balls swept the *Shrewsbury*'s deck, ripping the left leg off Captain Robinson and killing the first lieutenant and 13 of the crew. Succeeding blasts from the *Pluton* killed 12 more of the *Shrewsbury*'s sailors and injured 46. The *Shrewsbury*'s mainmast and mizzenmast were shot through, and her sails and spars were so riddled and shattered that she had to fall out of the line.

When Captain Anthony Molloy tried to bring the second British ship, the 64-gun *Intrepid*, to the *Shrewsbury*'s support, he came under even heavier fire from the French 74-gun *Marseillais*. With her main-topmast nearly cut in two, her sails in tatters, her rudder damaged, 19 shot holes between wind and water, and 21 killed and 35 wounded, the *Intrepid* also drifted out of the line.

De Grasse's ships did not escape without damage. A broadside from the *Princessa* in the British van swept the decks of the *Réfléchi*, killing the captain. And the *Auguste* ran into a withering fire of British musketry as well as cannon. The *Auguste*'s foretop bowline was shot away, threatening to send the foretop crashing down to the deck. Two French sailors were shot as they climbed up to repair the bowline. A third Frenchman thereupon scrambled to the foretop, repaired it while shot flew around him, and then slid safely back to the deck. Admiral Comte Louis Antoine de Bougainville summoned the young man to the quarter-deck and offered him his purse. But the sailor replied: "You need not pay me for doing my duty, Admiral."

The opening guns of the battle had fired just after noon of September 5. It was almost dusk before Graves lowered his "Line Ahead" signal, which then permitted his captains to turn toward the nearest enemy. But it was too late. The faster French ships were in the Atlantic; de Grasse had escaped what should have been a calamitous trap without the loss of a single ship. In killed and wounded, he had inflicted 336 casualties on the British, while suffering 230 casualties himself.

The British were seething with recrimination. In an angry post-mortem aboard his flagship, the *London*, Graves demanded to know why Hood had not turned out of the line to engage the enemy.

Hood coldly replied, "You had up the signal for the line."

Graves turned to the man who had led the van into action: Rear Admiral Francis S. Drake, a descendant of the great Elizabethan hero. Why, Graves asked, had Drake engaged the enemy?

"On account of the signal for action," Drake replied.

Graves triumphantly turned back to Hood and asked, "What say you to this, Admiral Hood?"

Sir Samuel said calmly, "The signal for the line was enough for me."

It did not help matters that Graves next allowed de Grasse to outmaneuver him again—this time to the disaster of Cornwallis and the British forces fighting at Yorktown. On September 6, seeking to prevent de Grasse from blockading Cornwallis, again Graves went after the French fleet, which was lying off Cape Henry. A merry chase it was. For five days, de Grasse led Graves on a wide circle out into the Atlantic and back toward Chesapeake Bay, slowing when the British fell behind,

speeding up when they began to close, always remaining temptingly and infuriatingly near. It was a superb strategem. For while de Grasse was playing hare and hounds, the eight warships of his comrade-in-arms, the Comte de Barras, arrived at Chesapeake Bay, as de Grasse knew they would, and proceeded to land their heavy artillery for the French and American troops besieging Cornwallis.

To make matters infinitely worse for the hapless Graves, he was now faced with 32 French ships of the line, most of them in better shape than his vessels. And now his fleet was down to 18; the *Terrible* had been so weakened by the battle and subsequent chase that Graves had ordered her scuttled. The crowning blow came when the French took up a blocking position across the entrance to the Bay.

There followed an icy exchange of notes between the *London* and the *Barfleur*. "Admiral Graves presents his compliments to Sir Samuel Hood," and "desires his opinion what to do with the fleet?" Reply: "Sir Samuel presents his compliments to Rear Admiral Graves," and "would be very glad to send an opinion, but he really knows not what to say in the truly lamentable state we have brought ourself." With resignation, Graves summoned another conference in his cabin. There was, all agreed, no alternative. The fleet would have to return to New York for repairs and reinforcements.

This sorry aggregation arrived on September 20. It was a month before a refurbished contingent of 25 ships of the line could sail again for Chesapeake Bay. They were too late. On October 19, just after the British fleet had departed New York, Cornwallis' band at Yorktown played "The World Turned Upside Down," and his troops marched out to surrender to General George Washington and his army.

The fighting on land continued for another year. But the war had been lost for the British at Yorktown, in considerable measure because of the failures of the Royal Navy and its outmoded line-ahead tactics. Yet even this catastrophe did not destroy the Admiralty's faith in traditional methods. For one thing, there seemed no suitable alternative—not one that the Admiralty wished to recognize, anyway. But in fact there was. In Edinburgh, Scotland, John Clerk, an amateur tabletop tactician, a landlubber playing with ship models, had already devised a new set of tactics that would help greatly in making the Royal Navy supreme once again—though it would take awhile for his theories to penetrate the upper echelons of the Naval establishment.

In all his life, John Clerk never went to sea. He was 10 years old before he even saw his first ship, in the harbor at Leith, the seaport for Edinburgh. But he had read the shipwreck saga *Robinson Crusoe* and had become

Nineteen British men-of-war, accompanied by smaller frigates (upper panel, right), maneuver into a precise line of battle as they approach Chesapeake Bay on September 5, 1781, allowing the French time to compose their own line before escaping in the opposite direction. When the laggardly British finally turned to close with the enemy (lower panel), they did so at such an awkward angle that the French rear was never even engaged.

fascinated by a ship model owned by some of his schoolmates. He soon thought of joining the Navy, but was forbidden to do so by his family, who, as he later explained it, "already had suffered heavy losses in both sea and land service."

Young John Clerk had to be satisfied with sailing small boats in Leith harbor and with hours spent on the pier studying the ways a sailing ship employed the wind. He returned home to build ship models, sail them on his father's pond and experiment with rudders and rigging. As he grew older, naval tactics became his hobby—and obsession. He covered his family's tables with charts and drawings of tactics. He carved dozens of wooden ship models, small enough to carry two fleets about in his pockets, so he could work out his formations whenever he found himself with a few spare moments and a table nearby.

He became an Edinburgh merchant. But he doodled endlessly with his battle diagrams, worked out innumerable combinations of ship-of-the line formations with his ship models, and analyzed and reanalyzed the *Fighting Instructions*.

With his fresh eye, John Clerk detected the most serious weakness in the line-ahead formation: it depended for success on the enemy's cooperation; he had to form a line of battle as well. For the most part, the enemy fleets had done so up to now. But with the French Navy adopting its new tactics of hit-and-run, unless the French had a numerical superiority, Clerk concluded that the time-honored line-ahead formation was usually worthless. And when he read about the widely publicized courts-martial of Keppel and Palliser after the Battle of Ushant, he was even more convinced. The issue at court was whether Keppel had formed a proper line ahead, while to Clerk it seemed clear that the French had escaped *because* Keppel had insisted on a line ahead and had waited too long to form it in any case.

This was too much for Clerk. He started to write a book decrying the old tactics and offering some novel ideas of his own. Entitled *An Essay on Naval Tactics*, John Clerk's study was intended as a textbook for Naval officers. It was packed with diagrams and charts, and its major proposition was concentration of fire—"directing the greater part of the force of fleet against a few ships, either in the van or the rear."

It was stunningly simple. Clerk advocated that instead of always parading properly and fighting one on one in gentlemanly fashion, the Navy concentrate on just a part of the opposing fleet, employing all of its ships against a few of the enemy's. The principle depended on a fundamental fact of fighting sail: a vessel's maneuverability was determined by the velocity and direction of the wind. Thus, for example, one could attack the rear section of a line of ships and devastate it before the leading ships could double back to the rescue. A ship of the line might take as long as half an hour or more simply to come about.

In the past, the ships in numerous sea battles had split into separate groups of combatants. But most of these situations had occurred by accident and not by design. The Admiralty had always felt uncomfortable about such instances.

John Clerk became a zealot. He traveled to London, and through friends of friends tried to peddle his ideas to the Admiralty and to any captain or admiral to whom he was introduced. Naval warfare was a popular subject in England in those days; any Royal Navy success brought cheering crowds into the streets, and a loss stimulated editorials, letters, petitions and similar outcries all across the country. Clerk began to attract attention—at least among civilians. Enough friends, acquaintances and Navy buffs were interested in his book to permit a limited printing. But the Navy was something else again. Copies were sent to the Admiralty and to many admirals, only to be greeted with studied disinterest.

Many of the recipients, when asked, said they had not bothered to read the book. Others denied that they had even seen it. One admiral who publicly acknowledged the work and actually went so far as to praise it, did so with the patronizing comment: "And when I reflect that its ingenious author is only a military seaman in theory, I cannot sufficiently express my approbation of it."

But a number of admirals and captains were quietly reading Clerk's book in the privacy of their cabins and studies. One of them was a man who would soon make naval history.

George Bridges Rodney was autocratic, sybaritic, profane—and brilliant. He had been Naval commander in chief in the West Indies before the War of Independence. He had served as governor of Greenwich Hospital for old and infirm seamen when it was described as "a hotbed of the dirtiest conceivable jobbery and thieving." By 1774 Rodney's gambling debts had grown so huge that in order to escape his creditors, he had fled to Paris during a rare period of peace between England and France. When more creditors in Paris threatened to close in on him, he was rescued by a friend: in a grand gesture of *ancien régime* chivalry, the wealthy Louis Antoine de Gontaut, Duc de Biron, proffered Rodney a loan that permitted him to return to London, where in 1779 the Admiralty reassigned him to the West Indies.

It was an even more important post than before. Not only was much of the naval warfare of the American Revolution being fought in the West Indies, but the area also served as the British base for naval actions off the North American coast. Rodney was therefore the recipient of much wellwishing and a great deal of well-meaning advice. According to John Clerk, it was through a mutual friend that Rodney was given a manuscript copy of Clerk's *An Essay on Naval Tactics*.

Admiral Rodney was a member of the conservative school of tactics and a supporter of the line-ahead battle formation. Yet he was also a man with an open mind. He did not comment directly to Clerk. But an acquaintance recalled an evening before Rodney's departure when the admiral sat at a dinner table demonstrating with cherry pits among the port glasses how he planned to break the French line. And when another friend asked Rodney what he thought of John Clerk's theories, the admiral had an oracular answer: "You shall see what I think of it the first time I meet the French fleet."

In fact, he did not employ Clerk's cut-the-line tactics the first time he met a French fleet—though he did depart somewhat from the orthodoxies of the day. En route to the West Indies with 22 sail of the line, he

First Position | Second Position in 2 Motions | Four   Balance   Motions | First Position | Third Position in 2 Motions | Three   Extension   Motions

encountered an enemy squadron off the Portuguese coast, just below Cape St. Vincent. It was the Spanish contingent of a force blockading Britain's base at Gibraltar. In the so-called "Moonlight Battle" on January 16, 1780, in wintry gale winds, Rodney did not wait for the Spaniards to form a line or to form one himself. Ill with the gout, an aged man at 61, he gave his commands from his berth: "Lay me alongside the biggest ship you can, or the admiral if there be one." He did not cut the enemy's line because there was no line to cut. But he routed the Spanish fleet, capturing or destroying seven of the 11 ships.

The blockade of Gibraltar was lifted. Rodney became a national hero and was knighted. He continued on to the West Indies, where he fought two inconclusive battles with the French; in neither of them did he have the opportunity to go for the enemy's line. He remained there for a year, during which he amassed a fortune in prize money from privateers and from a looting expedition against the rich Dutch island of St. Eustatius in the Leewards. Then in the summer of 1781, in great discomfort from the gout and chronic prostate trouble, he returned to England to take advantage of the healing waters of Bath.

By December 1781, as all England was agonizing over the Navy's sorry performance at Chesapeake Bay and the subsequent surrender of Cornwallis at Yorktown, Rodney prepared to return to the West Indies, and went aboard the *Formidable,* a 90-gun ship of the line. But westerly gales delayed his journey and he went ashore to wait the storm out at Cawsand Bay. The son of port Commissioner Paul Ourry later remembered when the admiral and the commissioner propped their gouty feet before the fire and he overheard Rodney declare, "Damme, Paul, if I get near that rascal de Grasse, I'll break his line."

In February of 1782 Rodney was back in the West Indies. His second-in-command was Sir Samuel Hood, who had helped to lose the Battle of Chesapeake Bay. The winner of that battle, Comte de Grasse, had also returned to the West Indies. Rodney and de Grasse finally met in April of 1782, off the island of Dominica.

De Grasse had 33 ships of the line to Rodney's 36. But the French Navy's orders were to avoid pitched battles whenever possible, and under these circumstances de Grasse was convoying an assault force to attack England's most important West Indies possession, Jamaica. Rodney had guessed de Grasse's target; when he had been warned that he should keep protective squadrons near Barbados, St. Lucia and Antigua he had answered, "Oh damn these islands! Jamaica is of ten times more consequence than all of them put together."

De Grasse turned north. Rodney followed. For four days he chased his

Without so much as toppling his topper, an exemplary seaman goes through the knee-flexing bends and lunges of a ballet-like drill designed to teach the fancy footwork that would make him deadly with a cutlass. Genteel as the exercises may appear in this diagram issued by the Admiralty in 1813, they were followed in grim earnest by sailors who knew their skill with a blade would mean life or death upon the call for "Boarders away!"

quarry along the westward shores of Martinique and Dominica. At this point de Grasse became the victim of bad fortune. It first took the form of a series of misadventures by the hard-luck French 74-gunner *Zélé*. On the night of April 10, after two days of chase, the *Zélé* collided with the 64-gunner *Jason*. Both were too damaged to keep up with the rest of the French fleet. The *Jason* was sent off to port for repairs, while the *Zélé*'s crew tried to make their repairs at sea. The next morning Rodney spotted the crippled *Zélé* and sent a few ships to take her. De Grasse countered by coming back to cover her. On the night of the 11th the *Zélé* collided with another French ship, the *Ville de Paris*, and put herself entirely out of action. De Grasse was forced to abandon her; he now had 31 ships, and Rodney, with his 36, was almost upon him.

Moreover, de Grasse found himself in a trap. His northward progress was blocked by a group of islets known as the Saints, between Dominica and Guadeloupe. He considered ducking through the passage between the two islands, but the wind was blowing through the channel from the east. His only open route lay to the south. He would have to double back on his pursuers. But at least—as at Ushant—it would be a passing engagement with the fleets on opposite tacks. They would sail past each other at a combined speed of four to five knots even in the dying breezes. The British gunners would be unable to concentrate on the French hulls, while the French could still cut up the British rigging; it took much pounding to damage stout oaken hulls, but one good broadside of flying chain and bar could slice through great areas of shrouds and braces. De Grasse turned south. And Rodney turned to meet him as he came past.

At first it looked like every other Royal Navy battle for the past century. In an unswerving line ahead, Rodney's fleet moved alongside the French fleet as it filed past. His gunners aimed at the French hulls as de Grasse's gunners sent chain and bar shot slashing through the British rigging; the topmasts of nearly every ship crackled and twisted as the flying shot cut them away.

But now de Grasse became the victim of foul luck from which there was no escape. The wind shifted. It hauled from east to southeast and hit de Grasse's line at the center. The French ships at the center and rear, already close-hauled, had to fall off slightly to keep their wind. Others were taken aback and stalled. Gaping holes appeared in the French line.

Had John Clerk been aboard Rodney's flagship, he would have cheered. Here was the perfect example he had hypothesized in so many diagrams and in so many tabletop maneuvers with his pocket models. The enemy line was open and waiting to be cut.

At this point, Rodney may or may not have suffered an attack of indecision. Only one record survives to tell what transpired on the *Formidable*'s quarter-deck during the next few minutes. Many years later, Sir Charles Dashwood, who had been a midshipman aboard Rodney's flagship, recounted a vivid scene. As he related it, Fleet Captain Sir Charles Douglas had climbed onto the hammock nettings at the forward rail of the quarter-deck to study the ships ahead, and saw the gaps in the French line. One gap was directly ahead. Climbing down, he asked Midshipman Dashwood, "Dash, where's Sir George?" Dashwood had just replied that the admiral was in his cabin when Rodney came on deck.

Doffing his hat, Douglas approached Rodney and urged, "Break the line, Sir George. The day is your own, and I will insure you the victory."

"No," said Rodney, "I will not break my line."

The two men paced the quarter-deck in opposite directions, turning and coming back toward each other. Douglas tried once more. "Only break the line, Sir George, and the day is your own."

This time Rodney replied with grudging permission. "Well, well, do as you like," he said, and went into his cabin.

Douglas immediately ordered the helm to port. The *Formidable* swung across the line of battle and moved through the French line, all guns firing as she went. In the hail of cannon balls from the British flagship the French warship *Glorieux* lost all her masts at once.

The *Formidable* flew no signal for breaking the enemy's line because there was none in her flag locker. And Rodney must have watched anxiously at his stern windows. Whether or not he had been talked into it, he had made a radical decision. The question was whether his fleet, still under "Line Ahead," would break precedent and follow his lead.

Within minutes Commodore Edmund Affleck in the 74-gun *Bedford* went through another opening, splitting it so that the entire British rear could follow the *Bedford* through. Captain Alan Gardner of the *Duke* had in fact preceded Rodney through the line by accident: the wind shift had pushed the French ship opposite him across the *Duke*'s bow. In horror at the thought of being cut off, Gardner looked to the flagship, which was next astern of him, and with vast relief watched the *Formidable* turn through the line. The *Duke* swung over and followed her.

Unlike his compatriot at the Battle of Chesapeake Bay, Rodney immediately hauled down his "Line Ahead" signal, keeping aloft the one for close action. Rounding up on the unprepared Frenchmen on their other side, the British ships isolated and surrounded small contingents of the disordered French line, concentrating four ships against three and in some cases three against one.

The French ship *Ardent*, carrying most of the siege artillery for the attack on Jamaica, struck her colors after a few exchanges of fire. Most of the French decks were crowded with soldiers for the Jamaica assault; they were mowed down by British shot. So many bodies were dumped over the French sides that the sea quickly became tinged with red, and schools of sharks moved in among the ships.

The dismasted *Glorieux* was taken in tow by a French frigate. British men-of-war moved in on them. On the *Formidable*'s quarter-deck, Fleet Captain Douglas, watching the pursuit, was reminded of Homer. As Rodney came back on deck, sucking a lemon, Douglas called to him: "Behold, Sir George, the Greeks and the Trojans contending for the body of Patroclus." Rodney snarled, "Damn the Greeks and damn the Trojans! I have other things to think about."

The 61-year-old admiral, exhausted by the tension of battle, ordered an armchair brought onto the quarter-deck and sank into it. Tossing aside his lemon, he asked a nearby midshipman to make him a lemonade. The midshipman went below and returned with the lemonade, stirring it with the only utensil he could find, a dirty knife. Rodney looked at the knife and said, "Child, that may do very well for the midshipmen's berth but not for an admiral; drink it yourself and go and call my steward to me."

The *Formidable* had gone through the French line at about 9 a.m. The swirling battle went on, with a pause during a flat midday calm, into the late afternoon. By then five of the French ships had struck their colors. The *Glorieux* was cut away from her tow by the British pursuers. The prize of the battle was the 104-gun French flagship, the *Ville de Paris*, on which half-a-dozen British ships concentrated their fire. As her hull splintered and her rigging disintegrated under the storm of shot, the French flagship's gun crews fought back until all their cartridges were gone and they had to ladle the powder into the gun barrels. By late afternoon, her rudder knocked out and her cannon balls used up, the *Ville de Paris* rolled helplessly in the sea as Hood's *Barfleur* came down and sent a last flaming broadside into her. On the *Ville de Paris*'s quarter-deck a tall figure stood by himself. Admiral de Grasse finally hauled down his flagship's colors. As he did, Rodney brought the *Formidable* alongside the *Barfleur,* and officers from both British ships were rowed to the French flagship to climb her side and accept de Grasse's surrender.

On the *Formidable*'s quarter-deck Rodney turned to Douglas and said, "Now, my friend, I am at the service of your Greeks and Romans, for the enemy is in confusion and our victory is secure."

To "that rascal de Grasse" Rodney was generous and courteous. The French admiral was given the run of Rodney's cabins, and professed himself in love with the Misses Rodney as soon as the portraits of Rodney's four daughters were restored to the admiral's cabin from the wine room, where they had been stored during the battle. During the pleasant, peaceful days following the battle, de Grasse strolled the *Formidable*'s quarter-deck, watching the sailors catch a shark and chatting with Fleet Captain Douglas; despite his stay in Paris, Rodney's French was limited, but Douglas was a French scholar. The French admiral confided that he had had to leave his private fortune, amounting to £5,000, in a chest aboard the *Ville de Paris*, and was concerned that the chest might be looted by his sailors. Rodney sent some British sailors over to the *Ville de Paris*; they returned with de Grasse's chest and a few others as well.

For weeks after the Battle of the Saints, and for more than a century since, controversy has persisted. Sir Samuel Hood argued that Rodney should have followed up his victory by pursuing the remainder of the French fleet. Rodney, however, had not slept for four nights. Darkness was falling swiftly, as it does in the tropics, and there would be no moon. The ships were not far from the shoals and reefs of the islands. The French had done their usual damage to the British rigging. Rodney had had enough, and he did not want to risk losing one of his ships—or any of the prizes he had captured. By next morning, when Hood came aboard the *Formidable* to urge a chase, the surviving ships of the French fleet were already below the horizon. "Come, now," said Rodney, "we have done very handsomely as it is."

With understandable satisfaction Rodney dispatched a fast frigate to London with the message: "It has pleased God, out of his Divine Providence, to grant to His Majesty's arms a most complete victory."

Englishmen reacted to Rodney's news with pent-up hysteria. It was

Rodney's flagship Formidable (flying the white flag, center background) smashes through the French line at the Battle of the Saints on April 12, 1782. The admiral's revolutionary maneuver set the French to rout and ushered in a new era of naval tactics. But on another level, the great victory was something of a disappointment: because Rodney managed to capture a mere five ships, his reward for the stunning victory amounted to only £5,016 in prize money.

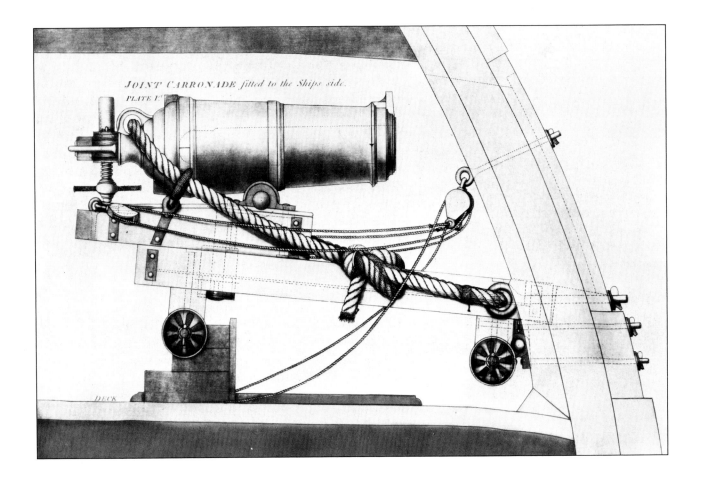

the Royal Navy's most decisive victory since the naval engagements of the Seven Years' War. Rodney was rewarded with a peerage and an income of £2,000 a year; Hood was also given a peerage, and two more of Rodney's captains were knighted.

At the Battle of the Saints, Rodney had launched a new day in naval warfare. Since the Seven Years' War, British admirals had fought the enemy in the line-ahead formation, and had never won so decisive a victory—until Rodney cut through the enemy's line off Dominica.

His victory was compounded of other elements besides the new tactics. A major contributor was Rodney's fleet captain, Sir Charles Douglas. Historians have questioned Midshipman Dashwood's recollection that it was Douglas who talked Rodney into adopting Clerk's tactics, but Clerk later claimed that he had personally demonstrated his maneuvers to Douglas in London before the Battle of the Saints. Douglas deserves much of the credit for other reasons. He was a brilliant innovator, who markedly improved the British rate of fire. Douglas substituted flannel for silk as a powder cartridge; flannel was more flammable than silk and thus left no smoldering remnants in the breech of the cannon, which in turn meant the elimination of the worming in order to extricate the still-burning cartridge fragments. Another Douglas innovation was to moisten the wads between powder and ball, also reducing the possibility of their igniting and the need for the worm.

Called "the smasher" by the British—and the "devil gun" by the French, who were its targets—the stubby carronade was designed for close quarters and in its biggest models fired an immense 68-pound ball propelled by five and a half pounds of powder. Introduced in 1779, it played a major role in the Battle of the Saints; the French did not devise anything equaling its powers of destruction until 1799.

Yet a third Douglas improvement was a perforated goose quill filled with powder; it could be thrust into the cannon touchhole much more quickly and efficiently than the old method of pouring a portion from a powder horn. Hundreds of these goose quills were ready for instant use in the Battle of the Saints.

Among the most important of Douglas' contributions was one that materially increased the rate of fire. He devised a system of lead springs and weights that worked to absorb the recoil of the cannon and made their return to firing position much easier and quicker. But the greatest Douglas invention was an intricate block-and-tackle arrangement that enabled a crew to aim a gun with greater accuracy and flexibility. Besides the wedges that had lifted or lowered the muzzle, Douglas' tackle permitted a wider arc when training the gun. Douglas' reforms enabled gun crews to aim as much as 45 degrees in either direction; when approaching an enemy, they could get in as many as three shots before the enemy was in position to reply—and when departing, they could deliver an equal sting after the enemy had been forced to cease fire. At the Battle of the Saints the gunners of de Grasse's flagship, the *Ville de Paris*, were dumfounded by the concentrated fire they were receiving.

The British had yet another surprise for the French. On his last visit to England, Rodney had been introduced to a devastating new weapon. It was a large, short-barreled gun called the carronade because of its origin at Scotland's Carron Iron Works. Mounted on a track that provided more friction than the wheels of a ship's gun, thus reducing the recoil, the wide-muzzled carronade could fire a monster 68-pound ball with a five-and-a-half-pound powder cartridge. The carronade was useless at long range but murderous close up. And because the island of Dominica prevented the French line from falling away, most of the Battle of the Saints was fought at close range. When the *Formidable* went through de Grasse's line, Rodney's carronades accomplished more damage and slaughter than a dozen big guns could have caused at a distance. Of the five French ships that were captured, three were the victims of carronades blasting into their sterns.

With the aid of these technological, strategical and tactical advances, Sir Charles Douglas, Lord Rodney and John Clerk had formed an unlikely triumvirate to alter the tactics of fighting sail forever.

Rodney praised Douglas but did not mention Clerk in his report on the Battle of the Saints. But on his return to London he acknowledged his debt to the amateur admiral of Edinburgh by contributing to an edition of Clerk's book a series of salty, self-revealing footnotes, among them: "The naval instructions want a thorough reformation; but 'tis not in the power of every commander-in-chief to make what additions he pleases." And, "There will ever be a manifest advantage in obliging your enemy to depart from their original intention, and attacking them in a different mode from that they offer you."

In a word: surprise. Splitting the enemy's line and doing the unexpected would be the tactic adopted by a new generation of fighting admirals who were only now stepping onto the quarter-decks of the Royal Navy. And it was just in time, because the Royal Navy's greatest challenge of all was about to arise.

Chapter 3

A bloody nose for Napoleon at the Nile

he little man on the quarter-deck could scarcely be seen over the high weather rail as the ships sailed past, each dipping its colors in salute in the pale light of the early morning. The *Orient*, armed with 120 guns and flagship of the French fleet, was positioned outside the harbor of Toulon while the ships filed into the Mediterranean. On her quarter-deck Napoleon Bonaparte, scarcely five feet three inches tall, watched his enormous fleet fall into formation in a freshening breeze: 13 great ships of the line, 42 frigates and other smaller vessels, plus 130 troop and supply transports. It was just after daybreak on May 19, 1798, and Napoleon's armada was embarked on a daring enterprise that he had concocted to befuddle and cripple the hated enemy, the English.

Though he was the strong arm of the Directory of revolutionary leaders who were ruling France, he was not yet the country's undisputed emperor. He was about to prove his strategic as well as tactical genius, he was certain, by using this armada setting sail across the Mediterranean. Napoleon's successful military campaigns on the Continent had persuaded him that England alone stood in the way of France's domination of all Europe. He was convinced that the one way to ruin England was to jeopardize the richest colony of her empire; and that colony, since the loss of the American possessions, was India.

The route to India lay through Egypt, and so Napoleon's fleet was bound eastward. Aboard the transports and crowding the men-of-war were 34,000 sailors and soldiers, 700 horses and more than 1,000 pieces of field artillery. In the Mediterranean, this host would be reinforced by three smaller contingents from other ports, increasing the total manpower to 55,000. With a force of this size Napoleon expected to overrun Egypt and strike overland through the Middle East to India before the British could mount a challenge.

It appeared that Egypt would be an easy conquest for the well-drilled troops of Napoleon's army. The country, under the nominal rule of the Sultan of Turkey, was actually governed by the Mamelukes, a military order descended from earlier slaves. Two Mameluke chiefs, known as beys, Murad and Ibrahim, ruled Egypt's peasants with a heavy hand, and Napoleon expected to have little trouble overthrowing them.

The whole plan was still a secret; Napoleon had shared it with only a few of the top officers in the fleet. Some of the civilians must have guessed, however. They made up their own small army of 500 experts and technicians whose findings they hoped would prove useful to any future French settlers in Egypt. Napoleon, who never thought small, intended not only to conquer the Egyptians but also to study their country and transform it into a valuable colony of France.

But his grand design was fraught with danger. Though his army was magnificently trained and equipped, the navy he commanded had only recently been brought back from the abyss of destruction. It had not been endangered by foreign enemies, but by the government itself.

After the French Revolution in 1789, the new masters of France had demolished the Navy as a matter of principle. Under Louis XV and his grandson, Louis XVI, the French Navy had belonged to the lesser aristocrats; one officer on the Navy List had as his sole assignment the task of

Resplendent in dress uniform after the Battle of the Nile, Nelson displays a chest sparkling with the rewards of gallantry in this 1798 portrait by Lemuel Abbott. But Nelson's hat bears the decoration that intrigued him the most—a diamond-studded aigrette from the Sultan of Turkey. The aigrette, according to Nelson, had "a radiant star in the middle, turning upon its centre by means of watch work which winds up behind."

certifying that applicants to the French Naval Academy were of noble birth. During the Reign of Terror from 1793 to 1794 three quarters of the Navy's proud officer corps had died on the guillotine or fled into exile. Aboard the ships, discipline disappeared; ordinary seamen voted on what orders they wanted to obey, and practical command fell to the demagogue with the loudest voice.

The ships themselves, though superior in design to those of the British, had suffered from the Revolution as well. Their arms were commandeered for revolutionary forces, as were all manner of stores. Furthermore, the Navy had to make do for repairs with whatever it could scrounge, and the canvas, timber and iron that it used for French men-of-war were often of inferior quality.

In time, the Directory that ruled the country recognized the error. France had embarked on a war of imperial conquest in 1792, fighting England, Austria, Prussia and Holland. While most of the early campaigns were fought in Europe, it eventually became obvious to its leaders that to achieve its real goals, France must conquer, or at the very least neutralize, the huge battle-hardened Navy of England. Thus, while Napoleon, a general at 28, had been leading his troops to victory in battles against the Austrians in Northern Italy, the Directory was attempting to restore the French Navy. Discipline and morale had been reestablished to some extent, largely through the efforts of a new generation of French Naval officers, which included some aristocrats who had been lured out of hiding by desperate members of the Directory. A new shipbuilding program had been started, though its results were not yet being felt.

Embarking on his Egyptian campaign, Napoleon was forced to rely mostly on repaired and refurbished ships of the line. He had serious reservations also about the abilities of the Naval officers he had inherited. Few of his fighting captains were as experienced as their Royal Navy counterparts; in fact, a number were recently recruited merchant masters, relatively unfamiliar with naval tactics, signaling and gunnery. Even had he been blessed with the best of officers, he knew that he was taking an enormous gamble in sending a fleet slowed by transports across the Mediterranean while the Royal Navy lay in wait. But Napoleon was nothing if not a gambler, and he watched with a steady eye as his vessels formed up off Toulon.

It took eight hours for all the ships to work their way out of Toulon and join the formation. The fleet did not sail directly to Alexandria, but first made for the island of Malta. This was one of the ingenious parts of Napoleon's grand plan. Malta was situated in the very heart of the Mediterranean; by controlling it France could control the entire sea and thus disrupt British communications with the Middle East.

Since 1530 the island had been ruled by the Knights of Malta, descendants of returning crusaders who had settled there after their exile from the Isle of Rhodes. The major business of the Maltese was petty piracy— and like pirates everywhere they understood overwhelming power. When Napoleon's forces arrived they had little trouble; there were a few pockets of resistance, then the Knights surrendered the island. For eight days the French soldiers and sailors, on a rare liberty, roamed the capital

city of Valletta, looted Malta's treasures and enjoyed its sweet oranges and willing women. For once there was no danger of large-scale desertions; where would a man go on that tiny island? At last, leaving behind a garrison of 3,000 men dumfounded at their good fortune, Napoleon on June 19 reembarked his troops and took his fleet into the Mediterranean. This time, he announced that their destination was Alexandria.

The grand fleet proceeded southeastward at the speed of the slowest transports, which was scarcely three knots. At that rate it would take the fleet two weeks to reach Egypt. As on the two-and-a-half-week voyage from Toulon to Malta, the soldiers aboard the crowded ships became seasick almost as soon as they cleared the harbor. Seasick and pale himself at first, Napoleon kept to his berth, his eyes closed, as his secretary read to him from the Bible and from the Koran, both of which Napoleon had listed in his traveling library under the heading of "politics." When he gained his sea legs after a few days, Napoleon climbed to the *Orient*'s quarter-deck to watch gunnery practice beside Admiral François Paul de Brueys, one of the survivors of the old Navy. Napoleon also felt well enough to conduct sessions on politics, economics and religion with his staff officers and civilian savants. In the evenings he engaged in card games, at which he typically cheated and then returned his winnings. However, he was restive and preoccupied. From the moment that the fleet had departed from Malta on its crawling passage to Egypt, fast frigates had been circling the convoy day and night on the lookout for the inevitable British pursuit.

The third night out was foggy, with virtually no visibility. But something was going on: in the distance Admiral Brueys could distinctly hear the booming sound of cannon signaling from ship to ship. By the number of shots, he surmised that it was a major fleet. In this part of the Mediterranean that could only be the Royal Navy.

The build-up at Toulon had not escaped the attention of the British Admiralty. But its purpose was puzzling. Where was the big fleet headed? For England's back door, Ireland? For the English Channel and Britain's own shores? There were many guesses, but few of them included Egypt. Earl Spencer, First Lord of the Admiralty, sent a worried message to John Jervis, commanding the British fleet off Cadiz that was blockading a force belonging to France's Spanish ally. Jervis should put a watch on Toulon and be prepared to intercept the fleet when it came out. If Jervis himself could not lead the squadron, Spencer had his own candidate: the up-and-coming Rear Admiral Sir Horatio Nelson.

The choice would bring recriminations from the many admirals senior to Nelson. But as if by telepathy Jervis had already decided on the same man. On May 2, 1798, the day Spencer sent his message, Jervis dispatched Nelson with three ships of the line, two frigates and a sloop to have a look at Toulon.

Nelson was 39 and had accumulated considerable experience—though not so much as he might have wished. After his two commands in the West Indies aboard the brig *Badger* and the frigate *Hinchingbrooke*, he had spent much of the decade of peace between 1783 and 1793 on the beach at half pay, as was customary in the Royal Navy. His

An imperious Napoleon Bonaparte comes ashore after accepting the surrender of Malta, a tiny but rich and strategic Mediterranean isle. Confronted by a "sea covered for miles with ships whose masts resembled a huge forest," the defending Knights of Malta, who were descendants of crusaders, offered only token resistance before bowing to the French, who not only set up a base but also looted the place of its ancient treasure.

duty in the West Indies had led to his marriage to Frances Nisbet, widow of a Nevis Island doctor. The couple returned home, Nelson chafing for action. He had spent some time in France seeking to learn the language, without much success.

At long last, in 1793, he had been recalled to command the ship of the line *Agamemnon*, which he termed "one of the finest 64s in the service," and from then on he was ascendant. Curiously, his first major action against the French was on land. While in the Mediterranean he was detached with a party of seamen and marines to build artillery batteries at Bastia and Calvi during the British attack on the French island of Corsica. At Calvi he had lost the sight of his right eye to a stone splinter during a cannonading of his fortifications.

Returning to sea in the *Agamemnon*, he played a gallant role in a battle against 15 French men-of-war in 1795, during which he outfought and helped capture the 80-gun *Ça Ira* off Toulon. He was named a commodore in 1796 and was put in command of the 74-gun *Captain*. And it was in this man-of-war that he scored his first truly great coup, being largely responsible for victory in the Battle of Cape St. Vincent, fought against France's ally Spain off the coast of Portugal on February 14, 1797.

In the *Captain*, Nelson was part of a 15-ship squadron under Jervis cruising the eastern Atlantic when they came upon a Spanish fleet of 27 ships of the line. Despite the heavy odds, Jervis immediately ordered an attack. The Spaniards had not yet formed a line but were bunched in two groups: a van of nine, followed by the main force of 18 ships. Diving into the gap between the two, the British line poured broadside after withering broadside into the main Spanish force. Jervis then planned to reverse course swiftly and return to close with this cluster of 18 enemy ships. But his line was slow in making the reverse turn. And now the Spaniards attempted to slide around the tail of the British line and form up with their nine-ship van, thus bringing their full number to bear.

Nelson, on the quarter-deck of the *Captain*, third from the last in the British line, instantly grasped the situation. Without a moment's hesitation he broke ranks, came about and threw himself across the bows of the 18 onrushing Spaniards.

It was a cardinal sin, an act of unprecedented insubordination; in the Royal Navy one followed one's admiral's orders. Yet Jervis, to his everlasting credit, acknowledged the courage and brilliance of Nelson's move and quickly ordered two ships to follow suit. The *Captain* was by that time in close action with the gigantic 130-gun *Santisima Trinidad* and six other Spanish vessels. With his wheel shot away and his foretopmast gone, Nelson plowed his wreck of a ship into the enemy throng and sent his marines piling over the rail onto the deck of the 80-gun *San Nicolas*. Boarding the enemy ship himself by means of an upper quarter-gallery window, Nelson fought his way to the deck, where the surprised Spanish officers surrendered.

Just at that moment a volley of small-arms fire rattled out from the stern of a second Spanish ship, the 112-gun *San Josef*, which in the melee had fouled the *San Nicolas* and was locked alongside. Nelson gathered his marines for another assault and jumped onto the main chains of the *San Josef*. But the Spaniards had no stomach for further

Beneath the ensnarled rigging of two Spanish ships at the Battle of Cape St. Vincent, Nelson (in white) and his marines, after crossing and capturing the 80-gun San Nicolas, cut their way directly onto the deck of the great 112-gun San Josef. On the poop deck above, a Spanish officer is about to surrender the ship. Nelson later lightly referred to this remarkable double catch as "Nelson's Patent Bridge for boarding First-Rates."

battle. As Nelson climbed onto the deck, an officer leaned over the rail and surrendered the ship. Thus the audacious young commodore had bagged two prizes with a single boarding party.

In the end, two more Spanish ships were captured and the fleet was put to rout without the loss of a single British vessel. For his gallantry Nelson was made an admiral and a Knight of the Bath. Equally important, he won the acclaim and gratitude of his commander, Jervis, who himself was created Earl St. Vincent because of the victory.

The audacity that marked Nelson at the Battle of Cape St. Vincent showed itself again within a few months—though this time with near-fatal results. The British had learned that a Spanish treasure galleon had put into Santa Cruz de Tenerife in the Canary Islands. Nelson suggested to his mentor, the newly created Earl St. Vincent, that he be allowed to go after it, and the earl readily agreed. On the night of July 24, Nelson descended on the island with four ships of the line plus three frigates

His right elbow shattered by a musket ball, Nelson is dragged aboard a landing boat after a disastrous amphibious 1797 assault on the island of Tenerife. His ill-conceived scheme to seize Spanish treasure ships in the harbor was foiled by adverse weather and staunch defenders. On his return to his ship, he shouted, "Tell the surgeon to get his instruments ready. I know that I must lose my arm, and the sooner it is off the better."

Nelson's combination knife and fork, shown here next to its case, made dining somewhat easier after the loss of his arm. The "left handed Admiral," as he took to calling himself, confessed that he had rather expected to lose a limb in the course of his career, but he was apparently much surprised by the slowness of his recovery. "He suffers a great deal of violent pain, and takes opium every night," a friend remarked two months later.

and a cutter. In order to capture the prize, it was necessary to secure the island. But nothing went right. Bad weather, tricky inshore currents and a stout defense by the Spanish garrison foiled the British landing parties. As Nelson personally led the assault, a musket ball shattered his right arm. "I am a dead man," Nelson cried. But seamen rowed him back to his ship, the *Theseus*, for this action, where the surgeon successfully amputated his arm. As he was recuperating at sea, Nelson despondently wrote Earl St. Vincent to say that "a left-handed admiral will never again be considered useful."

Injuries aside, he was the frailest admiral in the fleet; he stood barely five feet seven inches and weighed no more than 130 pounds. Moreover, he suffered periodic fevers brought on by malaria contracted in Central America during his tour of duty in the Caribbean. Cold nights on deck brought on racking coughs; nervous anxiety caused him sleeplessness and weakness from loss of appetite; and most of the time—an awful fate for a sailor—Nelson was seasick.

Yet there was something altogether exceptional about the man that had made Lord Spencer and Earl St. Vincent, each acting on his own, reach down through the admirals' list for Nelson at a critical moment. This one-armed, one-eyed, emaciated little man was transformed by battle. He was a brilliant tactician, and the sound of guns, the smell of smoke, the presence of death turned him into a fearless, savage and relentless fighter. If anyone could be counted on to track the Toulon fleet, intercept it and pound it to destruction, St. Vincent reasoned, it was Horatio Nelson.

But Nelson's mission got off to an almost disastrous start. His three ships of the line—his own *Vanguard*, Captain Sir James Saumarez' *Orion* and Captain Alexander Ball's *Alexander*—were east of Gibraltar bound for Toulon when on May 20 a gale surprised them and dismasted the *Vanguard*. Under a spritsail, Nelson for two days clawed off a rocky shore. When the gale abated somewhat, Ball brought the *Alexander* alongside and took the *Vanguard* in tow. The three ships struggled toward safety in Sardinia, but heavy swells threatened to drive them ashore. At last, believing that the *Vanguard* was lost and that the *Alexander* could still escape, Nelson ordered Ball to cut loose and save himself. Through his speaking trumpet, Ball shouted: "I feel confident that I can bring her in safe. I therefore must not, and by the help of Almighty God I will not, leave you!" Ball was right. They made it to the Sardinian island of San Pietro, and Nelson went aboard the *Alexander* to thank his savior. If the proverb he quoted was a cliché, the gratitude it expressed was real. "A friend in need," he told Ball, "is a friend indeed."

It was May 27 by the time the *Vanguard* had her new masts and she and the *Orion* and *Alexander* were ready to go to sea. To sea they immediately proceeded, and the following day encountered a merchantman from Marseille, from whose captain they extorted the information that the Toulon fleet had already sailed.

Where to? Nelson could only guess. He had no fast frigates to send scouting for them. There had been frigates in his little fleet before the storm, but their commander, seeing the damage to the *Vanguard* as he himself was driven away, had assumed that Nelson would return to Gibraltar for major repairs and had taken the frigates there. But Nelson did not know that this had happened. Thinking that his frigates were still at sea, he headed for a prearranged general rendezvous that was some distance from Toulon, where he hoped to find his swift scouting craft and send them out reconnoitering for Napoleon.

Reaching the spot, Nelson found no sign of the frigates. But the following morning he received welcome news, brought to the rendezvous by Captain Thomas Hardy in the brig *Mutine*. St. Vincent had gotten reinforcements and had immediately sent off a frigate and 10 ships of the line to reinforce Nelson's meager squadron. Their captains were among the elite of the Royal Navy; most of them were old friends of Nelson's. On June 7 they arrived. There were many greetings and a council of war was convened, in which all agreed that they should proceed eastward without delay to search for the Toulon fleet.

Off Naples they halted long enough to discover that the French fleet was headed for Malta. Nelson altered his course for Malta. But off Sicily they hailed a passing ship whose master reported that the French had already captured the island. What now?

Nelson polled his captains. Most believed that if the French were not at Sicily, which was obvious, Napoleon's destination most likely was Egypt. And one of them even divined Napoleon's grand strategy. Wrote Thomas Troubridge, captain of the *Culloden*: "I am led to think Egypt is their present destination, as their getting possession of Alexandria or any part of Egypt will put our possessions in India in a very perilous situation." Off Nelson raced in hot pursuit.

He had a plan, brilliant, unconventional and likely to bewilder the French. Instead of the usual unwavering line-ahead formation, Nelson had divided his own fleet into three groups. Two groups would drive down onto Napoleon's warships from different angles, scatter them and concentrate on a few ships at a time. The third section would wade in among the transports, picking them off while their protectors were fighting for their own lives.

But it was a plan never tried. The same impetuosity that made Nelson irresistible on the attack made him vulnerable in the chase. In his anxiety to find his quarry, he raced past it. While the Toulon fleet crawled through the fog, its admiral anxiously listening to the British signal guns, the English ships sped past toward Egypt. The pursuer preceded the pursued all the rest of the way across the Mediterranean. On June 28 Nelson's ships backed their mainsails off Alexandria. There was no sign of the French. Nelson now wondered if he had been devastatingly wrong. Had the passing captain been mistaken or lying? Had the Toulon fleet sailed west instead of east? Was it even now on the other side of the Strait of Gibraltar and headed for the English Channel? In desperation Nelson ordered full sail back across the Mediterranean—and thereby compounded his first error.

In laying his course for Alexandria the youthful Napoleon had not relied on fog alone; he had also depended on his wits. Instead of sailing in a direct line from Malta to Alexandria, the Toulon fleet took a more roundabout course, picking up the coast of Crete before turning southeast for Egypt. After a two-week passage, the fleet reached Alexandria on July 1, two days after Nelson's departure, and Napoleon was told that a large British fleet had just departed the area.

Now Bonaparte faced the problem of the landing. In a council of war held aboard the *Orient,* everyone agreed that it would be suicidal to attempt a landing inside Alexandria harbor. The good weather had given way to a gale coming from the north. Alexandria's defenders were waiting; both entrances to the harbor were narrow, and the French forces would be slaughtered as they tried to enter the harbor. Admiral Brueys voted for an overnight wait for the storm to subside and a landing at nearby Abukir bay. However, Napoleon would not wait. "Admiral," he said, "we have no time to waste." He ordered a landing on a beach at Marabut, a village eight miles to the west of Alexandria.

Through a wild night of storm and surf, with boats capsizing and smashing on the rocks and men drowning in the surf, Napoleon's troops were landed. Without waiting for horses, artillery, food or even water, Napoleon led his soldiers across the desert and at eight the next morning attacked the city. By 11 a.m. Alexandria had fallen. One French officer wrote home: "I can assure you that it was thirst that inspired our soldiers in the capture of Alexandria."

Before going ashore to lead his troops, Napoleon had another disagreement with Admiral Brueys. It ended in a compromise. Napoleon wanted his fleet to anchor in Alexandria's harbor as soon as he had taken the city. Brueys wanted to return to Toulon or to the island of Corfu instead of sitting in Alexandria waiting for the British to pounce on him. He finally agreed to remain in the area, though not in Alexandria's bottlenecked harbor. Taking the fleet 23 miles east, he went into Abukir bay—the spot where he had wanted to land in the first place.

In Brueys's opinion, Abukir was a much more readily defensible area. The bay extended 30 miles in a long curve, ending at one of the two mouths of the Nile, near Rosetta. Eons of silting from the river had created a maze of channels and shoals throughout the bay, making it a trap for any ships unfamiliar with its soundings. Brueys improved on the natural defenses by mounting a battery of four guns and a mortar on an island inside the bay's entrance. Then he anchored his ships in a line alongside a shoaling sandbank, as close to the shelving shallow water as he dared. He ordered the upper yards of the ships brought down; at anchor there would be no need for sails, and with the spars down there would be no danger of their toppling onto the gun crews if there was a battle. Brueys's line of ships therefore made a formidable floating fortress: they were backed up close to the sandbank, with 500 guns aimed outward, ready to shatter any fleet that attempted to come in after them. Satisfied that his position was impregnable, Brueys settled down to wait for the British—if they could find him.

Nelson's fleet reached Syracuse on July 19. There was no news of the Toulon fleet. After three days of reprovisioning, he extended his search to Greek waters. Then on July 28, in the Gulf of Koroni, in southern Greece, he received his first real news in a month from two vessels that had sighted the French fleet off the coast of Crete four weeks earlier,

In his newly learned left-handed scrawl, Nelson lists his various hurts and wounds for an unknown admirer. Nelson, who endured more operations than any other flag officer of his time, sums up all his injuries with the quip, "tolerable for one war." In fact, Nelson, plagued throughout his adult life by headaches, seasickness and fevers, was rarely free from suffering.

Wounds received by Lord Nelson
His Eye in Corsica
His Belly off Cape St. Vincent
His arm at Teneriffe
His Head in Egypt.
Tolerable for One War

Written in 1803, by Lord Nelson, at the request of a gentleman who wished to have a statement of his wounds

headed southeastward. The same day, Ball in the *Alexander* captured a French prize with similar information. The French fleet had in fact gone east; the British had somehow missed it twice. In a fury of frustration, Nelson was determined that he would not miss it again.

Throughout the fruitless chase to Alexandria and back, Nelson had kept everyone ready for action at any moment. Now the tempo and the tension increased. Gun drill was held each day. The crews stood ready to clear for action. In the admiral's cabin or on the quarter-deck of the *Vanguard*, the conferences continued; in them every possible battle situation was proposed and the tactics for each were discussed.

The conferences were a Nelsonian innovation. The admirals of the earlier generation had kept their own counsel, and orders were given by flag signals, such as they were, during the battle itself. Nelson not only knew that he did not intend to fight by the book; he was also well aware that the Royal Navy's signal system was still crude and subject to misunderstanding. He intended something more, and this was his most important innovation. More than any other 18th Century admiral, Nelson believed in sharing tactical options with his captains, discussing every possible situation and emphasizing that when battle was in progress, every captain would be on his own. If a captain saw an opportunity to do damage to the enemy, he was free to attack without awaiting signals from the flagship's masthead. The old line-ahead dogma of each ship's blindly following the leader was not only dead, it was replaced by something previously unheard-of in the Royal Navy: delegation of authority.

Not surprisingly, the Naval officers with whom Nelson thus shared his problems and responsibilities felt that they were something special—as indeed they were. Nelson unabashedly called them his "Band of Brothers." With an equal lack of embarrassment they called themselves "The Chosen Band." As they sat around the admiral's table in the *Vanguard*, under a ceiling dancing with sunlight reflected from the Mediterranean, they made an oddly assorted group.

Sir James Saumarez of the *Orion,* tall, erect and slightly supercilious, contrasted with Nelson's flag captain, Sir Edward Berry, slight, wiry and peppery, who knew little about complicated tactics and cared even less; Berry was a fighter, pure and simple. Alexander Ball of the *Alexander* had a large domed forehead and the mannerisms of an Oxford don and was given to orotund pronouncements. Ralph Miller, New York-born son of an American Loyalist, had a devilish imagination: the *Theseus* had only two tiers of guns, so he painted a line of fake gunports above the upper deck to give her the appearance of a three-decker. The prescient Thomas Troubridge of the *Culloden* was the son of a London baker and became the founder of a dynasty of admirals. Sam Hood of the *Zealous* was a hulking giant who could not stand upright on the gun decks; Thomas Foley of the *Goliath* was a round-faced Welshman who kept a good captain's table and enjoyed dirty stories. Bluff Ben Hallowell of the *Swiftsure* had once quelled a mutiny with his fists; he was the only officer in the Royal Navy known to have given the imperious old Earl St. Vincent a resounding clap on the back.

Aristocrat and plebian, bantam cock and bear, all were united in undying devotion to the soft-spoken, generous, vain and spellbinding little

Three mutinous cheers and a fleet in rebellion

Battle sustained the British tar. Even blockade duty with its implicit promise of a fight—and prize money—was bearable. But harbor or guard duty close off the English coast without any excitement to relieve the monotony brought home as nothing else did all the hateful aspects of the Royal Navy: tyrannical officers, thieving mates, foul quarters, inedible food and wages so shamefully meager that sailors' families often had to beggar themselves to survive.

On Easter morning, 1797, all the pent-up resentment overflowed among the crews of 16 ships of the line anchored at Spithead, just outside Portsmouth harbor. The men deposed 65 of the most detested officers, climbed the fore shrouds of their vessels, roared out three mutinous huzzahs and refused to put out on patrol as ordered.

The men demanded a modest pay raise of a few shillings a month, better food, improved care for the sick, occasional leave to see their families, a royal pardon for their action and a promise that the worst officers would not return. For a month they held out. Finally the authorities granted a pay raise and a few other demands, including a pardon.

But in the meantime the trouble had spread to the Nore at the mouth of the Thames where a dozen vessels were anchored. This was a more sinister affair. The ringleader was a former schoolmaster named Richard Parker, who not only wanted higher pay and all the rest but also urged a blockade of the Thames to enforce the demands. However, this was calling for an act of treason that few sailors could condone. Rioting broke out, and as ship after ship deserted the cause, Parker surrendered, five weeks after his mutiny had begun.

From his jail cell, Parker wrote to a friend, "Remember never to make yourself the busy body of the lower classes, for him whom they have exalted one moment as their demagogue, the next they will not scruple to exalt upon the gallows." Two days later, true to his own prophecy, Richard Parker—along with 28 of his mutineers—swung from the highest yardarm in the fleet.

The DELEGATES in COUNCIL or BEGGARS on HORSEBACK.

Mutineers heckle their admiral in this cartoon as anarchists under the table claim undue credit for the 1797 Naval revolt at the Nore.

one-armed genius who was seeking to lead them into battle against the Toulon fleet, if only they could find it.

On the morning of August 1 the Pharos Tower of Alexandria came into view again. But now the harbor was full of French transports, and the French flag flew from the harbor's battlements. Still there was no sign of warships. Single-mindedly, Nelson turned to search for them, setting his course along the coastline east of Alexandria.

At noon the drummers announced dinner. Nelson would not go; anxiety kept him from eating. His captains sat down to eat in their separate dining cabins. Throughout the fleet the stewards were pouring the last of the wine when a signal rippled to the masthead of the *Zealous*: "Enemy Discovered." Napoleon's fleet was anchored in Abukir bay.

The hour was 2:30. Nelson studied the signal through his telescope, snapped it shut and called for the signal "Prepare for Battle." Then he decided he would have some dinner after all.

Below Nelson as he dined, the guns rumbled out on their carriages. On the upper decks, the stubby carronades, the devastating "smashers" that fired huge 68-pound cannon balls at short range, were being uncovered. From the stern windows of the *Vanguard* the long line of towering ships presented an impressive parade, their clouds of sails filled by a light "topsail breeze" from the northwest, their round bows parting the sea in a creamy foam, their sides jagged with rows of cannon poking out.

Certainly it was an impressive sight to French Admiral Brueys as he watched from the quarter-deck of the *Orient*. It was now late afternoon. The admiral had a bellyache, probably as a result of an attack of dysentery. But he was satisfied with the tactical position of his fleet. He expected the British to wait for him outside the bay, or to set up a blockade. A ship of the line drew up to 30 feet of water, so Brueys was confident that the enemy would not attempt to enter the shoal-ridden bay in the approaching darkness. He was thus utterly stunned to see the British ships approaching the bay. Nelson, characteristically, was determined to give battle, and the sooner the better. He knew that the bay was treacherous, and that the French would doubtless seek to take advantage of the shoals. But he was willing to bet that a way could be found to get at the anchored enemy. And so on he came, his men at the bow ready to take soundings and call back the depths as the fleet entered the bay.

Once within range, Nelson was certain that he could destroy the French. In his cabin conferences he had planned the tactics even for such a situation, and his captains knew exactly what to do. The fleets were evenly matched: 13 British ships of the line against 13 more heavily gunned French ships. But Nelson was upwind. If he concentrated all his ships on the enemy's van and center, the upwind ships of the French line, he could change the odds to nearly 2 to 1 in his favor: the downwind Frenchmen would be unable to beat upwind to join the battle. Only after knocking out the French van and center did Nelson plan to slide down the line and pick off the ships of the French rear.

Nelson felt remarkably chipper. He was banking on his Band of Brothers, and on his men. When he saw the French masts, he later told a friend, "I could not help popping my head every now and then out of the window, although I had a damned toothache, and once, as I was observing their position, I heard two seamen quartered at a gun near me, talking, and one said to the other, 'Damn them, look at them. There they are, Jack, if we don't beat them, they will beat us.' I knew what stuff I had under me, so I went into the attack with a few ships only, perfectly sure the others would follow. I knew my captains.''

It was now 5:30 p.m. The sun had become a huge red ball touching the sand dunes to the west. The British ships approached Abukir Island, at the bay's entrance, giving it a wide berth because of a long shoal reaching out toward them. The small French battery emplaced there by Brueys opened fire, but the range was long and the shots ineffective. The British ignored them. On board the ships the only sounds were the flutter of the signal flags, the wash of the water alongside, the creak of a block overhead or a gun's restraining gear below, and the soft chant of the leadsmen calling the depth. On the *Goliath,* leading the British line, John Nicol, a Scotch cooper who had been impressed four years earlier, was studying the countenances of his shipmates. "A serious cast was to be perceived on every face," he remembered later, "but not a shade of doubt or fear. We rejoiced in a general action; not that we loved fighting; but we all wished to be free to return to our homes, and follow our own pursuits. We knew there was no other way of obtaining this than by defeating the enemy. 'The hotter the war, the sooner peace,' was a saying with us.''

At the entrance to the bay the *Vanguard* moved alongside the *Zealous.* Nelson was beginning to forget his toothache. He called across to Hood to ask if there was enough water under their keels. Hood replied: "I cannot say, sir, but if you will allow me the honor of leading into battle, I will stand in and try."

"You have my leave," Nelson called to Hood. "I wish you success." Nelson raised his hat.

Hood raised his in reply, and a wind gust took it from his hand. "Never mind, Webley," he said as his first lieutenant scrambled for it; "there it goes for luck. Put the helm up and make sail."

But Thomas Foley of the *Goliath* had other ideas. One of his midshipmen had been first to sight the French fleet, but the *Goliath's* signal halyards had fouled and the *Zealous* had raised her signal first. Foley was not going to let the *Zealous* beat him again. He had his studding sails and staysails ready, expecting the next command from Nelson; the moment he saw it fly to the *Vanguard's* yardarm—"Form Line of Battle as Convenient" —he let go his extra sails and forged ahead. Hood saw the *Goliath* move away and said, "Well, never mind. Shorten sail and give him time to take up his berth. We must risk nothing that will tend to the enemy's advantage, and we shall all soon have enough to do."

Hood's decision was the right one for another reason. Foley, it happened, had the only good map of Abukir bay. It was in a 20-year-old French atlas titled *Bellin's Collection,* and it showed the soundings of the bay. With this map Foley was able to confirm what he had already observed: Brueys had made a major miscalculation.

By anchoring his ships only at the bow, Brueys had invited defeat. The French ships had been anchored up against the shoals of the west bank while the wind was from the east. But now the wind was from the north-northwest; the ships had swung around so there was deep water between

Admiral François Paul de Brueys, French commander at the Nile, was aware of a fundamental weakness in his fleet. "The crews of our ships," he wrote Napoleon, "are composed of invalid soldiers, young and insubordinate. In the choice made for your army we were left with the worst."

As Egyptians look on, the French fleet (center line), anchored in Abukir bay, near Alexandria, meets the British onslaught. Captain Thomas Foley (inset) led his squadron between the enemy and the shore and caught the French by surprise.

them and the shoals. Had they been anchored at the stern as well as the bow, they would not have swung. Foley's map confirmed his assumption that there was deep water between the French line and the shallows inside the line. Foley knew what tactic to use, and he did not bother to query the flagship because he was sure that Nelson had spotted Brueys's mistake just as he had.

He was right. The *Vanguard*'s flag captain, Sir Edward Berry, later recorded that Nelson studied the French line "with the eye of a seaman determined on attack; and it instantly struck his eager and penetrating mind that where there was room for an enemy's ship to swing, there was room for one of ours to anchor."

Nelson now sent up his favorite signal, a red pennant over a blue flag: "Engage the Enemy More Closely." The cheers could be heard through the fleet and across the bay. Some French sailors tried to answer, but their cheers sounded half-hearted, and they also could hear the derisive laughter from Nelson's men.

Listening to this exchange, Nelson realized that while the French tactic of firing at the British rigging and then making an escape had its merits in preserving ships, it had the disadvantage of breeding the attitude of the prey instead of that of the predator. He hoisted no more signals. No more were needed.

Aboard the *Goliath* Foley gave a quick order to his helmsman. The *Goliath* went across the bow of the leading French ship, the *Guerrier*. Raking her with the first broadside of the battle, Foley rounded the French line, turned and went in between it and the shore.

He discovered that the *Guerrier*'s captain had compounded his commander's mistake. Expecting to be attacked only on his outward side, he had let his crew stack piles of crates, gear and other impediments on his landward decks. The French sailors scrambled to clear the landward guns. While they did, Foley let go another rain of cannon balls, smashing the *Guerrier*'s sides open, knocking out most of her landward guns and killing most of their crews with a shower of splinters from the crates.

Foley's plan was to drop a stern anchor alongside the *Guerrier*, but his anchor cable ran out too far, and the *Goliath* moved down the line until Foley drew up opposite the next ship in the French line, the *Conquérant*. He opened fire on her. And in perfect coordination Nelson's other captains adapted their tactics. Around the head of the French line came the *Zealous* and the *Theseus*. The *Zealous* dropped anchor alongside the still-reeling *Guerrier*. Miller in the *Theseus* ordered his guns loaded with double and triple the regular single round of shot and rode across the *Guerrier*'s bow until her masts were in line. "We then opened," he wrote later, "with such effect, that a second breath could not be drawn before her main and mizzen masts were gone." Miller then deftly took the *Theseus* around the anchored *Zealous* and *Goliath* to attack the third French ship, the *Spartiate*, before directing his guns to the *Aquilon* and the *Conquérant* on either side of the *Spartiate*.

Saumarez' *Orion* added to the damage to the *Guerrier*, sending another broadside into her splintered bow before running inside and down the French line to anchor on the quarter of the *Peuple Souverain* and on the bow of the *Franklin*, sixth in the French line.

Battle of the Nile

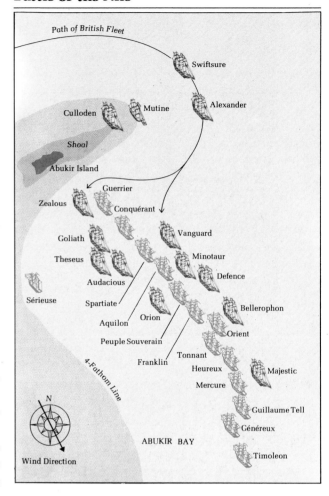

The British fleet (red) begins its attack on the anchored French fleet (blue) at the Battle of the Nile. As Nelson in the Vanguard leads the main frontal assault, Captain Thomas Foley in the Goliath slips in behind to close with the Conquérant, while the rest of his squadron leapfrogs down the back of the French line. The French supposed themselves safe to the rear because of the shallowness of the water, but they had swung fatally far from the four-fathom line, thus giving the British room to maneuver.

Wounded in the head by a piece of flying metal, Nelson is tended by a surgeon's mate in the cockpit of the Vanguard at the height of the Battle of the Nile. Though the injury was superficial, Nelson thought he was dying. Nevertheless, he ordered the surgeon (left foreground) to tend first to a seaman, saying "I will await my turn with my brave followers."

As surprised by the British tactics as the men aboard the *Guerrier*, the captain of the French frigate *Sérieuse*, lying in the shallow water next to the shore, made a desperate attempt to foil the British maneuver: he opened fire on the *Goliath*. It was a rash intervention; frigates were used as scouts and message carriers and did not usually add their meager firepower to that of the ships of the line. The *Sérieuse* paid for her captain's sin. Foley was outraged by the impertinence. "Sink that brute!" he ordered. His guns opened fire on the frigate, followed by the guns of the oncoming *Orion*. The *Sérieuse* slowly sank, her men scrambling up the rigging as the hull settled in the shallow water.

To make the envelopment perfect, after the *Audacious* had rounded the French line to the inside, Nelson and the rest of his fleet attacked the French on the outward side. The van and center of Brueys's line were thus surrounded and attacked from both sides. And the entire British fleet was concentrated on the forward half of the French line.

The entire British fleet except one. In the most frustrating episode of his career, Captain Troubridge took the *Culloden* too close to the shoals of Abukir Island at the bay's entrance and ran aground. For the rest of the night he fought his own battle with the shoal and did not get free until morning. His only consolation was that in the darkness his lights served as beacons to keep the other ships from running onto the same shoal.

The rest of the British were earning their victory. The French had been hurt badly in the first hour of the battle; every one of the first eight ships in the French line was raked by two British ships. But Napoleon's navy fought back with desperate determination. Aboard Foley's *Goliath* the thump of cannon balls followed by the showers of splinters rocked the ship and cut down most of the men on the upper deck. Below on the gun decks the acrid smoke soon made everything nearly invisible. The smoke spread across the water, and the enemy ships could be seen only by the flashing red tongues of fire from their guns. Below the gun decks John Nicol, the cooper, had been assigned to help pass out the powder instead of manning a gun—an assignment he regarded as "wounding to my feelings and trying to my patience." Deep in the orlop deck he could only listen to the roar and crash of the battle above.

There were some women on the *Goliath,* smuggled on board by their husbands and lovers. Nicol recalled that they "behaved as well as the men." One of them was the gunner's wife, who did her part by bringing "her husband and me a drink of wine every now and then which lessened our fatigue much." A woman from Leith was killed. Another from Edinburgh, no doubt stimulated by the excitement, went into labor. While lives were being snuffed out on the decks above, a new life was born below; it was a boy, a true son of a gun. A woman named Nancy Perriam helped the surgeon in the cockpit of the *Orion.* She never forgot the young midshipman, a protégé of Captain Saumarez, who was brought below with his arm blown out of its socket. "The boy bore the operation without a murmur," she wrote later, "and when it was over turned to me and said, 'Have I not borne it like a man?' Having said this, he immediately expired."

Nicol remembered two other gruesome oddities. A young gunner was about to light his match to a gun when he was hit by a ball that came right through the *Goliath*'s gunport. The shot "took off his arm," Nicol recalled. "It hung by a small piece of skin, and the match fell to the deck. He looked to his arm, and seeing what had happened, seized the match in his left hand and fired off the gun," then staggered off to the surgeon in the cockpit below.

The other boy Nicol noticed was sitting on a cartridge chest and did not jump when ordered to. The gunner gave him a shove, and the boy tumbled onto the deck and lay still. He had been killed by the percussion of a cannon; there was not a mark on him. The body was dumped overboard and the firing went on.

On the quarter-deck of the *Theseus* Captain Ralph Miller had a bad moment when he realized that the broadsides of three French ships of the line bore directly on his ship. "Happily the enemy made no use of the opportunity," he remembered, and added, "I was resolved to remain quiet as long as they." His gunners belowdecks puzzled over the order to cease fire, until another British ship came to the *Theseus'* support.

By 9 p.m. the French van was all but out of action. The *Conquérant* had struck her colors, and the dismasted *Guerrier* was about to. Darkness had settled over the bay, shattered by the stabbing light of gunfire and illuminated by an occasional flaming sail or a fire on deck. Most of the ships

The Navy man's lust for loot

Patriotism, loyalty, glory, courage, comradeship, hatred, fear, all played a role in motivating the men of the Royal Navy. But one of the strongest spurs to a seaman was the promise of prize money. The plunder of victory had long been an honored institution among fighting mariners everywhere. But in the British Navy of the 18th Century, the distribution of prize money was as carefully orchestrated as the *Fighting Instructions* for conducting a naval battle.

Every captured enemy ship, with its cargo, was put before the High Court of Admiralty, which most often condemned it for sale and share-out. Naturally the court took a small percentage, but the rest went to the lucky Navy men involved. The captain of the victorious man-of-war got a share of three eighths; he gave one eighth to his fleet or area commander and pocketed the other two. His officers divided two eighths, the midshipmen and warrant officers got one, and the rest of the crew split the final two eighths.

In Nelson's day the admiral in command of a rich area such as the West Indies could routinely count on earning £100,000 in the course of a half-dozen years. Even a lucky captain could do almost as well. On October 17 and 18, 1799, the British frigates *Ethalion, Naiad, Alcmene* and *Triton* captured two Spanish frigates laden with specie. When the prize was shared out, each of the four captains received more than £40,000.

Of the thousand or so crewmen on the four frigates, every man received £182—or the equivalent of 16 years' wages for the work of an afternoon. A few wise sailors used such prize money to purchase their release from Navy service. But most were content to blow it all on a stupendous drunken bash that they aptly termed a "Bob's-a-dying."

Curiously, this universal lust for loot seems not to have affected Horatio Nelson—at least not to a great extent. Loud were the groans through the British fleet in the Mediterranean in 1798 when Nelson was so busy searching for the French that he refused even to take half an hour off to scoop up a passing fleet of fat Spanish merchantmen.

British tars issue a sour commentary on the Royal Navy's distribution of prize money in this cartoon, published in 1805.

EQUITY or a Sailors PRAYER before BATTLE. *Anecdote of the Battle of Trafalgar.*

were hidden in the roiling clouds of smoke, with only their masts visible in the flashes of light. The British had an extra advantage because Nelson had had the foresight to order white instead of blue ensigns and a horizontal row of blue lights at the mizzen of each of his ships, for easier identification in the darkness. Still, the smoke swirled over all of the ships in blinding banks, and to a gun-crew captain the scene was often merely a cloud of smoke out of which the ghostly form of a ship might suddenly appear. A red moon appeared over the eastern sand dunes. As it rose, it revealed an inferno of smoke and fire in which the British and French kept up their cannonade.

Brueys's flagship, the *Orient*, was in the center of the line; the British attack was now closing on her, and her decks were whistling with shot. A sliver of shrapnel had struck Brueys in the head. It was a flesh wound, and he used his kerchief to wipe away the blood. Another piece of shot hit him in the body. Then a cannon ball ripped off his left thigh, nearly cutting him in two. Still he would not go below. He ordered his aides to prop him up against a chest, saying, "A French admiral should die on his quarter-deck." He continued to direct the defense, but gradually weakened until he fainted from the loss of blood. He died shortly after, according to one of his ensigns, "with the same tranquillity of soul that he had shown in combat."

Just before Brueys received his first wound, Nelson paced his own quarter-deck and the *Vanguard* exchanged broadsides with the *Spartiate*. Even though the French ship had been attacked on her other side by the *Theseus*, her gun crews fought so well that the *Vanguard* was badly mauled. Then the *Minotaur* came to the *Vanguard*'s aid. It took the three British men-of-war to subdue the *Spartiate*.

Nelson was already planning his attack on the rear of the French line. He stopped pacing to study a crude map of the bay and at that point was hit in the forehead by a piece of langridge, the scrap shot fired by the French to cut up the enemy's sails. He started to fall and was caught by Berry, his flag captain. Spluttering through the blood that gushed down his face, Nelson cried, "I am killed! Remember me to my wife." Berry led his blinded commander down the ladders, through the smoky, echoing gun decks, to the cockpit. The surgeon looked up from his operating table and started toward them. But Nelson had regained his composure. He waved the surgeon away, saying he would await his turn.

When the surgeon did get to him, he found the wound bloody but superficial. The piece of iron had laid bare Nelson's cranium for an inch over the unseeing right eye. But the wound was three inches long, and a flap of flesh had fallen over the good eye. The surgeon folded the flap back in place, used strips of adhesive to hold it, and wound a bandage around Nelson's skull. Berry led the admiral into the bread room, a cavernous storage space near the cockpit, and told him to lie down.

Nelson was still convinced that death was near. "This is the hundred and twenty-fourth time I have been in action," he said, "and I believe it is now nearly over with me." He asked again that his last words be conveyed to his wife. He sent for Captain Louis of the *Minotaur*. When Louis arrived, Nelson held his hand out to him, saying, "Your support prevented me from being obliged to haul out of the line. Farewell, dear Louis. I shall never forget the obligation I am under for your brave and generous conduct; and now whatever may become of me, my mind is at rest."

For a while he lay quiet, but within minutes he was asking for John Campbell, his secretary, to take down his report on the battle. Campbell had himself been wounded, and the sight of Nelson with the reddened bandage around his head was too much for him; his hands shook so that he could not write. Nelson sent him away. He asked for Comyn, the chaplain, who arrived to find Nelson, with the bandage pushed up from his good eye, scrawling: "Almighty God has blessed His Majesty's arms in the late Battle. . . ."

At 9:30 Berry came below again. The battle was a magnificent sight at this point, he reported. There were fires throughout the French fleet, and the biggest fire was on the *Orient*. Nelson got to his feet and insisted on going on deck. Berry led him up the ladders, past the thundering guns and cheering gunners, and onto the *Vanguard*'s quarter-deck.

The scene was undeniably spectacular. An acrid yellow cloud hung over everything, and the falling ashes of a hundred fires made a gritty sound underfoot as Nelson and Berry walked on the deck. Around them the water was filled with spars, barrels and bodies, and the sound of guns was punctuated by the splash and hiss of cannon balls hitting the water.

But the focus of the conflagration was the towering *Orient*. On the afternoon before the battle, her crew had been painting her, and they had not had time to jettison all the paint buckets. So the first few broadsides had ignited fires all over the ship. As she began to burn, five British ships within range directed their fire at her. The flagship's tall mainmast crashed over the side in a geyser of water. The mizzenmast followed. As Nelson looked across the water at her, the *Orient* seemed to be consuming herself. It would not be long before the fire reached her powder magazines; at that point, she would explode like a gigantic bomb.

Clearly her officers and crew realized this too. An ensign named Lachenède later recalled: "After incredible but futile efforts, we left the bridge deck, which was covered with flaming corpses. The ship was burning fore and aft, and already the flames were reaching the 24-pounder battery. And yet in the 36-pounder battery, the men seemed to be unaware of the danger, and they continued to fire vigorously."

With Brueys dead, his chief of staff on the *Orient*, Admiral Honoré-Joseph-Antoine Ganteaume, assembled the remaining officers. While fires crackled outside the admiral's cabin, they agreed to flood the *Orient*'s hold. But the fire moved faster than the water came in. Ganteaume gave the order to abandon ship; the wounded men were left to burn.

From the *Vanguard*'s deck the abandonment of the *Orient* was an odd sight, the lowest tier of guns still firing as a rolling carpet of humanity poured over the ship's side into the water. Nelson asked if any of the *Vanguard*'s boats were still serviceable. Only one was. He ordered it sent to pick up survivors from the *Orient*. At that point the fire reached the *Orient*'s powder magazine.

The explosion shook every ship in the bay. The *Orient* became one huge ball of fire. There was a stunning stillness; every gun fell silent as the gunners watched the spectacle of burning spars, sails and bodies showering into the hissing water.

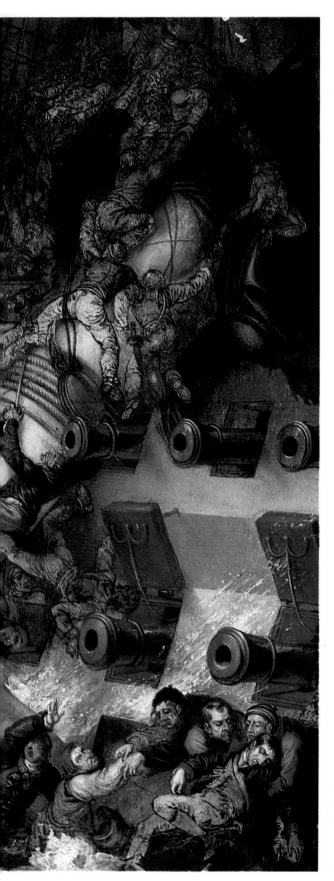

After some minutes, guns took up again and the battle continued. Amid the floating wreckage and bobbing heads where the *Orient* had been, a few British boats tried to rescue survivors. Of the *Orient's* 1,000 men, only 60 were saved.

One survivor made it on his own. Captain Ben Hallowell of the *Swiftsure* was taken aback when confronted by a dripping man, naked except for a French cocked hat on his head. "Who the deuce are you?" he growled. Lt. Charles Berthelot of the *Orient*, the man replied, explaining that he had been commanding the lower-deck guns when the overhead beams fell through. After stripping and abandoning ship with the gunners, the lieutenant had climbed back through another gunport and found his hat; without it, he reasoned, he would not be recognized as an officer and a gentleman.

The Battle of the Nile went on through the night, with the French fighting bravely and in desperation. Captain Alexandre Thevenard of the *Aquilon* lost both legs to one cannon ball. Captain Aristide Dupetit-Thouars of the *Tonnant* also had both legs shot off. He refused to go below, ordered tourniquets put on his stumps and had a barrel of bran brought on deck. Seated in the barrel, he continued to give orders while his life blood seeped away. Finally he said to a lieutenant, "I might lose my head along with my blood and do something foolish if I keep the command. It is time I gave it up." With his pistol he blew out his brains. The *Tonnant's* men fought on without him until she was a mastless hull, with 120 men killed, 150 wounded and 1,600 survivors of other French ships crowding her decks.

Shortly after dawn the last guns ceased firing. Sunrise revealed a watery battlefield of smoking wreckage. Where the evening before there had been two stately lines of warships, there was now a tangled mass of jagged masts and floating hulks. John Nicol, climbing on deck from his post below, was awed. "The whole bay was covered with dead bodies," he recalled, "mangled, wounded and scorched." Of Napoleon's grand fleet, six ships of the line had struck their colors, the flagship was on the bottom of the bay and four others were grounded on the beach. Two more, which had been stationed at the rear of the French line and were therefore undamaged, now made their escape. Hood in the *Zealous* tried to go after them, but no other ship was in condition to assist in the chase, so he was recalled. One of the fugitives was the *Guillaume Tell*, flagship of Rear Admiral Pierre Villeneuve, commander of the French rear. Villeneuve would meet Nelson again, at Trafalgar.

By contrast, not a single British ship had been lost. But there was scarcely one with all its masts.

Desperate French sailors scramble aboard nearby ships as the Orient, flagship of the French fleet at the Battle of the Nile, is sundered by a colossal explosion in her powder magazine. The huge, 120-gun Orient sank, carrying a vast sum in treasure that was earmarked to help finance Napoleon's Egyptian adventure.

The stiff human price, paid by both sides, amounted to nearly 2,000 dead—including at least 1,700 French and more than 200 British. Abukir Island, the site of Brueys's useless battery, was used for a burial ground where French and British, including the woman killed aboard the *Goliath*, were buried together in the armistice of death and all commemorated with a single cross.

It was more than two weeks before all the British ships were repaired, many of them with parts salvaged from the wrecked enemy vessels. At last, on August 17, Nelson sent seven of the British ships and six of the French prizes to Gibraltar under the command of Saumarez. Two days later, with two of his men-of-war, Nelson took the *Vanguard* to Naples. Three ships were left behind to continue the blockade of the harbors and keep the trap sprung on Napoleon.

Months later, Nelson received a ghoulish souvenir. Captain Hallowell sent aboard the flagship a handsome coffin, built from pieces of the *Orient*'s mainmast that Hallowell's boats had salvaged. Nelson was delighted with it. He had it stood on end behind his chair in his dining cabin until his manservant Tom Allen could stand it no longer. He persuaded Nelson to have it stowed below until it could be taken home to England to wait for him there.

The Battle of the Nile was the most devastating naval victory of the 18th Century. Tactically it demonstrated that England's new admirals and captains were revolutionizing the old methods of naval warfare. Strategically it proved that the Royal Navy was at last rising to the challenge that had been mounting since 1770. The challenge would continue to rise and would threaten England's very shores. But in the Mediterranean, at least, the tide had turned in Britain's favor.

It was 13 days after the battle before the news reached Napoleon on the edge of the Sinai Desert. Upon hearing the news, Napoleon dismounted from his horse and walked out alone into the desert, where he stood gazing in the direction of the coast. As he walked away from them, his aides heard him say, "So this is the end of my navy. Can it be that I am fated to perish in Egypt?" Shortly thereafter he walked back to his assembled officers and attempted to make light of the situation, exhorting his troops to greater efforts on land.

Of Admiral Brueys, Napoleon said, "He did well to die." On August 19, the same day that Nelson sailed for Naples, Napoleon wrote a letter of consolation to Brueys's widow: "He died honorably, and without suffering, as every soldier would wish to die. Your sorrow touches me to the quick. I want you to count as of some value my friendship, and the lively interest that I shall always take in the wife of my friend." On the same day he also wrote to the Directory in Paris, blaming the disaster on the incompetence of Admiral Brueys.

There remained a final British gesture to compound Napoleon's humiliation. Deciding to console himself with one Pauline Fourès, a petite blonde who had stowed away on the ship of her cavalry-lieutenant husband, Napoleon sent the lieutenant off to France with dispatches. The British blockaders caught the ship—and, instead of imprisoning Fourès, sent him back to Alexandria.

The bittersweet life of a midshipman

"Good heaven! And is this to be my future residence?" exclaimed one persnickety teenager on a day early in the 19th Century as he cast his eyes about the dark and squalid cockpit of a Royal Navy warship. "Better go back to school; there, at least, there is fresh air and clean linen."

It was a first impression shared by many an English schoolboy who won through his family connections a berth on a Naval vessel as a midshipman—a seaborne apprentice training to be an officer in His Majesty's Navy. For these sons of the landed gentry and the professional classes, it was an apprenticeship marked by privation and privilege, as depicted in the accompanying sketches, dated 1820, by Captain Frederick Marryat, a graduate of the midshipman's mill. Done for his own amusement, the caricatures are sometimes waggish, yet they accurately reflect the midshipman's life with all its hopes and dreams of glory.

The neophytes ate and slept in the cockpit of the orlop deck, a foul den below the water line of the ship where the odors of rancid butter and cheese from the purser's stores

As his mother weeps for his fate, a British imp in a new midshipman's uniform takes time out from packing his sea chest to prod his sister playfully with his dirk, one item in an array of fancy new gear with which he will launch a career as a Naval officer. The head of the household watches his son's fanciful antics impassively.

mingled with the stench of the bilges sloshing just beneath them. Their dining table also served as the surgeon's bench, and only the more experienced, it was said, could distinguish the gravy stains from the dried blood.

This was no place for a weak or sensitive boy. The horseplay was rough, and the rule of the fist prevailed. The less assertive among the midshipmen were incessantly bullied and intimidated; their hammocks were cut down as they slept, their clothes were stolen and their food was pilfered.

But as fledgling officers, the youngsters were expected to endure such travail, and in the process to learn the jobs of nearly everyone aboard ship, including the dangerous work aloft. Despite their youth, they were granted most of the privileges of officers. They held absolute authority—which they often abused—over the ordinary seamen aboard ship. Many a brave and brawny tar was forced to submit to shrill obscenities and stinging slaps from some smooth-cheeked young tyrant. There was no recourse to higher authority. "By the god of war," one officer roared to his seamen, "by the god of war, I'll make you touch your hat to a midship-

His mouth agape, a new arrival on board ship drops his hat in amazement at the sight of the cramped midshipmen's berth, his home for the next six years. The older midshipmen are at their rum, noisily proposing toasts and piping tunes, while one youngster blacks his boots and another snoozing shipmate is about to have a prank played on him.

Having lashed himself to the topmast crosstrees to keep himself from falling, this midshipman dozes peacefully through a mild form of punishment called "mastheading," an exile aloft for a few hours that most youths considered relaxing—except during foul weather.

As his vessel rolls wildly in heavy swells and loosed cannon balls careen dangerously about the tilted deck, a midshipman braces himself against a stanchion near the mainmast and watches shipmates struggle to keep their balance.

man's coat, if it's only hung on a broomstick to dry!"

It did not matter that some midshipmen were even more tender than their ages would indicate. At least one was so infantile that he still sucked his thumb. Another, an 11-year-old, was humiliated when his father, the ship's captain, spanked him in full view of the crew.

Not all midshipmen were young. Some were nearer 50 than 15. These were the failures who had botched the examination for a lieutenant's commission, given after the first six years' service. They remained midshipmen their entire careers, consigned to berth with raucous striplings.

From this division in age and aspiration a ceremony evolved. Each evening shortly after supper, one of the aging midshipmen would plunge a fork into an overhead beam. It was a signal for the youngsters to take to their hammocks, slung in a curtained-off area of the cockpit, perhaps to dream of promotion, and leave those who had not made the grade to their rum, their tales worn smooth from the telling, and their complaints as burnished as the ship's brass.

On a stormy night a drenched and miserable midshipman (foreground) stands a desultory watch as sheets of rain slant across the upper deck. A messboy with a warming jug of rum scurries toward an officer. Other crewmen on the watch hug themselves against the piercing cold.

As a midshipman brings him a cup of tea, a lieutenant, his telescope under one arm, oversees the morning scrubbing of the deck from his seat atop the capstan. A clutch of ragtag sailors on their hands and knees are pushing sandstone blocks— called holystones because they were about the same size as a Bible—to grind away dirt from the oaken planks.

Once a midshipman was promoted to lieutenant, he could participate in boisterous drinking bouts such as this one under way in the officers' mess. Three officers have been rendered unconscious by an excess of spirits. And another, in a fit of drunken pique, is rearing back to throw his goblet at an errant messboy.

Chapter 4

Battle, blockade and chase

With broadsides booming, Nelson's ships of the line (center) fire on the vessels of the Danish fleet in Copenhagen harbor in 1801.

n September 22, 1798, Nelson's battered flagship *Vanguard* was towed into the bright Bay of Naples. The fleet had been caught in a fierce storm on its return passage across the Mediterranean after the great victory at the Nile, and the elements had done almost as much damage as the French. But that only heightened the drama and emotion of the occasion. The *Culloden* and the *Alexander* had preceded the *Vanguard* into port by a few days and had given notice of Nelson's approach. Now, as the flagship and her admiral entered the mirror-smooth bay, against the backdrop of a slowly smoking Vesuvius, all of Naples seemed to erupt in joyous welcome.

Cheering, singing throngs, beggars and highborn alike, lined the wharves and filled the rooftops; birdsellers released a rainbow of buntings from wicker baskets. Across the water came a cacophony of music as bands and orchestras, even one from the opera house, boomed forth with "Rule Britannia" and "See the Conquering Hero."

An armada of 500 pleasure boats filled with celebrants put out from shore. Among the welcomers was King Ferdinand IV of the Two Sicilies, which included the island of Sicily and the lower half of the Italian boot; the monarch embarked in a great gilded state galley with spangled awnings and was rowed out to greet Nelson. He clasped the admiral's hand as he boarded the *Vanguard* and called Nelson his "deliverer and preserver." His Queen, Maria Carolina, sister of the recently guillotined Marie Antoinette, was too spent with emotion to leave the palace. At the news of Nelson's triumph over the despised French, she had, according to an observer, "wept, kissed her husband, her children, walked frantically about the room, burst into tears again, and again, kissed and embraced every person near her, exclaiming, 'O brave Nelson! O God! bless and protect our brave deliverer! O Nelson! Nelson! what do we not owe you! O conqueror—savior of Italy! O that my swollen heart could now tell him personally what we owe to him!' "

They owed Nelson much—as did every Mediterranean kingdom and principality. In the months before the debacle at the Nile, the French had been casting openly covetous eyes on the Kingdom of the Two Sicilies. The royal court at Naples had been trembling for its very existence; the French had promised that they would "revolutionize" all Italy. No wonder then that Maria Carolina had written her minister in London after the Nile: "The whole of the sea-coast of Italy is saved; and this is owing alone to the generous English. This battle, or to speak more correctly, this total defeat of the regicide squadron, was obtained by the valor of this brave admiral, seconded by a navy which is the terror of its enemies."

For the Royal Navy and Nelson, Naples was an ideal base from which to consolidate the newly powerful British position in the eastern Mediterranean. It was perfectly situated to isolate the French garrison on Malta, cut the lines of communication between France and Napoleon's army in Egypt and generally keep France on the defensive in an area the French tended to regard as their own sea. Naples was also the best place for Nelson to repair and refit his storm- and combat-weary squadron, and for the admiral himself to get some much-needed rest and recuperation.

Better still, Nelson had friends in Naples. On a previous visit, he had been entertained by the British Minister, Sir William Hamilton, and his wife, Lady Emma. They had got on famously, and Sir William had written Nelson upon hearing the glorious news of Abukir: "Come here, for God's sake, my dear friend, as soon as the service will permit you. A pleasant apartment is ready for you in my house, and Emma is looking out for the softest pillows to repose the few wearied limbs you have left."

It all sounded perfectly innocent, as the 68-year-old Sir William undoubtedly believed it to be when he penned his note. But it was the start of a scandal that would set tongues wagging from Naples to London, and bring rumblings of disapproval from the Admiralty itself. Sir William's wife, the 33-year-old Lady Emma, was a woman with a checkered past, and she remained as notorious as she was beautiful. Mistress to a number of prominent Englishmen, she had been married to the last of them, Sir William, for seven years. She was now one of the most noticeable figures on the Neapolitan scene, a great favorite of King Ferdinand and Queen Maria Carolina and a party-giver of spectacular tastes and unflagging energy. The chief attraction at these gatherings was Emma posing in Roman costumes in order to demonstrate her classical beauty. After seeing her on one of these occasions during a visit to Naples, Germany's great man of letters Goethe described her as the finest treasure in Sir William's collection of *objets d'art*—"a masterpiece of the arch-artist." A more mundane visitor wrote: "Sir William has lately got a piece of modernity which will fatigue and exhaust him more than all the volcanoes and antiquities in the Kingdom of Naples."

While Nelson was still at sea, Lady Hamilton had written her own note of effusive congratulation: "If I was King of England, I would make you the most noble, puissant Duke Nelson, Marquis Nile, Earl Alexandria, Viscount Pyramid, Baron Crocodile and Prince Victory." And when Nelson's *Vanguard* entered Naples, she was among the first to board the ship. Nelson, perhaps naïvely, reported the scene in a letter to his wife, Fanny, in England: "Up flew her ladyship, and, exclaiming 'O God, is it possible?' she fell into my arm more dead than alive." She appeared to be on the verge of swooning with emotion, and in any case wept copiously, for Nelson added, "Tears, however, soon set matters to rights."

Nelson accepted Sir William's offer of an apartment in his townhouse, the richly furnished Palazzo Sessa, and was soon spending many an evening on Emma Hamilton's balcony, overlooking the harbor. On Nelson's 40th birthday Emma gave one of her grand parties. Nelson wrote to his wife: "The preparations of Lady Hamilton for celebrating my birthday tomorrow are enough to fill me with vanity. Every ribbon, every button has 'Nelson' etc., Songs, sonnets are numerous beyond what I ever could deserve." Emma Hamilton told her diary: "My dress from head to foot is *alla Nelson*. Even my shawl is blue with gold anchors all over. My ear-rings are Nelson's anchors; in short we are all be-Nelsoned."

While other British visitors referred to Lady Hamilton as "bold, forward, coarse, assuming and vain," Nelson described her, again to his wife, in very different terms. She was, he said, "one of the *very* best women in this world. She is an honour to her sex."

Of Naples, Nelson at first thought little, describing it to Earl St. Vin-

A dark incident in a lustrous career

"To advance (trusting to God for His blessing on a just Cause), to die with sword in hand,—or remain quiet and be kicked out of your kingdoms." Thus did Horatio Nelson lay out the options for King Ferdinand IV of Sicily and Naples in November 1798.

Ferdinand was the last free-ruling monarch in all of Italy, but he was paying a heavy tribute for the privilege to France, which controlled the rest of the peninsula. The British victory at the Nile had given him courage, and at Nelson's urging he finally sent his ragbag army to march against the French garrison in Rome. After an initial success, the Neapolitans were routed. Ferdinand himself crept home in disguise —and as the French marched on Naples, Nelson evacuated the entire royal court, plus £2.5 million in treasure, to Sicily in British warships. By January 1799 the French tricolor was flying over Naples; the city-state was proclaimed a republic and was to be ruled by a puppet government.

One man who stayed behind was Commodore Francesco Caracciolo, the most eminent officer in the small Neapolitan Navy. Caracciolo had no love for the French; in fact, he had fought alongside Nelson in 1795, commanding the only Neapolitan ship in a British fleet action against the French off Genoa. But like many other Neapolitans, he regarded Ferdinand with disgust—both for his craven flight and for his unenlightened rule. Caracciolo decided to join the Republicans and accepted command of their navy.

The Neapolitan republic was short-lived. On June 20, with aid from Russian and Turkish allies, resurgent royalists recaptured the city. Under terms of the surrender, all French and rebel troops were promised safe conduct to France. But now Nelson came on the scene once again. Arriving with 18 warships, he unilaterally annulled the safe-conduct agreement and demanded unconditional surrender. With satisfaction, Nelson wrote: "The rebels came out of their castles as they ought, to be hanged or otherwise disposed of as their sovereign thought proper."

Caracciolo was found hiding at the bottom of a dry well. He was brought directly before Nelson, who ordered a court-martial. Caracciolo was quickly found guilty of treason. That very evening he was hanged from the yardarm of his former flagship, the *Minerva*, and then was cut down to splash into the water like so much garbage.

A few days later, Caracciolo's bloated corpse bobbed to the surface of the water near Nelson's flagship—to the consternation of the recently arrived King Ferdinand (*below*), who had reluctantly given up grouse hunting in Sicily to reclaim his capital.

Nelson and Lady Hamilton peer past King Ferdinand IV and a chaplain at the body of rebel officer Francesco Caracciolo as it bobs to the surface several days after Nelson had presided over his court-martial and execution. One witness recalled that the King turned pale and "uttered an exclamation of horror."

cent as a kingdom of "fiddlers and poets, whores and scoundrels." But he was willing enough to meddle in Neapolitan affairs. He tried his hand at military strategy on land but succeeded only in persuading Ferdinand to engage in a disastrous campaign against French forces in northern Italy. In December 1798, under pressure of an advancing French army and revolutionary actions from within, Nelson sailed the Hamiltons and the Royal Family from Naples to Sicily. The evacuation of the Royal Family and all their dependents was carried out with the minimum of fuss. The grateful Ferdinand awarded Nelson a substantial Sicilian estate in the foothills of Mt. Etna. The region was called Brontë, and Nelson was created Duke of Brontë. He liked the name because it was Italian for "Thunder," and he afterward signed himself "Nelson and Brontë."

In June 1799, while further repairs were being made to the *Vanguard*, Nelson shifted his flag to the *Foudroyant*, an 80-gun ship of the line. In April of 1800, Nelson took Emma, Sir William and a number of other guests on a cruise off Malta, which was still being gamely defended by its French occupiers. While the *Foudroyant* lay at anchor too close to Valletta, the French fired a shot at her. Humiliated before his guests, Nelson was "in a towering passion," a midshipman later recalled, "and Lady Hamilton's refusal to quit the quarterdeck did not tend to tranquilize him." Before the ship could get under way, her fore-topmast was hit and Nelson insisted that Emma go below.

But aside from that exciting divertissement, all was very relaxed; later Nelson commented on the "days of ease and nights of pleasure" of this voyage. During it Emma conceived Nelson's child.

Sir William Hamilton could hardly have failed to notice during the many months of Nelson's sojourn in Naples the growing attachment between his wife and the Hero of the Nile. From the start, his attitude toward the affair had been more avuncular than uxorious. At his advancing age, he was pleased to find an outlet for his wife's boundless energy, particularly when she had made such a catch. But Nelson's captains were not so tolerant. One of them, Thomas Troubridge, who had commanded the *Culloden* at the Nile, was frank. "I beseech your lordship leave off," he wrote. "I wish my pen could tell you my feelings, I am sure you would oblige me." Nelson did not bother to answer the note. His lack of response led Troubridge to write a young lieutenant who had applied to sail with Nelson that "between ourselves I do not think he will serve again"—meaning that Nelson was so enslaved by Emma Hamilton that he could no longer muster the will to fight. It was the beginning of a permanent break between Nelson and one of his favorite captains. In the words of another observer, "the Lord of the Nile seemed as clumsy and dim on land as he is adroit and notable at sea."

In due course, Nelson received two letters that told a great deal about discipline and loyalty in the Royal Navy. One was from the First Lord of the Admiralty. Lord Spencer was polite but his command was unmistakable. "I believe I am joined in opinion by all your friends here, that you will be more likely to recover your health and strength in England than in an inactive situation at a Foreign Court, however pleasing the respect and gratitude shown to you for your services may be."

The second letter was a scrawled note that Nelson received as he prepared to obey his orders for recall. "My Lord, it is with extreme grief that we find you are about to leave us. We have been along with you (although not in the same ship) in every Engagement your Lordship has been in, both by Sea and Land; and most humbly beg of your Lordship to permit us to go to England as your Boat's Crew in any ship or vessel or in any way that may seem most pleasing to your Lordship. My Lord, pardon the rude style of Seamen, who are but little acquainted with writing, and believe us to be, my Lord, your ever humble and obedient servants—BARGE'S CREW of the *FOUDROYANT.*"

Nelson had no need for a barge crew. He went home by land, via Leghorn, Vienna, Prague, Dresden and Hamburg. It happened that Sir William's tour of duty as ambassador was over, so the Hamiltons accompanied Nelson—which may not have been what the Admiralty had in mind. Everywhere they caused a great gabble of gossip, but if Nelson was aware of it he gave no sign. In Vienna, Lord Minto, the British Minister, said: "She goes on cramming Nelson with trowelfuls of flattery, which he goes on taking as quietly as a child does pap." At another point in the trip, General Sir John Moore noted in his diary: "He is covered with stars, ribbons and medals more like a Prince of an Opera than the Conqueror of the Nile. It is really melancholy to see a brave and good man, who has deserved well of his country, cutting so pitiful a figure."

At Hamburg, Nelson hired a packet for a stormy five-day trip across the North Sea to Yarmouth, and a hero's welcome home from the waiting dockside crowd. A wildly cheering assemblage took the horses from the homecoming hero's carriage and pulled it themselves to the local inn. When the landlady asked Nelson if he would approve of her changing the name of her inn to The Nelson Arms, he replied, "That would be absurd, seeing that I have but one." In London, the reception was mixed. Englishmen flocked around him in the streets. But the puritanical King George III, although he was persuaded to invite the admiral to a levee, greeted Nelson coldly, asked him about his health and turned away before Nelson could answer.

The meeting with Lady Nelson was, understandably, even chillier. As she had during his previous absences at sea, Fanny Nelson had been living alone in the Nelsons' home outside London, awaiting his occasional letters, which continued to be affectionate during his Naples sojourn. But rumors and messages from mutual friends had forewarned her, and she was hardly in a welcoming mood. It soon became obvious that Nelson's marriage was at an end. He openly joined a *ménage à trois* with the Hamiltons in London. The gossip mills hinted that the illustrious admiral had been seduced into abandoning his career.

At that point Napoleon came to Nelson's rescue.

For eight months after the defeat at the Nile, Napoleon remained with his army in Egypt. The French legions took Cairo and advanced north along the coast into the Levant. But the army was much reduced by disease, and there was increasingly hard fighting in prospect as the Sultan of Turkey marshaled troops for a counterattack against the invaders. Moreover, with the British in control of the Mediterranean, there was little hope of reinforcement from France; in fact, a British expeditionary force

The estimable Fanny

"My love is founded on esteem, the only foundation that can make passion last," young Horatio Nelson earnestly assured the 26-year-old Frances Nisbet (*above*) a short time before they were married in 1787.

Fanny was well cast as the wife of an ambitious young Naval officer. She was pleasant-looking, gracious and intelligent, and possessed an independence of spirit that Nelson admired. For a time they seemed quite happy. But Nelson's long sojourn in Italy after his victory at the Nile in 1798 proved a heartbreak for the estimable Fanny. At first, when his letters home ran on and on about the beauteous Emma Hamilton, wife of the British ambassador to Naples, Fanny kept her aplomb, and gave no sign of being the injured wife. But it was another story altogether when the involvement became a scandal that rocked all England.

Too proud to accept the ugly humiliation but too gentle to cause a public scene, Fanny quietly removed herself from Nelson's life. There was never a divorce or a legal separation; Nelson continued to send her money for her support until his death, after which the British government granted her a generous pension until she died in 1831 at the age of 70.

captured the strategic island of Minorca from the French, and for Napoleon's lonely garrison on Malta surrender was only a matter of time.

By mid-1799, Napoleon had no choice but to forget all thought of attacking India. Abandoning his army to its fate (of the 34,000 men, nearly all eventually suffered death or capture), he hastened home to France. On August 22 he slipped aboard the frigate *Muiron* so secretly that his army commander, General Jean-Baptiste Kléber, did not know that he had been left in charge until after Napoleon's departure.

Sneaking through the blockading British ships only because the lookouts mistook the *Muiron's* lights for those of one of their own frigates, Napoleon landed at Fréjus, in the South of France, in October 1799. So emotional was his reception by Frenchmen longing for a decisive leader that within four weeks Napoleon had contrived to overthrow the Directory—"that ridiculous bunch of lawyers," as he called them. On November 9, 1799, he became First Consul and unchallenged dictator of France. He was also accorded a new opportunity to strike at the British. Despite the effective loss of the Mediterranean, France was still supremely powerful on land, and Napoleon now accomplished something of a diplomatic coup. Influenced by France's awesome army, the Baltic states of Russia, Prussia, Sweden and Denmark entered into a League of Armed Neutrality, which, while not declaring war on Britain, nevertheless cut off trade and in effect closed the Baltic Sea to British shipping.

The treaty was signed in December of 1800. It was a serious blow to England—most particularly to her navy. The Baltic states were essential suppliers of Britain's flax and hemp. Moreover, the Royal Navy depended on the Baltic countries for much of the timber for its masts.

Britain reacted angrily, but preliminary overtures accomplished little. The British again turned to their admirals. This time the combination was to be a fighting admiral and a diplomatic admiral. The latter was Sir Hyde Parker, a veteran of four years in command of the West Indies station, and presumably wise in dealing with the islands' touchy governors; unquestionably he had made a fortune from prizes taken in the area (*page 81*). The target of the naval action would be Denmark, which lay athwart the entrance to the Baltic and could thereby deny the sea to British ships. Sir Hyde Parker's mission was to take a fleet to Copenhagen and present a firm demand that Denmark quit the alliance. If the demand was refused, Sir Hyde was to turn loose his fighting admiral.

That, of course, would be Horatio Nelson, now honored with the title Baron of the Nile and of Burnham Thorpe, as well as Duke of Brontë. And for the 42-year-old Nelson, idling in London with Lady Hamilton, this recall to the quarter-deck could not have been better timed. Despite his infatuation with Emma Hamilton and the approaching birth of their child, Nelson was growing restive. He had already asked the Admiralty for a new command. He accepted this one with alacrity, even though he was to be second-in-command.

Now the tables were turned: Nelson, who had had to be summoned from his Neapolitan lotus land, was anxious to get into action and became impatient as Sir Hyde Parker appeared to dawdle; every day that passed provided the Danish Navy with more time to get ready. A widower, the 62-year-old Sir Hyde had on his return to London taken an 18-

year-old bride. It was February 1801, a whole month after receiving his commission, before he and the new Lady Parker journeyed to Yarmouth and took a suite in the Wrestler's Arms. Weeks passed as the preparations for the expedition dragged on. In the midst of all this, other concerns afflicted Nelson. In late January, Emma had given birth to their child, a daughter. Nelson and Emma conspired to pretend that the parents were a Mr. and Mrs. Thompson, and the baby was sent to a wet nurse in London. But Emma could not resist calling her Horatia.

There was something else as well. Just before the birth and for many weeks after, Nelson was consumed by jealousy. The Prince of Wales, a notorious womanizer, had told friends "how Lady Hamilton had hit his fancy," and had attempted several times to dine with her. The advances had been rebuffed at Nelson's insistence and the Prince eventually lost interest. But Nelson was in a fury while it lasted.

The combination of anxieties was too much for Nelson. When he heard that the fleet's departure would be further delayed because of a ball planned by the young Lady Parker, he sent a confidential note complaining to the Admiralty, where his friend and mentor, the Earl of St. Vincent, had been appointed First Lord. Sir Hyde immediately received a letter from the crusty old St. Vincent: "I have heard by a side wind that you have an intention of continuing at Yarmouth until Friday, on account of some trifling circumstance. I really know not what they are, nor did I give myself the trouble of inquiring into them. I have, however, upon consideration of the effect of your continuance at Yarmouth an hour after the wind would admit of your sailing would produce, sent down a messenger purposely to convey to you my opinion, as a private friend, that any delay in your sailing would do you irreparable injury."

Sir Hyde sent Lady Parker back to London and, without even waiting for fresh provisions, took his fleet of 23 sail of the line to sea. In the Channel they were met with gales and blizzards. Decks were coated with ice, and sails and lines were frozen stiff. Lieutenant George Elliott of Nelson's flagship, the St. George, wrote that one morning, "it took us nearly an hour at daybreak to shovel down the snow from our tops and yards." Navigating in near-zero visibility, the ships were driven southward by the gales. Half the men in the fleet were coughing and everyone's hands were bleeding from working the icy rigging by the time the ships reached the Skagerrak. Sir Hyde anchored and sent the frigate Blanche ahead with England's ultimatum.

Nelson was as impatient with the delays of diplomacy as he had been ashore waiting for Sir Hyde to get the fleet under way. He had not even wanted to attack the Danes, but to bypass them and wipe out the bigger Russian fleet. With Russia out of the League, he was convinced, the other nations would quickly capitulate. But Sir Hyde did not want to go into the Baltic Sea and leave his rear undefended. In fact, he would not even approach Copenhagen until he had an answer from the Danes. Nelson's scornful reaction, in a letter to a friend, was: "I hate your pen and ink men; a fleet of British ships are the best negotiators in Europe. The Dane should see our flag waving every time he lifts up his head."

In any case, Nelson was not disappointed. The Danes rejected the ultimatum; and the rest of the mission, in effect, was left in his hands.

In this British cartoon a craven Napoleon Bonaparte turns his back on his French army slumbering beneath the Pyramids of Egypt and steals away in the night. The soldiers subsequently perished, but to Napoleon their fate was of no moment. "A man like me does not care a damn for a million lives," he once declared.

No doubt mostly because of Nelson's infectious aggressiveness, Sir Hyde was persuaded to follow his deputy's plan of attack. It was dangerous but, Nelson was convinced, necessary. The situation was reminiscent of the Nile. A large enemy force—at least 25 ships and floating batteries—was arrayed in line along the wharves of Copenhagen harbor. They were tightly packed together and supported by shore batteries above and behind them. There was less room for maneuver in Copenhagen harbor than there had been in Abukir bay. Down the middle of the approach to the harbor ran an enormous sandbank called the Middle Ground; to attack the Danish fleet the British would have to sail into the channel between the sandbank and the defending ships.

From the Danish point of view, it appeared to be an almost unassailable arrangement. They believed that the British would be forced to parade down the Danish line to get into position; thus the British van, the leading ships, would be subjected to the fire of virtually every Danish ship as they ran the gauntlet. But as at the Nile, Nelson had conceived a tactic to cope with this massed firepower. There were two approaches around the Middle Ground to the Danish position—one from the north, one from the south. The northern approach had a wider, deeper channel, but was covered by the heavy guns of many forts. The southern channel was narrower and shallower, but was less well defended. This was the route Nelson chose. He persuaded Parker to let him take it, while Parker stood by to support him if necessary from the northern approach.

Because of the shoals they would encounter, Nelson had transferred his flag from the *St. George* to the *Elephant,* which had a shallower draft. He had asked Parker for 10 ships and had been given 12. Now he gathered his captains around him in the low-ceilinged dining cabin of the *Elephant,* and described the tactics he had worked out.

The captains included only three of his original Band of Brothers—Foley, Thompson and Hardy. Nelson's second-in-command was Rear Admiral Thomas Graves, cousin of the man who had lost the Battle of the Chesapeake but himself a competent and respected commander. Nelson also had such fighters as Captain Thomas Fremantle, who had been with him at Tenerife and Captain William Bligh, a martinet who had suffered an infamous mutiny but a brave and expert seaman nonetheless. In addition, Nelson had Captain Edward Riou, whom he had not met before but who had a reputation as the Navy's finest frigate commander.

The plan Nelson described was complicated, because for once the enemy's position could be foretold—most of the Danish ships were anchored or settled on mud. Thus every attack maneuver could be planned in advance, and this time there was no need to delegate authority. The details were complicated also because Nelson had taken into account the comparative firepower of each of the enemy's ships and each of his own.

Yet the basic tactic was devastatingly simple. In a word: leapfrog. There was just enough room in the King's Channel, as it was known, between the Middle Ground shoal and the Danish line for two ships to pass abreast—which meant that there was enough room for one British ship to anchor and for another to sail between it and the Middle Ground. That was what they would do.

Allowing for comparative firepower, Nelson planned to have the first ship in the British line pass only four ships in the Danish line and anchor alongside the fifth. His next ship would run down past the first four Danes and outside the first British ship, to anchor opposite the sixth Danish ship. And so on—several more following the first two with the same leapfrogging tactic. By then the first four Danes would have been softened up by the fire of the passing British men-of-war, and should be easy prey for a direct assault by the next four British ships. Then, after engaging the first four, the remaining British ships would pass down the line until all 12 were fully engaged. It was a brilliant plan. No British ship would be exposed to the fire of more than a few Danish ships while getting into position. And by the time the 12 British ships were in their proposed line, they would be in range of only 16 of the 25 Danish ships. Moreover, the British attack would be before the wind, as at the Nile— they would simply wait at the southern end of the harbor until the wind went into the north. So even if some of the remaining Danish ships could weigh their anchors, they would be more paralyzed than the French at the Nile, with a head wind and less room to maneuver.

Stimulated by the plan, Nelson's enthusiasm and the free-flowing wine, his captains toasted victory and went back to their ships. Nelson kept Foley and Riou to help copy the details of the plan on sturdy cards

A fishy stratagem that carried the day

One of the marvels of fate is the disguises it assumes. Horatio Nelson carried the day at Copenhagen at least in part because of the intervention of a turbot—a small, delicious flatfish related to the halibut.

The tale begins with Nelson fuming mightily as His Majesty's fleet approached the Baltic. The commander, Sir Hyde Parker, planned to send an emissary ahead to present an ultimatum to the Danes, rather than attack straightaway, and Nelson thought that tactically and psychologically unwise. "What nonsense," he scoffed. "How much better could we negotiate was our fleet off Copenhagen, and the Danish minister would seriously reflect how he brought the fire of England on his Master's fleet and capital."

Nelson was determined to change Parker's mind, but Parker was feeling none too kindly toward his ambitious subordinate. In fact, he disdained even to communicate with him.

The old admiral was vulnerable on one count—his love of good food. Nelson waited impatiently until his ship, the St. George, heaved up on the fishing grounds of Dogger Bank. Though the night was inky black and the seas were running high, he dispatched a boat over the side to go in search of a fine turbot for the admiral's evening meal. When, after some difficulty, the piscatory prize was finally secured, the crew was instructed to deliver it to Sir Hyde with Nelson's compliments.

Precisely what passed through Parker's mind will never be known, but one of Nelson's lieutenants had no doubt about the salutary effects that the gesture produced. As the officer was to remind Nelson years later, "Sir Hyde condescended to return a civil note; without which opening Your Lordship would not have been consulted and without such intercourse Your Lordship would not have got the detached squadron; without which there would not have been any engagement, and consequently no victory."

SIR HYDE PARKER

to be delivered to each captain in the morning. As they worked, Nelson's servant Tom Allen clucked at him and brought hot drinks. It was a frigid night; cakes of ice could be heard bumping against the hull, and in the lantern light the men could see their breath. Allen finally lugged Nelson's cot into the after cabin. Nelson climbed into it but could not sleep. His own Captain Hardy—who was serving aboard the *Elephant* as a volunteer—left to recheck the soundings; the captains were worried about the reliability of the pilots they had brought from England, merchant sailors who had experience in these waters but who were beginning to evidence signs of fright. Nelson kept calling from his cot, asking how the copying was proceeding and what the wind direction was. The wind was hauling into the south. Hardy returned to report that he had rowed through the ice with muffled oars and had taken soundings right up to the bow of the nearest Danish ship: there was water enough.

The next morning was April 2, 1801. The wind was out of the southeast in exactly the direction Nelson wanted. But the pilots panicked at the sight of the bristling guns along the Danish shore and refused to take their positions by the ships' wheels. Nelson later noted how he suffered "the misery of having the honour of our Country entrusted to pilots who had no other thought than to keep the ships clear of danger, and their own silly heads clear of shot." Despite the soundings, and because of a strong current, three ships went onto the Middle Ground at the outset. Nelson's agitation was extreme when he saw himself deprived of a quarter of his strength. Nevertheless, with great skill he managed to bring his remaining nine ships into close action just as he had planned, each leapfrogging into position and anchoring opposite an enemy.

The first broadside was hurled across the water shortly after 10. The cannonading reached a shattering crescendo by noon, and continued unabated into the afternoon. Positioning himself ninth in line, Nelson had anchored his *Elephant* opposite the Danish admiral's flagship, the *Dannebrog,* and was engaged in a murderous slugging match. As the battle raged around him, reported an observer, "his countenance brightened and he became joyous, animated, elevated and delightful."

The situation looked anything but delightful to Sir Hyde Parker, four miles away at the other end of the harbor. After three and a half hours of fearful battle most of the southern section of the harbor was obscured by smoke, but it seemed to him that Nelson was getting the worst of it. Sir Hyde could not make headway against the wind, and thus could not go to the rescue. He finally said to his fleet captain, "The fire is too hot for Nelson to oppose." So he signaled: "Discontinue the action."

At this point Nelson was pacing the poop deck as usual. A piece of enemy shot sent a shower of splinters past him. He smiled at one of his officers and said, "It is warm work, and this day may be the last to any of us at any moment," then paused as he reached the gangway and shouted above the din, "but mark you, I would not be elsewhere for thousands!" That was when his signal lieutenant reported, in some dismay, the signal that was flying on Sir Hyde's flagship.

Nelson's immediate reaction was a flash of anger at the signal lieutenant. "Mr. Langford," he shouted in his high, squeaky voice, "I told you to look out on the Danish Commodore and let me know when he sur-

rendered. Keep your eyes fixed on him." Nelson resumed his pacing.

The signal officer knew his duty. As Nelson came back, the lieutenant asked if he should repeat the signal, as called for in the signal book.

"No," said Nelson. "Acknowledge it." The lieutenant ran down the steps to the quarter-deck and gave the order. As he returned to the poop, Nelson asked if his own signal, "Engage the Enemy More Closely," was still hoisted. The lieutenant said yes. Nelson said, "Mind you keep it so." He knew he was committing an act of grave insubordination. Sir Hyde had not only raised his "Discontinue" signal but had also fired two guns; that meant an order to the entire fleet. Clearly he intended to resume command to order every ship to withdraw.

What Sir Hyde could not see through the haze and smoke was that at this point in the battle virtually every Danish ship was so damaged that surrender was a matter of time. What is more, most of the British ships, while less damaged than the Danes, were so crippled in their topmasts and unmaneuverable that to attempt to disengage through the narrow King's Channel under fire would amount to suicide.

Beside Nelson was his old friend Foley, captain of the *Elephant* and formerly captain of the *Goliath*, the first ship to round the French line at the Nile. Foley knew Nelson's agitation from the way Nelson waggled his "fin," the stump of his right arm. Nelson turned to Colonel William Stewart, commander of a detachment of troops aboard, and asked what

On the eve of the Battle of Copenhagen, Nelson and his captains lift their glasses in a toast to a leading wind and success the following day. Colonel William Stewart (left of the pole), who led the soldiers assigned to the fleet, wrote that at the end of the feast aboard the Elephant, "every man separated with anxious impatience to follow their great leader to the approaching battle."

must at that stage have been a rhetorical question: "Do you know what's shown on board of the Commander-in-Chief?" The officer, unfamiliar with naval signals, asked what it meant. "Why, to leave off action," cried Nelson. "Leave off action! Now damn me if I do!"

He went over to Foley and looked up at his tall friend's face. "You know, Foley," he said, "I have only one eye—and I have a right to be blind sometimes." Taking his pocket telescope, he whipped it out and put it to his blind eye. "I really do not see the signal," he said.

He snapped shut the telescope and continued his pacing. Foley could hear him muttering, "Damn the signal! Keep mine for closer battle flying! That's the way I answer such signals! Nail mine to the mast!"

One captain who did obey Sir Hyde's signal was Riou. His frigate *Amazon* was near the north end of the line, closer to Sir Hyde's flagship. Riou had been wounded in the head. As he gave the order to cut the *Amazon*'s cable, he said, "What will Nelson think of us?" The frigate momentarily swung, enabling the Danes to rake her deck. Riou was cut in half by flying shot.

Nelson, having defied his superior officer in battle, now usurped Sir Hyde's diplomatic function. Under a flag of truce he sent a message to the Danish Crown Prince Frederick, who was directing the defense. Using the casing of the *Elephant*'s rudderhead as a desk, Nelson scrawled an ultimatum, addressed "to the Brothers of Englishmen, the Danes."

"Lord Nelson has directions to spare Denmark, when no longer resisting; but if the firing is continued on the part of Denmark Lord Nelson will be obliged to set on fire all the batteries he has taken, without having the power of saving the brave Danes who have defended them."

At that stage, Nelson had not yet actually "taken" any of the Danish ships. But the blunt threat was enough to bring about a cease-fire. The most important link in the Baltic league was broken.

Sir Hyde Parker knew the seriousness of Nelson's disobedience. However, he was grateful for the victory and he doubtless realized how embarrassing court-martial proceedings would be for him. He overlooked the incident. Already Nelson was urging Sir Hyde, with his relatively undamaged squadron, to race on eastward and attack the Russians; Sir Hyde delayed and asked London for orders. The Admiralty called him home and put Nelson in command.

By now Nelson had managed to effect some repairs, and he immediately took his fleet to the Russian harbor of Revel in the Gulf of Finland. But there was no more need for fighting. In fact, had the wind not turned south in Copenhagen harbor on April 2, and had the news from Russia traveled fast enough, there would have been no need for the Battle of Copenhagen and the loss of more than 250 English lives and more than 1,035 Danish dead and wounded. An assassin had murdered Czar Paul I of Russia on March 24. The League of Armed Neutrality died with him, for although he had been particularly sympathetic to Napoleon, his successor, Czar Alexander I, regarded France with a deep suspicion.

When Napoleon heard of the Battle of Copenhagen he threw a tantrum, screaming and stamping his feet. On calmer reflection he concluded that his first instincts had been correct: he must deal with England directly.

Edward Riou, ill-fated leader of the British frigates at Copenhagen, had earlier made a gallant name for himself when in 1789 he battled the terrible storms off the Cape of Good Hope for two months. He kept his frigate afloat and his crew alive by sheer force of character, until he finally brought them to safe haven.

That, of course, meant dealing with the Royal Navy. But how? It was obviously impossible to conquer the British in any sort of general naval campaign. The French Navy had fallen into calamitous decline over the long years of war; the once proud service had lost more than 50 per cent of its ships to enemy action or other causes. By 1801, France had only 39 ships of the line and 35 frigates, a number of them unfit to fight.

Since the Battle of the Nile, the French Navy had been virtually imprisoned by the Royal Navy—which by contrast had expanded prodigiously. The Royal Navy now counted an overwhelming 180 ships of the line and 213 frigates, manned by about 130,000 keenly trained men.

If this awesome force could not be faced head on, it must somehow be circumvented. That was the foundation of Napoleon's newest and most daring plan of conquest. The way to deal with England was to strike at her heart. England lay across the Channel. Napoleon need only leap across this narrow stretch of water to reach London. It was a gamble of desperation, the sort of gamble only Napoleon would make, and the sort only he could win.

It would start with the assembling of a huge flotilla of landing barges at Boulogne, less than 30 miles from Dover. An army of 161,000 soldiers was to be gathered for an invasion so overpowering that it could sweep up to London within days of landing on Britain's shores (*pages 121-125*). Napoleon calculated that he would have to control the Channel just long enough to get his flotilla across. The strategy for that part of the plan could wait. At the moment Napoleon had another diversionary ploy. With his invasion troops massing at Boulogne and all England hastily assembling armies of defense, Napoleon suddenly proposed peace.

A few members of the British Admiralty recognized Napoleon's move for what it was—a brief respite during which France could attempt to rebuild her shattered navy. But most Englishmen were too war-weary, and Britain agreed to the Peace of Amiens on March 25, 1802. It was to last only a year and two months; in the interim Napoleon continued his ominous build-up at Boulogne, and the British soon realized that the war with France was far from finished.

During the Peace of Amiens, Nelson had his longest home leave. Acting for him, Emma Hamilton had purchased a 70-acre estate at Merton (*pages 108-110*), eight miles outside London, and Nelson, both Hamiltons and Horatia moved in. Nelson took his seat in the House of Lords and harangued the Admiralty for additional decorations for his Copenhagen veterans (he himself had been created a viscount).

At Merton, Nelson reveled in the role of country squire. He took pains to stop and chat with the tradespeople and, with Emma, regularly attended the local church. Emma made a great point of including Nelson's relatives in the constant stream of guests invited to Merton. "Here we are as happy as Kings and much more so," she wrote a friend. For a time, old Sir William seemed content as well, enjoying the fishing in nearby streams. Eventually, however, life at Merton began to wear on him, and he moved back to London. When he died on April 6, 1803, at the age of 73, Emma and Nelson were with him. He expired in Emma's arms, and with his hand in Nelson's.

Little more than a month later, Nelson's home leave came to an end.

Among Nelson's captains at Copenhagen was William Bligh, whose 56-carronade Glatton set the Danish flagship afire. Twelve years earlier, Bligh had made history of a different sort when the crew of his Bounty mutinied off Tahiti and cast him adrift in an open boat similar to the one shown in this engraving. Displaying real navigational genius, Bligh sailed the craft almost 4,000 miles to safety.

On May 18, 1803, England declared war on France again, and Nelson was recalled to duty.

Now the Admiralty intensified its strategy of blockade against France. The lesson of the American War of Independence had finally been learned: even the largest of navies could not protect all of England's far-flung possessions. The proper defense was a strong offense, and the offense consisted of pinning the French Navy to its major Naval bases —at Brest on the Atlantic coast and Toulon in the Mediterranean.

Blockading was difficult and grueling work. In the course of the long earlier war against France the Royal Navy had lost not a single capital ship to enemy action. But it had had to replace 350 vessels—ships of the line as well as smaller frigates and cutters—lost in wrecks and other accidents. Off the French Atlantic ports powerful tides swept blockaders onto the rocks; in both the Atlantic and Mediterranean, storms dismasted the sturdiest men-of-war and blew them onto the French shores.

Even the most stalwart captains hated blockade duty. Cuthbert Collingwood, who would be with Nelson at Trafalgar, was normally an imperturbable character who felt more at home at sea than on land, but following a long stretch on blockade he wrote home to his wife: "I have hardly known what a night of rest is these two months; this incessant cruising seems to me beyond the power of human nature."

Nelson, too, had served his share of blockade duty. And characteristically, on one occasion he had tried to seize the initiative by going in after the enemy. This was in 1801, during Napoleon's first build-up at Boulogne. On the night of August 4, he had bombarded the harbor for 16 hours, inflicting damage on both the French warships and the assembled flotillas of landing craft. Eleven nights later, he ordered up an assault force of 57 boats manned by ax-wielding sailors and marines with the objective of cutting loose the enemy's landing craft and towing them back to England. But the French were ready, and Nelson's men had to retreat after losing 44 of their number.

By the summer of 1803, when hostilities were renewed after the Peace of Amiens, Nelson was in the Mediterranean commanding the blockade of Toulon. His flagship was the 104-gun Victory, pride of the Royal Navy. After the Battle of Ushant she had been flagship for Admiral Lord Howe off Gibraltar and for Admiral Sir John Jervis at the Battle of St. Vincent. She had been refitted for her Mediterranean duty and her admiral's quarters were comfortable almost to the point of luxury.

On summer blockade in the Mediterranean the worst enemy was boredom. Nelson tried to forestall it by keeping in constant touch with his officers. Only two of his Band of Brothers from the Nile were with him —Hardy and Fremantle. "I am with perfect strangers," he wrote, "although I believe very good men." He set about knowing them better.

A daily routine developed. In the morning the admiral frequently invited groups of midshipmen to breakfast. He had a cup of tea and a bit of toast while they enjoyed some meat as well. Nelson was his cheeriest at these breakfasts; many of the midshipmen later recalled his joviality. By 7 a.m. he was on the quarter-deck, pacing back and forth. At midmorning he was back in his cabin reading dispatches, or at his special desk, built to fold for stowage during battle and containing the desk and

Palmy days at Paradise Merton

Bedizened as always with his chest full of medals, Nelson posed for the pastel at top in 1800 after the Battle of the Nile. The pastel of Emma, above, by the same artist, is a somewhat idealized view of the voluptuary once described as "a Whapper! with her manner very vulgar." But Nelson thought it a fine portrait and carried it onto the Victory, where he gave it a place of honor in his quarters.

"*Tria juncta in uno*"—Latin for three joined in one—was how Horatio Nelson, Lady Emma Hamilton and Emma's husband, Sir William, dubbed their ménage as they settled into Merton Place, Surrey, in 1801.

Almost since the beginning of his sojourn in Naples two years before, Nelson had been wildly in love with Emma, who, for all her wanton ways, at 33 retained the fresh beauty of a schoolgirl. For his own reasons, the aging Sir William acquiesced to his wife's affair with the great naval hero, seeming to regard Nelson almost as a son. But while the gossips might be ignored in Naples they could not be disregarded in England, and the three of them sought respite from the public eye on their return.

Nelson had borrowed £9,000 to buy the 70-acre estate about an hour by carriage from London. Emma was given carte blanche in decorating what she called "Paradise Merton." Emma was an inveterate party-giver, and with the eminent Nelson at her side she was soon assured a continuous stream of distinguished weekend guests. Visitors were both fascinated and repelled by the arrangements. Lord Minto, an old friend of Nelson, found the atmosphere "disgusting" and "ridiculous," and reported: "The whole house, staircase and all, is covered with nothing but pictures of her and him."

But Nelson reveled in Emma's treatment and his happiness was made complete when Horatia, officially the Hamiltons' infant adopted daughter but clearly the love child of Nelson and Emma, arrived in 1801. Lord Hamilton seemed untroubled by the addition. He had long held deep respect for Nelson. But as he advanced in age, even the philosophical Sir William could not tolerate such spirited living. In March 1803, exhausted by the trio's long trips and desiring the tranquillity of museums and his club, he moved back to London, leaving Nelson and Emma to more energetic pleasures.

An accomplished diplomat, an eminent volcanologist and art historian, Sir William Hamilton was the epitome of those qualities admired in the Age of Reason when Joshua Reynolds portrayed him in 1777. But after his marriage to Emma, most Englishmen called him "old Antiquity."

Evening entertainment at Merton revolved around extravagant meals and lively card games. Emma, seated here behind the candelabra, was a passionate gambler and she thought nothing of staking as much as £500 at a sitting, dipping into both Sir William's and Nelson's purses for funds.

Nelson's desire for "a little farm" where he could live with Emma and Sir William produced this imposing country estate near Wimbledon. Although both men left her generous bequests when they died—Sir William in 1803 and Nelson in 1805— the legacies were inadequate to keep the spendthrift Emma solvent, and Merton Place was sold in 1808 to repay debts.

Whiling away the weeks and months of
Nelson's sea duty, Lady Hamilton
recalled their good times together in this
silk-embroidered rondelle. The scene,
with Merton Place in the background, is an
adaptation of one she found in a novel.

Emma's embroidered petticoat hem celebrates the dukedom of
Brontë, bestowed on Nelson by the King of Naples after the Nile.

Sir William Hamilton left this miniature
enamel of Emma to Nelson, whom he
called "the most virtuous, loyal, and truly
brave character I ever met with."

Horatia, Nelson's darling and his
unacknowledged daughter, was as a ruse
"adopted" by Lady Hamilton and
brought to live at Merton after spending her
first few months with a wet nurse.
Watercolorist Thomas Baxter depicts
her here at the age of four as an equestrian.

chair in one piece and—hidden under it—the admiral's chamber pot.

At 2 p.m. the *Victory*'s band struck up a tune and the fifers at 2:45 launched into the familiar "Roast Beef of Old England" to announce midday dinner, which was served precisely at 3 p.m. Nelson invited his captains to dinner in rotation according to their seniority. The dinner included three main courses—a fish, a roast, a vegetable—fresh fruit for dessert, three or four wines, sometimes including champagne, and finally coffee and liqueurs. Nelson ate little because of his tendency to seasickness—perhaps a chicken wing with a bit of macaroni and a glass or two of wine. His servant Tom Allen kept diluting his wine with water, and reminding him, "You will be ill if you take any more." But Nelson made sure that for his officers it was the high point of the day. Dinner lasted as late as 5 p.m., and as the fleet surgeon described it, "If a person does not feel himself perfectly at his ease, it must be his own fault, such is the urbanity and hospitality which reign here."

Most of the diners then took a postprandial stroll on the quarter-deck while the ship's band serenaded them. At 6:00 came tea and biscuits in the admiral's dining cabin, followed by punch and cake at 8:00. There was much genial conversation in Nelson's great cabin, with its candles at the sweeping stern windows, the mahogany desk, chairs and tables, the wide sofa, the silver bowl full of fruit, the Wedgwood spittoon—and prominently overlooking all, the wistfully smiling portrait of Nelson's love, Emma Hamilton. By 9 p.m. the captains climbed down into their waiting gigs to be rowed back to their ships.

Even under such pleasant circumstances the tedium was oppressive. One captain fought boredom by growing mustard plants and watercress. Another maintained an aviary. Yet another brewed spruce beer.

The boredom belowdecks was equally oppressive and more difficult to deal with. Besides inviting midshipmen to breakfast, Nelson tried to improve morale with occasional rewards. When a midshipman dived overboard to save a seaman from drowning, Nelson promoted him to lieutenant. Then, in an attempt to counter excessive expectancy among the other midshipmen, he leaned over the poop-deck rail and addressed them: "Mr. Flin has done a gallant thing today, and he has done many gallant things before, for which he has now got his reward. But mind, I'll have no more making lieutenants for men falling overboard."

Nelson made a fetish of caring for the physical well-being of his crews. To a doctor friend at home he wrote, "The great thing in all military service is health, and you will agree with me that it is easier for an officer to keep men healthy, than for a physician to cure them." He described the means he used, sending his supply vessels to Sardinia, and the captured islands of Minorca and Majorca for "*onions*, which I find the best thing that can be given to seamen; having always good mutton for the sick & cattle when we can get them, and plenty of fresh water."

Boats were sent out fishing for tuna and anchovies to supplement the meat. Nelson was particularly anxious to secure fruit juices as a guard against scurvy; he sent to Sicily for 50,000 gallons of lemon juice; each of the 8,400 men in the fleet got a pint a day.

He supervised the smallest details of supplies for his men, ordering flannel blouses with extra-long shirttails for the foretopmen who had to lean out over the yards, and complaining angrily to the Admiralty about a shipment of jerseys and trousers "of coarse wrapper-stuff." He was proud of the resultant high morale among his men. "We are healthy beyond example, and in great good humour with ourselves," he wrote home to Emma, "and so sharp-set, that I would not be a French Admiral in the way of our ships for something." When a new surgeon joined the Victory after she had been on station 20 months, the doctor reported with astonishment that of the 850 men aboard the flagship only one was sick in bed, and that the same good health was to be found on the other ships.

The condition of the men became much more important when summer gave way to the winds of autumn. The northerly gales that swept over France at that time of year were funneled by the Alps and Pyrenees and sent howling down across the Gulf of Lyons. Nelson wrote home in September that "such a place as the Gulf of Lyons for gales of wind from the N.W. to N.E. I never saw." As early as September, he reported, there were "three days' gale of severe blowing weather which frequently comes on suddenly." And he was one of the worst sufferers. The cold nights on deck gave him a hacking cough and aggravated the rheumatism in the stump of his right arm (he found that it worked well as a barometer). He had recurrent attacks of gout. Toothaches continued to plague him; most of his uppers were gone by now. He was seasick much of the time. His remaining eye was troubling him and he became convinced that he was going blind; the ship's surgeon blamed it on overuse of the one eye and prescribed a green eyeshade, but it did little to help.

His multilingual secretary, Dr. A. J. Scott, who was also the Victory's chaplain, read to Nelson from French newspapers sent out by British spies. But Nelson insisted on personally reading most of the voluminous correspondence entailed in the management of a fleet of men-of-war. He slouched in his favorite upholstered armchair, designed for him with an "in" pocket for arriving correspondence under the left arm and an "out" pocket under the right, and read until his eye throbbed and he could no longer see. When he dozed off, Scott would sneak some of the bulkier and less important documents from the "in" pocket to the "out" pocket.

The most difficult time for Nelson was night. The anxiety of waiting for the Toulon fleet to come out was almost too much for him; it made him dyspeptic and gave him chronic headaches. He could not sleep for more than two hours at a time. But he tried. Regularly at 9 p.m., as soon as his captains had returned to their ships, Nelson would take off his admiral's coat, britches and shirt, and in his underwear kneel at prayer beside his bed. The bed was more like a box, designed to be suspended like a hammock and to swing with the ship. Nelson would ease into the bed, under the quilt made for him by Emma, and try to sleep. After an hour or two he would be wakened by coughing spasms and would climb from the bed, slip into his buckled shoes, throw his greatcoat over his shoulders and go out onto the quarter-deck. The officers on deck would step respectfully to the lee rail. Nelson would nod to them and take up his pacing along the weather rail. He would walk for hours at a time. He averaged 15 miles a day on the quarter-deck of the Victory, waiting and hoping for some signal that would end the monotony of patrol.

So anxious was Nelson to lure the enemy out of Toulon that he adopt-

The Great Terror: England awaits invasion

"Let us be masters of the Straits for six hours," proclaimed Napoleon Bonaparte in 1804, "and we shall be masters of the world." Across the narrow Straits of Dover the First Lord of the British Admiralty remarked, "I don't say the French can't come. I say they can't come by sea."

The superiority of the Royal Navy was undeniable, and yet there was an aspect of chilling horror in Napoleon's bragging. If, perchance, he managed to span the Channel with his army, Napoleon could be in London within days. The prospect produced what came to be called The Great Terror.

Scarcely a week passed without an invasion scare; entire coastal towns were evacuated in panic. What if the French did not come by sea? Rumors of French tunnelers boring their way under the Channel or of an airborne descent by gas balloon bred general pandemonium. Every visitor from the continent was scrutinized suspiciously. In Wales it was actually believed that Bonaparte himself had already arrived in disguise and was lurking about in the Cambrian Hills while he waited for his troops.

But the English, for all their fright, intended to sell their land dear. The press whipped the populace into a fury with incendiary attacks on the French. A blizzard of morale-boosting caricatures (like those below and on the following pages) appeared featuring Bonaparte as the archtyrant being

An unflappable, pipe-puffing John Bull, England's personification of itself, exchanges unpleasantries across the Channel with a dwarflike Napoleon. The "wooden walls" of which Bull speaks—England's fleet of fighting ships—were her best defense against an invasion.

CONVERSATION across the WATER

Napoleon appears as a nasty little insect poking away and claiming the food of a corpulent John Bull in this 1803 cartoon. Under the terms of the short-lived Peace of Amiens, Britain was to surrender the island of Malta, seized from Napoleon in 1800. Britain's refusal to do so led to a resumption of the war.

The hop, step and jump of Napoleon's career, from his humble origins in Corsica, to France and the pinnacle of power, and from there to an imagined downfall on the point of John Bull's sword, is satirized in another 1803 drawing.

bested by England's stout John Bull. Customarily shopkeepers hung prints of these in their windows by day and then lent them out for the evening to be collected in portfolios and passed about at social gatherings.

In churches all over England, pastors preached *dulce et decorum est*— that it was sweet and proper to die for one's country. Rare was the service that did not invoke divine aid against Napoleon; one pastor at Colchester finished his prayer with the devout sentiment, "O Lord God, be pleased to change his wicked heart, or stop his wicked breath."

As Londoners laid by stocks of food in case of siege, the regular British Army of 139,000 men was mobilized to resist any French assault on the capital. The rest of the country was to be defended by hastily recruited but ardently patriotic local units consisting of more than 360,000 volunteers scattered throughout the towns and villages. Along the Channel coastline a series of 74 forts resembling huge inverted flowerpots was constructed and manned by eager volunteers.

At Buckingham Palace, King George III announced that if the French landed on England's shores, "I shall cer-

HOP

Step

Jump

From indigence in Corsica To Affluence in France

From aspiring ambition To the summit of Power.

From Calais to Dover Where little John Bull does the Corsican over.

Pub.d by T.Tegg 111 Cheapside Jan.y 1

Jan. 1803

HOP STEP and JUMP

Pub by Roberts 28 middl row

The French invasion fleet, an immense flotilla of barges, pinnaces and gun sloops, is reduced to size in this caricature of Napoleon floating on a flimsy clothing box. "We can tell him," blustered one contemporary magazine, "the only fear that Englishmen experience is the fear that he will not venture out of port."

tainly put myself at the head of my troops and my other armed subjects to repel them"—no doubt to the distress of His Majesty's generals. But he relieved their anxieties somewhat by refusing any rank higher than colonel to his wastrel son, the Prince of Wales.

On hilltops stretching from London to the coast, a chain of great semaphore stations stood ready to transmit messages and alarums. These towers had six movable shutters that indicated coded letters of the alphabet and that were always manned during daylight hours. At night Englishmen prepared

to spread the alarum with fire beacons made of piles of tar-saturated wood.

All England was on the alert. Even the toddlers were on their mettle. For British mothers took to crooning such chilling bedtime lullabies as:

Baby, baby, naughty baby,
Hush, you squalling thing, I say;
Hush your squalling, or it may be
Bonaparte may pass this way.
Baby, baby, he will hear you
As he passes by the house,
And he, limb from limb, will tear you
Just as pussy tears a mouse.

ed a dangerous tactic. He took his blockading fleet out of sight of the port, leaving only a few frigates to report to him if the French admiral ventured out of the harbor. It was a cat-and-mouse game, with Nelson hiding just over the horizon and waiting to pounce on his quarry. As he explained it later to an Admiralty member, "I beg to inform your Lordship that the port of Toulon has never been blockaded by me; quite the reverse. Every opportunity has been offered the enemy to put to sea, for it is there we hope to realize the hopes and expectations of our country."

And so the long, dreary duty continued. The British sailors renamed the port "Too-Long." Nelson had arrived in the summer of 1803. By autumn of 1804, he had become so exhausted that the ship's doctor persuaded him to ask for sick leave. But then in December, Spain joined the war on the side of France. Nelson forgot about going home.

Now, with the availability of Spanish vessels, Napoleon finally worked out his plan for temporarily clearing the Channel for his landing barges. It was Napoleonic both in scale and in complicated detail.

The French admiral in charge of the Toulon fleet was Pierre Charles Villeneuve, who had managed to slip out of Abukir bay and escape after the Battle of the Nile. Napoleon ordered Villeneuve to depart from Toulon with his 11 ships of the line and seven frigates at the first opportunity and to sail not for England but for the West Indies. En route he was to call on the Spanish commander at Cadiz and there he subsequently added nine ships to the Combined Fleet. Meanwhile, Admiral Honoré-Joseph-Antoine Ganteaume at Brest was to sneak his 22 ships by the Royal Navy's blockade and head for the West Indies. All 40 or more ships were to rendezvous at Martinique, the most important French stronghold in the area, where they would be joined by still more French ships on the Caribbean station.

But—and here was the key to Napoleon's plan—the reinforced Combined Fleet was not to attack British possessions in the West Indies; instead it was to head straight back to Europe. With this diversionary move Napoleon hoped to distract the Royal Navy into rushing to the defense of England's rich West Indies possessions. And while the British ships were decoyed across the Atlantic, looking around the West Indies for the French, Napoleon's Combined Fleet would race back to clear the Channel for the invasion of England.

On January 19, 1805, at three in the afternoon, Nelson's fleet was anchored in Madalena Roads more than 200 miles from Toulon, taking aboard supplies, when his two lookout frigates came rolling in before a gale. Whipping at their yardarms were flags signaling, "French Fleet at Sea." By six that evening, Nelson's fleet was in pursuit.

Admiral Villeneuve, on receiving Napoleon's orders, had waited for a gale in order to make as good time as possible before Nelson could pounce on him. He misjudged the severity of this one and, more important, the softness of his crews after months in port. The storm succeeded not in driving him toward Gibraltar but in damaging so many ships and injuring so many men that Villeneuve had to creep back into Toulon.

Nelson did not know this, nor did he guess it. When he found that the Toulon fleet had not cleared the Strait of Gibraltar, he again turned his search eastward. A pair of frigates reported sighting the French on an easterly course; from this Nelson concluded that their destination was either Naples, Sicily or somewhere in the eastern Mediterranean. He rushed all the way to Egypt without finding the foe. His embarrassment on racing back to find that Villeneuve had returned to Toulon was exceeded only by Napoleon's delight at so easily luring the great admiral off on another fool's chase. He cackled gleefully at Nelson's "immense stupidity" and said, "the man has a mania concerning Egypt." But Napoleon's pleasure was combined with outrage at Villeneuve. "What is to be done," he asked, "with admirals who allow their spirits to sink, and determine to hasten home at the first damage they receive? All the captains ought to have had sealed orders to meet off the Canary Islands. The damages should have been repaired en route. A few topmasts carried away, some casualties in a gale of wind, were everyday occurrences. But the great evil of our Navy is that the men who command it are unused to all the risks of command."

On this point Nelson and Napoleon were in agreement. After Villeneuve's return to Toulon, Nelson wrote: "Bonaparte has often made his brags that our fleet would be worn out by keeping the sea; that his was kept in order by staying in port; but he now finds, I fancy, if *Emperors* hear truth, that his fleet suffers more in one night than ours in a year."

Villeneuve managed to redeem himself somewhat in Emperor Napoleon's eyes on March 30, when he again slipped out of Toulon, choosing a dark and stormy night to slide unseen past Nelson's frigates. And again, when Villeneuve was found to have escaped, Nelson guessed wrong as to the Frenchman's direction. Once more the British set off in pursuit to the east—as Villeneuve fled westward. By the time Nelson realized his error, and turned west, the French fleet was through the Straits of Gibraltar and out into the broad Atlantic. By the time Nelson reached Gibraltar the winds had shifted into the west, blocking the passage and effectively bottling his fleet in the Mediterranean. Nelson bewailed the winds as "Foul, Dead Foul!" Yet there was nothing he could do but wait nearly two weeks until they shifted around into the east again and he could take his fleet through the narrow corridor.

Off across the Atlantic Nelson sailed, dropping south to pick up the trade winds and setting a course for the British island of Barbados. Once the fleet reached the trades, the winds held steady and Nelson began to gain on the French fleet. This despite the fact that the better-designed French ships were inherently faster and Nelson's storm-weakened vessels in bad shape; the *Superb*, for example, actually had cables wound around her hull to keep her seams from parting. However, the same storms had, as Nelson knew, toughened and sharpened the men to the point where British sail-handling and helmsmanship were vastly superior. The *Superb*'s Captain Richard Keats kept all sails flying and the studding-sail booms lashed to the yards while his men worked constantly at the pumps. Nelson sent him a message: "My dear Keats, be assured I know and feel that the *Superb* does all which is possible for a ship to accomplish, and I desire that you will not fret upon the occasion."

Villeneuve had picked up seven Spanish ships at Cadiz. With a fleet of 18 ships of the line, he arrived at Martinique on May 14, three days after

Nelson had started in pursuit. There was no sign of Ganteaume; in fact, Ganteaume had told Napoleon that the only way he could get through the close British blockade off Brest was to take his 22 ships out fighting. That was not part of Napoleon's plan; he wanted no battles until his force had been assembled in the West Indies. He ordered Ganteaume to keep waiting until he could sneak past the blockade. Ganteaume never did.

Nelson's majestic men-of-war—his "grey geese," as he liked to call them—plowed along at an average speed of four to five knots as they entered the cobalt-blue waters of the Caribbean. On the morning of June 4 the lookouts sighted Barbados, and at noon the fleet anchored in the roadstead off Bridgetown. While Villeneuve had taken 34 days for the crossing, Nelson had taken 24. At Barbados he was told that Villeneuve's targets most likely were Tobago and Trinidad to the south. His own hunch was that Villeneuve might still be somewhere near to Martinique to the north. But considering how wrong his hunches had been recently, he went south—and was wrong again. Villeneuve had indeed been near Martinique and Dominica, waiting for the other French fleet that never came and sending ashore 1,000 sick. Had Nelson gone north from Barbados instead of south, he would have met Villeneuve for a second British-French battle where Rodney had beaten De Grasse 23 years earlier.

Upon reaching Trinidad and finding no sign of the French, Nelson turned back north. But he was too late. As soon as Villeneuve heard that Nelson was in the West Indies, he decided to stop waiting for Ganteaume and set sail back across the Atlantic. Five days after Villeneuve's departure, Nelson reached Martinique and, discovering the enemy gone, set out in hot pursuit to the east.

Nelson guessed that Villeneuve was returning to Toulon and laid a course for Gibraltar and the Mediterranean. He sent his fastest frigate, the *Curieux*, direct to London with reports on the chase. Captain Bettesworth of the *Curieux* did better than that. One morning as he flew northeastward, his lookout hailed the deck. There they were, the entire Toulon-Cadiz fleet, headed not for the Mediterranean but north in the direction of the Channel.

Bettesworth reached England on July 8. His news electrified the Admiralty. Reacting to Napoleon's feint, the British had already begun to move to the defense, shifting more ships to a protective ring around England. Bettesworth confirmed the wisdom of the precautions. And with Nelson racing his fleet back across the Atlantic the prospects seemed good for a climactic battle.

Nelson in fact reached Europe before Villeneuve did. On July 20 he took his ships into Gibraltar for reprovisioning after two months at sea on his 14,000-mile chase, and stepped ashore himself for the first time in just under two years.

Two days later Villeneuve and his Combined Fleet, inching through one of the notorious fogs off Cape Finisterre, came upon Sir Robert Calder and part of the Channel fleet. Calder had been alerted by the Admiralty after the news from the *Curieux* and was watching for Villeneuve. In the fog Villeneuve could not make out how many British ships there were. His men were sick with scurvy and exhausted, and his ships were trailing underwater gardens of weed from the tropics. His flagship, the *Bucentaure*, had recently been struck by lightning. There was a brief engagement. Two of the seven Spanish ships that had joined at Cadiz were captured by Calder. Villeneuve slid off through the fog. He ran into Vigo Bay and then on to Ferrol, where he arrived August 1 to repair his ships and tend his sick.

At Napoleon's frantic urging, Villeneuve came out 12 days later and headed for the Channel again. By now nearly 30 British men-of-war stood between him and the Channel. Expecting to find just such a force, Villeneuve was not surprised when he saw a long row of lights ahead of him. He did not know that it was a convoy of merchantmen. He put about and went south again, this time all the way down to Cadiz, at the entrance to the Straits of Gibraltar. On patrol off Cadiz was Collingwood, who graciously moved aside until Villeneuve had taken his entire fleet into Cadiz harbor, and then clamped shut his blockade.

"Ships and seamen rot in harbour," Horatio Nelson once wrote. The experience of Admiral Villeneuve and his Combined Fleet, locked in Cadiz in the early autumn of 1805, provided vivid proof of this dictum. It was even worse than Nelson imagined. Cadiz seethed with animosity. Andalusia was recovering from an epidemic of yellow fever that had killed thousands of people and much of the area's livestock. The sudden demands of the Combined Fleet were more than the region could meet. The ships needed everything from spars to handspikes, as well as food and clothing. One report reaching London had it that even the public water fountains at Puerta Santa Maria, across the bay from Cadiz, "have been put in requisition for the use of the fleets."

The local Spanish authorities were so begrudging of supplies to their arrogant and unpopular allies that Villeneuve actually had to appeal to Madrid at one point. Only then were the goods forthcoming. But the troubles the French were having with the Cadiz townspeople were the least of their problems. Far more serious and demoralizing to all concerned was the brooding hostility between the French and Spanish officers of the Combined Fleet. The Spanish had a long history of seafaring. Their naval architects were among the world's best, and Spain's men-of-war were well built and powerfully armed. In Cadiz the queen of the Combined Fleet was Spain's *Santisima Trinidad*, largest warship in the world, a four-decker carrying 130 guns and towering over every other vessel in the harbor.

Spain's naval officers also had a proud tradition, perhaps too proud and too jealously defended; their tradition had not been interrupted by revolution as had been the case in France. But Spain's great weakness was in the quality of its ordinary seamen. The Spanish people had little taste for naval life and fled into the rugged hills in droves at the approach of a press gang; to fill the continual shortages, the Navy had to press foot soldiers who might know how to fire a gun but knew nothing about the sea or a man-of-war. When Nelson heard that France might be gaining some Spanish ships, he joked, "I take for granted not manned, as that would be the readiest way to lose them."

The inefficiency of Spanish crews was one reason why two Spanish ships had been lost in the brush with the British off Cape Finisterre. But

An enemy host of Napoleonic proportions

On August 3, 1805, Napoleon Bonaparte staged a grand review of the invasion force that was poised at Boulogne across the English Channel from Britain. There were, as one recorder put it, "nine miles of soldiers." Possible exaggeration aside, it was a fearsome host that Napoleon had gathered—and it was lusting for conquest.

Though some troops had arrived in Boulogne by 1798, the major build-up began in 1803 after Napoleon concluded that the only way to defeat the British was to capture their homeland. Soon there were four camps spread across acres of beach, holding 161,000 troops. The equipment and provisions that Napoleon had ordered for this mighty force included 15,000 bayonets, 21,000 muskets, nine million cartridges, 960,000 rations of biscuits—and 438,000 rations of brandy. Drawn up on the beaches and moored in orderly ranks in the harbor were 2,300 boats of all kinds to transport the fighting men and their impedimenta to the other side of the Channel: praams, caïques, shallops, corvettes, packets and flat-bottomed gunboats.

As always, the Emperor had personally supervised every aspect of his army, from its superb provisioning to its razor-keen training. The officers never knew when their master might descend on them for a surprise inspection. Though the business of government often kept him in Paris, Napoleon loved to slip away at night and go pounding down the highroad to Boulogne in his four-horse coach. At headquarters he would change into his gray riding coat, cut with extra-large armholes to accommodate his epaulets,

"Conquest has made me what I am, and conquest alone can maintain me," declaimed Bonaparte in 1797 after he defeated the Austrians in Italy. But all his subsequent designs were thwarted by the British, forcing him to conclude that he must invade England itself.

and don his favorite black felt hat with its tricolor cockade. Then before dawn he would sweep through the camps.

A typical tour might start as early as 2 a.m. with an inspection of the harbor guns and a visit to a landing barge. Next might come a round of the docks, a ride along the beach to survey one of the camps and a test firing of heated shot at a flammable target set up at sea. There was sometimes a visit to a second camp before Napoleon returned to headquarters at 10 a.m.

During the day, Napoleon habitually spent much time in a council room in a pavilion he had ordered built atop the Odre Cliff overlooking the Channel. The place was nearly bare, furnished with a single horsehair-stuffed green leather chair and a table covered with green cloth. The only decoration in the room was a big map of the Channel. A painting on the ceiling portrayed golden clouds in an azure sky and an eagle carrying a thunderbolt and flying in what could very easily be the direction of England, guided by Napoleon's star.

At staff meetings, some of which lasted four hours or even longer, the Emperor would sit in the only chair while his officers stood around him, leaning on their sword scabbards as they strove to answer his innumerable questions. From headquarters, memorandums spewed forth: "Let me know what distance a gunboat and a shallop can cover in half an hour by rowing, without sails, and at flood tide." "The uniforms of that battalion are worn out, they must be replaced." "It is imperative to discover which of the contractors have supplied bad drinks."

The Emperor was meticulous about equipping his soldiers with all new ar-

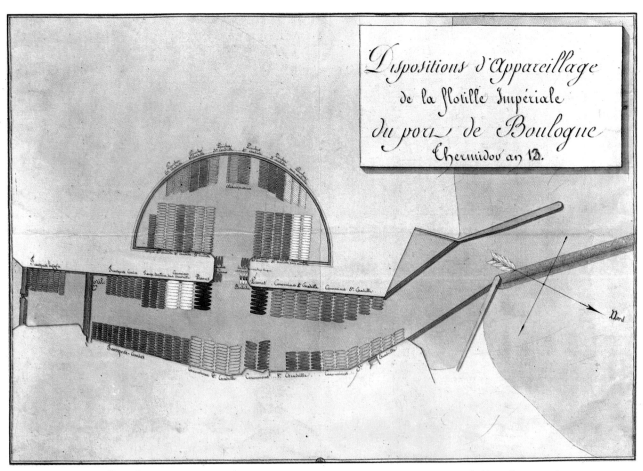

Napoleon's invasion fleet of troops, cavalry and artillery transports, plus gunboats and supply craft, jams the banks and docking basin of the River Liane at Boulogne in this 1805 watercolor plan, which was apparently drawn to be used by the French military staff.

Attended by aides, Napoleon stares across the Channel at England. It was an oft-repeated scene—but fanciful in this 1902 painting by the French artist Maurice Orange: the ships being constructed are not barges but deep-keeled warships, which would hardly be built on a beach.

mament: bayonets, muskets, cannon, mortars. He loved to engage in personal tests. On one occasion he insisted on firing the first shot of a monster battery of mortars he had ordered installed as a defensive precaution atop the Odre Cliff; the largest mortars ever cast, they took 45 pounds of powder and threw a 600-pound shell more than a mile. The thunderclap explosion made him deaf for two days, during which time his temper was so bad that everyone tried to stay away from him.

Still, these guns, this army, were his pride and joy. His navy, from the land-ing craft to the men-of-war of the fleet that must escort him safely across the Channel, was his trial and his frustration. He was forever voicing impatience with his Naval Officers, whom he accused of inertia, and he did not understand the vagaries of the sea.

On July 20, 1804, as he set off on a morning ride, Napoleon casually ordered a general review of the ships in Boulogne harbor to be held on his return. But a vicious storm was in the offing, and the officer in charge of the invasion fleet, Vice Admiral Eustace Bruix, an independent-minded sort, had no compunction about countermanding the order. On his return, Napoleon was in a fury. He sent for Bruix and almost struck him with his riding crop when Bruix flatly refused to obey.

But Bruix was subverted by Rear Admiral Charles Magon, his second-in-command, an ambitious officer who during the confrontation ordered the review to commence. For the rest of that rain-swept day the crews struggled to get back to their anchorages. Napoleon paced the beach, his head bowed into the gale and his arms folded. At one point he tried to climb into a

lifeboat to help but succeeded only in getting soaked by the surf and losing his hat. As the storm finally weakened, most of the ships made it back to their moorings. But next morning the beach was littered with more than 200 bodies—and Napoleon's hat.

Napoleon's account of the event to Empress Josephine was typical of the man: "Last night the wind freshened, and one of our gun-boats in the roads dragged her anchor, and ran on the rocks off Boulogne. I was afraid she would be a total loss, both men and gear; but we succeeded in saving them all. It was a magnificent spectacle: the reports of alarm-guns, watch-fires all along the shore, the sea raging and roaring, and all night the anxiety as to whether the poor fellows could be rescued or would perish before our eyes!"

It was a fable. As the months wore on, the Emperor was forced to recognize that his grand scheme was only a dream. Many times at Boulogne he had looked across the Channel through his special telescope. "One could pick out the houses and see people moving about," he wrote one of his consuls. "The Channel is a mere ditch and will be crossed as soon as someone has the courage to attempt it." But none of his soldiers ever crossed that ditch. Napoleon Bonaparte was forced to turn his violent ambitions elsewhere—because of the Royal Navy and Horatio Nelson.

Fantastical as it might seem, the design at top right for a 600-foot-long raft to be powered by windmills was submitted in 1798 as a prototype for Napoleon's invasion barges. The plan included an armored citadel, drawbridges fore and aft, and stables for horses to drive the paddle wheels if the wind died. Among the landing craft actually built were the sturdy, flat-bottomed, 120-foot-long pinnaces shown at right. They held two 18-pounder cannon, 18 pairs of oars, leeboards to enable the craft to stay on course and a drawbridge in the bow.

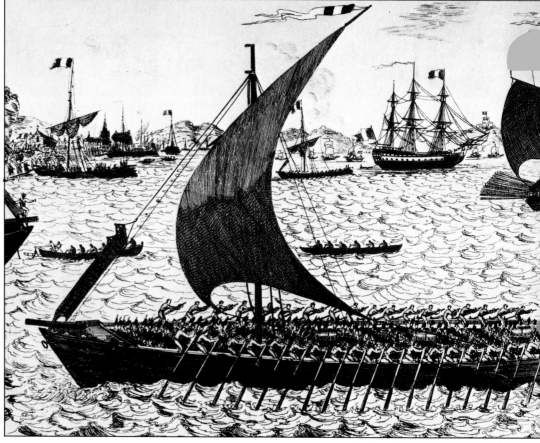

the Spanish officers felt that the French were to blame for lack of support. They charged bitterly that the two ships had been "deserted in action and sacrificed." There was open talk among the Spanish officers of "treachery" on the part of their French allies. So enraged was Vice Admiral Don Federico Gravina, commander of the Spanish squadron, that he stormed up to Madrid and tendered his resignation. After considerable effort the Prime Minister managed to calm him down and send him back to Cadiz to assist the French.

Villeneuve was having no easier a time of it with his own officers. Rear Admiral Dumanoir Le Pelley, descendant of a wealthy family that had already given two admirals to the French Navy, felt that he should have been chosen commander of the fleet and did not bother to hide his resentment. There were also dark mutterings from Rear Admiral Charles Magon, an impetuous officer who had been appalled by Villeneuve's headlong retreat at the engagement off Finisterre—so much so that when Villeneuve in the *Bucentaure* had passed his ship, Magon in a fury had thrown his spyglass and even his wig across the water at the flagship.

But Villeneuve had lost far more than just the confidence of his officers. He had lost the faith of his Emperor. Napoleon had reacted with volcanic rage to the news that his fleet—the fleet that was to open the English Channel for his invasion army—had slunk into Cadiz harbor. To his Minister of Marine, Vice Admiral Denis Decrés, he railed, "I don't believe Villeneuve has enough character to command a frigate. The man has no energy, no moral courage." He called Villeneuve "a coward and a traitor. A wretch who ought to be ignominiously cashiered. He would sacrifice everything to save his own skin."

And now Napoleon made a fateful decision. After waiting all those months with mounting frustration, he finally concluded that he could remain idle no longer and planned a new military adventure. Believing himself betrayed by his navy, he turned inland again—to the east where his old enemies in Austria had been moving against him. Almost overnight, his Grand Army of England, gathered over four years at vast expense, broke camp and on August 29 began the march toward Austria. From Boulogne, Napoleon wrote his Foreign Minister Talleyrand, "I am off at full speed. I am striking camp, and replacing my fighting battalions with reserves, which in any case give me a formidable enough army at Boulogne." The invasion was suspended, at least for the winter. It need not be canceled so long as there was a Combined Fleet in being.

On September 28, Villeneuve was informed of Napoleon's abrupt change of plans in a message from Decrés, who also advised the unhappy admiral that he had "much to do to regain His Majesty's confidence." Villeneuve's new orders were to take on board a contingent of French and Spanish soldiers quartered in Cadiz and pick up a Spanish squadron at Cartagena, and ferry them all to Naples, where they were to reinforce Napoleon's Italian operations. Villeneuve was to take the entire Combined Fleet out of Cadiz, sail to Cartagena and Naples, then return to the great French base at Toulon where he would await further orders.

Villeneuve loyally replied that he would do his best to execute Napoleon's orders. His Combined Fleet had now grown to 33 ships of the line with the addition of four more Spanish vessels in Cadiz. He made plans to embark the troops and sail as soon as possible. Somehow he must either evade or fight his way past the British fleet lurking offshore. Though the main enemy force was usually out of sight, everyone could see the watching frigates patrolling back and forth and knew that the capital ships could not be far off. But how many there were, and who was in command, Villeneuve could not know for certain. There was a report, by way of Lisbon, that the British admiral was Horatio Nelson.

On October 8, Villeneuve called his senior captains together aboard the *Bucentaure*, and the full depth of the Spaniards' disaffection immediately became apparent. They virtually refused to sail, coldly stating that their ships were unready and adding, as if Villeneuve could not read a barometer, that a storm was in the making. At one point the hot-headed Admiral Magon uttered a sneering remark about the courage of Spanish officers and almost provoked a sword fight with a Spanish commodore. As the argument about the weather continued, even the normally polite Villeneuve snapped: "It is not the glass but the courage of certain persons that is falling."

White-faced, trembling with fury, the Spanish Admiral Gravina replied: "Whenever the Spanish Fleet has gone into action, side by side with allies, as has often happened, it has ever borne its part valiantly and led the way, the foremost under fire. This, sir, as you yourself must admit, we fully proved to you at the recent battle off Finisterre." He then turned to his captains and roared: "*Mañana al mar!*—Tomorrow to sea!"

After the meeting, Villeneuve wrote a report to Decrés, stating that in his opinion the Spaniards were "quite incapable of meeting the enemy."

The next day there was a stirring parade of men-of-war as the Combined Fleet, 33 fighting ships, moved through the narrow inner-harbor entrance past the walled city. The plan was to clear the harbor and anchor in the roadstead outside to await the first favorable wind to make for the open ocean and head for the Straits of Gibraltar. But scarcely had the fleet dropped anchor before the predicted storm came howling down upon it. On and off for a week, the gales battered the ships. Villeneuve held two meetings with his French admirals to discuss the anticipated battle and hoped-for breakthrough to Naples. The veteran of Abukir offered his guess as to the tactics they would confront. "The British fleet will not be formed in a line of battle, parallel with the Combined Fleet, according to the usage of former days," he predicted. "Nelson, assuming him to be, as reported, really in command, will seek to break our line, envelop our rear, and overpower with groups of his ships as many of ours as he can isolate or cut off." But Villeneuve could offer no novel suggestion for defense against such an attack—he planned to proceed by the book, in traditional line of battle.

At last, on October 17 the storm abated, but now the winds were unfavorable. As Villeneuve impatiently waited for the winds to shift, he received a heartening bit of intelligence. The lookout posts along the Spanish coast reported that four British men-of-war escorting a troop convoy had been spotted sailing eastward into the Mediterranean from Gibraltar. Two more warships were in Gibraltar for water and minor repairs. Villeneuve concluded that all six had been detached from the blockading fleet—which would improve his odds considerably.

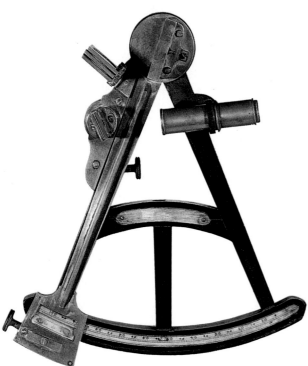

Nelson's quadrant—used to determine a ship's position relative to the equator— became more of a keepsake than a working instrument for the naval hero. Because of his brilliance as a commander, Nelson was promoted so swiftly that he lacked experience in navigation and ship handling and was never accomplished in those arts. As a fellow officer bluntly put it, "Lord Nelson was no seaman."

By 6 a.m. on October 19, 1805, the wind was light but from the right direction: the east, which would enable the fleet to clear the headlands enclosing the roadstead and make for the open sea. The signal rose to the *Bucentaure's* yardarm: "Make Sail and Proceed." Slowly the Combined Fleet moved out, drifting with the tide, fighting the crosscurrents and trying to keep off the shoals dotting the roadstead. By midday, with only seven ships clear of the roadstead, the wind died to a near calm. The ships that had made it to the open sea inched northward along the coast and anchored to wait for the others.

Through Saturday evening, October 19, strings of ships' boats towed the rest of the Combined Fleet toward the sea. On Sunday morning a fresh breeze came out of the south-southeast. The entire fleet of 33 ships of the line was in the open sea by noon.

As the ships worked their way out, tearful crowds watched along the walls of Cadiz and filed into the churches to pray for their relatives going into battle. At the Iglesia del Carmen, Cadiz' favorite church of mariners, there were so many worshippers that they were admitted in relays. On land and on board ship alike, the atmosphere was one of impending doom. The Spaniards were still bitterly complaining that their ships were poorly equipped, the men insufficiently trained and, "in short," as one officer put it, "the fleet was not in a state to perform the services appointed to it." With a show of bravado Villeneuve attempted to encourage his seamen with the message: "Nothing in the sight of an English Squadron should daunt us. They are skilled in seamanship; in a month's time we shall be as skillful." But everyone realized that even if this were true, which it was not, his men had only a few days at most, instead of a month, before confronting the gun crews of the Royal Navy obviously lying in wait for them somewhere nearby. Indeed, Admiral Magon believed that his only hope was to get close enough to a British ship to board it and try to capture it in hand-to-hand fighting. To spur his men, he had offered an expensive silver-mounted belt he had been awarded for past services to "the first man to board an enemy."

Aboard the French ship *Redoutable* another Frenchman, Captain Jean Lucas, grimly confronted the prospect of battle. During the confinement in Cadiz he had perfected his own special tactics, drilling his men with grappling irons, hand grenades, bayonets, pistols and muskets, and teaching his sharpshooters to fire from the *Redoutable's* tops onto the enemy's quarter-deck. He was aware that he would probably go down to defeat—likely even death. But Lucas was determined that he would take some Englishmen with him.

At the horizon, aboard the British frigate *Euryalus,* the attitude was exactly the opposite of that in the Combined Fleet. After weeks and months of patrolling and fighting storms, the moment the British had hungered for had come. Like the tails of wolves outside the fold as the sheep straggled out, the British frigates' signal flags flicked in the breeze. Across the water to Nelson's *Victory* beyond the horizon went the message. *Euryalus* to *Phoebe:* "Enemy Are Coming Out of Port." *Phoebe* to *Mars:* "Enemy Are Coming Out of Port." *Mars* to *Victory:* "Enemy Are Coming Out of Port."

And *Victory* to the British fleet: "General Chase, Southeast."

Friends and foes: the captains at Trafalgar

The Royal Navy's proud professionals

When the Royal Navy confronted the French-Spanish Combined Fleet at Trafalgar, a vast assembly of proud and mighty officers came together, representing a combination of social luster and professional talent. Friends or foes, they had one thing in common: they were gentlemen.

The Spaniards—with princely and ducal connections—had the bluest blood, and might look down their aquiline noses at the French, whose aristocratic ranks had been decimated by the Revolution. But egalitarian parvenus had not altogether swamped the French Navy; the commander in chief, Admiral Pierre Villeneuve, had an Eighth Century ancestor who had fought with Charlemagne, and among his officers were some with pedigrees reaching back to the 12th Century. If the British gentry who served the Crown afloat were newcomers by that time standard, they nevertheless had plenty of knights and lords-to-be among their officers—and the same unabashed reverence for the niceties of class as their national foes.

Indeed, that veneration often transcended national enmity. It was a matter of gracious routine for a conquering captain to exchange civilities and handsome tributes with the officer whose ship he had captured and perhaps offer him a convivial brandy as well. But toward his own crewmen a captain's stance was nothing short of Olympian. A seaman removed his cap when addressing his captain—just as he did when he entered a church. He might speak of his captain as a friend—as did some who served under Cuthbert Collingwood (right)—but he had in mind a patron, not a comrade. And well he might, for on the captain depended the very life of the crew. "He is a Leviathan," wrote the 18th Century satirist Ned Ward, "or rather a kind of Sea-God, whom the poor tars worship as the Indians do the Devil."

British, French or Spanish, a captain set the tone of his ship; afloat he answered to no one save his admiral, and whether the rule was strict or lax, cruel or benevolent was his to determine. The captains at Trafalgar had tastes ranging from horticulture to hydrography, and temperaments varying from impassive to incendiary. Each with his own idiosyncrasies put his stamp on the ship he commanded.

VICE ADM. CUTHBERT COLLINGWOOD of the Royal Sovereign was a gentleman-farmer ashore—he had a passion for planting oak trees—and was gentle with his men afloat. "I cannot for the life of me comprehend the religion of an officer who could pray all one day and flog his men all the next," he wrote.

CAPT. SIR THOMAS MASTERMAN HARDY of the Victory signed on at age 12 and showed promise at once; his first captain wrote his parents: "Thomas is a very good boy, and I think will make a complete seaman one day." Since 1798 he had served as Nelson's flag captain—and was his closest comrade afloat.

CAPT. RICHARD KING of the Achille had the Royal Navy in his veins: he was the son of one admiral, would soon become one himself and would sire still a third.

CAPT. ROBERT MOORSOM of the Revenge was known for his courtliness. When a woman was discovered aboard a prize he once took, he was "not wanting in civility to the lady," he wrote. "I ordered her two purser's shirts to make a petticoat."

CAPT. SIR EDWARD BERRY of the Agamemnon was one of the most handsome of Nelson's captains—and one of the best. When King George III met Nelson at a London levee after the Battle of Tenerife and noted that the admiral had lost his right arm, Nelson promptly replied: "But not my right hand, Sir, as I have the honour of presenting Captain Berry."

CAPT. PHILIP DURHAM of the Defiance almost missed the battle because his ship was not ready. But Nelson, who regarded him highly, intervened with the Admiralty, and the Defiance was soon fit to fight.

CAPT. ELIAB HARVEY of the Temeraire was relatively new to command but a cocky sort on whom fellow officers lost no love. "His head is turned," wrote Captain Thomas Fremantle. "Never having been in action before he thinks every Ship was subdued by him, and he wears us all to Death, with his incessant Jargon."

CAPT. EDWARD ROTHERAM of the Royal Sovereign donned a gold-laced hat and heavy gold epaulets for Trafalgar—defying a warning about enemy sharpshooters. "Let me alone!" he snorted. "I've always fought in a cocked hat and always will!"

CAPT. WILLIAM HARGOOD of the Belleisle rode into the Battle of Trafalgar astride a carronade. One lieutenant remembered: "An awful silence prevailed in the ship, only interrupted by the commanding voice of Captain Hargood. 'Steady! Starboard a little! Steady so!' "

CAPT. GEORGE DUFF of the Mars was the scion of a noble Scottish clan and had run away to sea at the age of nine. At Trafalgar he had three youthful kinsmen on board: his 13-year-old son, Norwich, as well as two young nephews.

CAPT. THOMAS FREMANTLE of the Neptune whiled away the long days of blockade by writing his wife, Betsey, affectionate letters detailing shipboard minutiae. Among other things, he recounted with amusement that the only goat on board fell through a hatchway during a storm, obliging him to drink his tea without milk.

CAPT. HENRY BLACKWOOD of the frigate Euryalus twice refused command of a ship of the line, preferring the dashing hide-and-seek of frigate work. Nelson exhorted him as he kept watch on the enemy in Cadiz harbor: "I rely on you, that we can't miss getting hold of them."

CAPT. JOHN STOCKHAM of the Thunderer—shown here in his lieutenant's uniform—by a stroke of fortune came to command a ship at Trafalgar; her captain had been called home to London to testify at an admiral's court-martial.

CAPT. JOHN COOKE of the Bellerophon, a conscientious and unorthodox officer, made an unusual arrangement on the eve of Trafalgar: with his next-in-command he took turns at the watch—a duty that senior officers seldom bothered with.

Leaders of the Combined Fleet

ADM. PIERRE CHARLES VILLENEUVE, commander in chief, was an aristocrat who survived the French Revolution. Collingwood found him agreeable: "He has nothing of the offensive vapouring and boasting which we, perhaps too often, attribute to Frenchmen."

REAR ADM. CHARLES MAGON of the Algésiras first saw action at 14 and had since proved so bold that Napoleon's aide-de-camp thought he should have been fleet commander.

CAPT. JEAN JACQUES MAGENDIE of the Bucentaure was Villeneuve's flag captain. A young midshipman of the British Euryalus, which took him prisoner, remembered him as "a short fat jocular sailor, who found a cure for all ills in the Frenchman's philosophy 'Fortune de guerre'—(though this was the third time the goddess had brought him to England as prisoner)."

COM. JULIEN COSMAO-KERJULIEN of the Pluton was called by his men "Va de Bon Coeur"—meaning "Goes with a Stout Heart." As a commodore he ranked between captain and admiral.

REAR ADM. DUMANOIR LE PELLEY of the Formidable at 35 was such an experienced officer, having captured 15 vessels by 1805, that Villeneuve chose him as second-in-command of the fleet.

CAPT. JEAN-JACQUES LUCAS of the Redoutable made such a hit in London after his capture that the sword he had surrendered was returned to him at a supper party hosted by a British admiral.

ADM. DON FEDERICO GRAVINA of the *Principe de Asturias* was commander of the Spanish division of the Combined Fleet. Self-assured and even-tempered, he was whispered to be the illegitimate son of the late King Carlos III of Spain.

COM. DIONISIO ALCALA GALIANO of the *Bahama* was known as "El Inclito Galiano," which translates loosely as "Galiano the Brilliant"—an epithet that suited both his fiery disposition and his field of expertise, which was astronomy.

VICE ADM. DON IGNATIO ALAVA of the *Santa Ana* exchanged compliments with Collingwood after the fight: Collingwood termed Alava's ship a "Spanish perfection," while the Spaniards averred that the Royal Sovereign was the Royal Devil.

CAPT. DON CAYETANO VALDEZ of the *Neptune* had won national adulation for bringing off the rescue of the *Santisima Trinidad*—the "Glory of Spain"—at the Battle of Cape St. Vincent.

COM. DON COSME DE CHURRUCA of the *San Juan Nepomuceno* was an authority on nautical engineering and so cool in combat that a shipmate recalled, "Shot flew round him without his ever once changing colour even."

Chapter 5

Trafalgar: the final kill

ven in the best of weather the sea off Spain's Cape Trafalgar heaves with swells that have come unobstructed across the entire sweep of the Atlantic. On the morning of October 20, 1805, there was a light breeze from the east, which had flattened the sea; the 10-foot swells were still formidable but gentle for the area. On board the *Victory*, Lord Nelson sent a dinner invitation to Vice Admiral Cuthbert Collingwood and a favored few of his other captains: "What a beautiful day! Will you be tempted out of your ship?" One of the captains invited to dine with Nelson that day was John Cooke of the *Bellerophon,* who ordered his ship to approach Nelson's *Victory.* While the *Bellerophon* was leaving her place in the line, her first lieutenant, William Cumby, spotted a signal flying at the masthead of the *Mars,* the nearest other ship of the line. He called it to Cooke's attention and they studied it through their telescopes. Cumby was certain it was signal 370: "Enemy Is Coming Out of Port." Cooke could not be sure; only the topsails of the *Mars* were visible over the horizon and the colors of her signal flags were difficult to make out against the sun. The *Mars* then made her "Distant" signal, which was designed to be seen at extreme long range and prescribed for just such a situation: a flag, a pendant and a ball that were hoisted at different mastheads. It was 370.

Just as the *Bellerophon* was about to relay the message, the *Victory* signaled acknowledgment to the *Mars,* having made out the signal herself. Another flag from the *Victory* canceled the dinner, and the next one called for "General Chase, South East." Cadiz roadstead was 50 miles away; the word that the Combined Fleet was leaving port had been passed all that distance in less than two and a half hours from the time the first British frigate had seen it happen.

Nelson had long been waiting for this moment. After his exhausting and fruitless chase across the Atlantic, he had stopped to rest for a few weeks in Gibraltar, then had applied for home leave. He took the *Victory* to Portsmouth and rode home to Merton through a night of driving rain.

He reached Merton at six in the morning on August 20, the same day that Villeneuve had taken the Combined Fleet into Cadiz. For almost a month he tried to relax while Emma coddled him and nursed him back to better health. But he could not unwind. He continued to rise at dawn or before. He walked for miles up and down beside the small garden stream, which he had nicknamed the Nile. He paced in his summerhouse, which he called the Quarter Deck, planning his tactics for the day when he would meet Villeneuve.

One of his callers at Merton was Captain Keats, whose leaky old *Superb* had made it to the Caribbean across the Atlantic and back and was finally brought in for overhaul. Nelson took Keats by the arm and guided

Surrounded by his captains, Nelson explains the tactics to be used in the Battle of Trafalgar. He called his ingenious plan to pinch off and destroy the enemy's ships piecemeal the "Nelson Touch."

him out to the Quarter Deck, where he outlined a plan for the confrontation of two great fleets at sea. "What do you think of it?" he asked, and then answered himself: "I'll tell you what I think of it. I think it will surprise and confound the enemy."

Nelson was pacing near the stream shortly before dawn on September 2 when a carriage rattled up the gravel drive. Captain Henry Blackwood, a veteran of the blockade and of the chase, stepped out. Before he could report his message, Nelson said, "I am sure you bring me news of the French and Spanish fleets, and I think I shall yet have to beat them." Blackwood did in fact have news of the enemy: he had come to let Nelson know that the Combined Fleet was in Cadiz, under loose surveillance by Admiral Collingwood.

Nelson followed Blackwood to London the next day and was given his orders by Lord Barham, new First Lord of the Admiralty. He was to take overall command of Collingwood's fleet and destroy the enemy should he dare to show his face. Nelson then returned to Merton and Emma for a final 10 days of leave.

On the evening of September 13 a carriage arrived from the Admiralty. Nelson had eaten little dinner. He and Emma had exchanged few words. He went upstairs to where Horatia lay asleep and knelt by her bed to pray. He did not wake her. He went downstairs, kissed Emma and climbed into the carriage. In a spray of gravel he was gone.

Late that night, waiting in a tavern at Guildford while his horses were being changed, Nelson let his emotions pour into his diary: "At half-past ten drove from dear, dear Merton, where I left all which I hold dear in the world, to go to serve my King and Country."

He had asked to have his devoted friend Hardy made captain of the *Victory*. The burly Hardy was ill with rheumatism, but the prospect of serving under Nelson again made him feel better. He was waiting at Portsmouth. So was the *Victory*, which had been cleaned and refurbished during the time in port.

In a futile attempt to avoid the crowds, Nelson and Hardy hurried down a flagstone alleyway into Penny Street and to the beach. But the waiting people immediately spotted the well-known little figure with the empty sleeve pinned up to the admiral's coat, and rushed down to the beach. Some reached out to touch him. Some knelt in the sand to pray. Others followed him, walking into the water as his barge pulled smartly away from the shore. There was waving and cheering as Nelson and Hardy were rowed across the harbor to the *Victory*. Years of war and hardship, fears of Napoleon and invasion, confidence in the one man they felt could meet the great challenge—all had turned the normally phlegmatic Britons into emotional hero-worshippers.

Nelson was nearly as moved as they. Waving his hat to the cheering throng in return, he turned to Hardy and made what evidently seemed to him an important distinction. "I had their huzzas before," he said. "I have their hearts now!"

The *Victory* sailed from Portsmouth on the 15th and with a fair, fresh wind was with the fleet off Cadiz by the 28th of September. Nelson took command from Collingwood and then commenced his vigil. While he

Nelson, aged 25 and the captain of the frigate Boreas, *wears a wig to cover temporary baldness that resulted from a bout of yellow fever contracted in the West Indies. The watercolor portrait, painted with remarkable skill on Antigua in 1784, was sketched by his good friend and peer, Captain Cuthbert Collingwood.*

Cuthbert Collingwood, sketched here with equal skill by Nelson when the two were in the West Indies, appears as a handsome 34-year-old with his hair tied back in a fashionable pigtail. A member of Nelson's original Band of Brothers, Collingwood was a vice admiral and Nelson's second-in-command at the Battle of Trafalgar.

waited, he prepared his officers and his men for the battle. Only four of the captains on the 27 quarter-decks of his fleet were from Nelson's Band of Brothers of the Nile. When one of them, peppery Sir Edward Berry, joined them in the *Agamemnon,* Nelson rubbed his "fin," his right stump, in anticipation and said, "Here comes Berry. Now we'll have a fight!" Sir Edward had a reputation for fighting with half-blind ferocity and had been in more fleet actions than any other captain in the Royal Navy. Indeed, Nelson, from the moment he had arrived in the *Victory* and had assumed command almost a month before, had been laboring to infuse that very sort of fierce fighting spirit in his officers and men. The *Victory* had scarcely joined the fleet on September 28 before Nelson invited his captains to dinner, half of them on September 29 and the other half the next day.

The first dinner was also a celebration of Nelson's 47th birthday and a festive occasion. Nelson had brought many messages from home. One was for Captain Edward Codrington, whom Nelson knew only by reputation. He made a point of greeting Codrington warmly and delivering a letter from the captain's wife, explaining that he had been entrusted with it by a lady and was therefore delivering it personally. Nelson then turned to Captain Thomas Fremantle, a cohort at Copenhagen. Mrs. Fremantle had been expecting a fifth child. Taking Fremantle aside, Nelson asked, "Would you have a girl or a boy?" With two of each, Fremantle had decided he would prefer a girl. "Be content," Nelson said, and handed him a letter from Betsey Fremantle's sister announcing the birth of a girl named Louisa.

Both dinners had the same pleasant, however calculated, air of informality, immediately endearing Nelson to his new captains and confirming what they had heard from those who had served with him. And at these dinners Nelson unveiled his plan for the battle.

Again, it was a generation removed from the old line-ahead tactics of the *Fighting Instructions.* Admiral Villeneuve, in his briefings of his French officers at Cadiz, had guessed its essentials: cut the enemy's line and concentrate on a part of his fleet at a time. But it was more than that. Instead of sailing alongside the enemy then turning to break through his line, Nelson planned to drive straight into it. Moreover, he would do it with two divisions of his fleet. He had originally planned three divisions, but that was when he thought he would have as many as 40 ships instead of his present 27; six more of his ships were at Gibraltar and in the Mediterranean reprovisioning, and he had not received as many reinforcements as he had expected.

One of his two divisions would sail at the enemy line at nearly a 90-degree angle, plow through between its rear and center, and concentrate on the rear third of the enemy fleet. The second division would cut the line between the center and van, concentrating on the ships in the center. Thus all of Nelson's fleet would attack two thirds of the enemy's fleet. And just as the enemy's rear at the Nile, anchored downwind, had not been able to beat upwind in time to aid the center and van, this time the enemy's van would have to circle back to help the rest of the fleet; by the time the French and Spanish could complete this difficult maneuver, Nelson was confident that it would be too late.

To the huzzahs of his countrymen, Nelson leaves for Trafalgar, descending the Portsmouth wharf steps in this turn-of-the-century painting by A. C. Gow. In fact, Nelson tried to avoid the crowds by embarking from the beach but was spotted and cheered to a frenzy— which secretly pleased him. "Why," Lady Hamilton had remarked a few days before, "you like to be applauded—you cannot deny it." Nelson had nodded and confessed, "I own it."

A silver-gilt cup was the parting gift that Nelson gave to little Horatia, his beloved illegitimate daughter by Lady Hamilton. Horatia returned her father's affection but confessed to her mother that her nursemaid had planted in her some misgivings concerning Nelson's profession: "I love my dear, dear godpapa but Mrs. Gibson told me he kill'd all the people, and I was afraid"

Like his previous tactical plans, this one was simple in concept but completely worked out in detail. It recognized the length of time a sailing warship took either to come about or to wear. It took into account the deterioration of French gunnery that went along with the general decline of the French Navy after the Revolution (the Spanish, for their part, had never been noted for either speed or accuracy). Against British gunners no attacker could sail straight at the line, limited as he would be to his bow guns. This plan of Nelson's also included an innovation like that at the Nile: delegation of authority. Collingwood was to lead the division attacking the enemy's rear; Nelson was to lead the attack on the center. From the time of signal for attack, Collingwood was to be on his own. Every other captain was to use his own judgment if he saw a chance to do more damage to the enemy forces. As Nelson put it, "in case signals can neither be seen or perfectly understood, no captain can do very wrong if he places his ship alongside that of an enemy."

The plan thus adapted itself to the Royal Navy's murderous weapon, the carronade, which could inflict its terrible damage only at close range. It also counted on not only the well-drilled British gun crews but also the new flintlocks, which sparked an instantaneous explosion in the cannon, thus permitting the gunners to choose the exact moment to fire during the ship's roll. With the old slow matches and trails of powder, gun laying was a matter of guesswork. There were other fine points of Nelson's plan. The van of both British forces, for example, would include powerful first-raters rather than the lighter ships that normally led the attack. By selecting the 100-gun *Royal Sovereign* and the 104-gun flagship *Victory* as the first in each of his divisions, Nelson would lead with his two most powerful punches.

No doubt partly because of the persuasive and dramatic way in which he presented it, Nelson's plan for the Battle of Trafalgar produced an emotional reaction. He wrote Emma Hamilton that "it was like an electric shock. Some shed tears, all approved—'It was new—it was singular—it was simple!' And, from the admirals downwards, it was repeated—'It must succeed, if ever they will allow us to get at them!'" To Emma but to no one else he called it "the Nelson touch."

While they waited to get at the enemy, Nelson spent the time refining, drilling and making sure everyone was superbly battle-ready. Part of the process, he knew, depended on morale belowdecks, and he made sure that it was as good as it could be. As usual, no detail was too small. One memorandum to his captains complained that the pursers were not providing enough fresh green vegetables for the soup. "It is therefore my positive directions that the Pursers are obliged to purchase vegetables for the Ship's soup when it is possible to procure them." When he discovered that the *Victory's* coxswain had been so busy filling the mailbags for home that he had forgotten to include his own letters and the vessel had sailed without them, Nelson ordered: "Hoist a signal to bring her back. Who knows that he may not fall in action tomorrow." He even asked a captain going to Naples to find if possible a young lieutenant who, as Nelson explained it in his note, "ran away with an opera-dancer from Malta," and was "very probably in prison for debt." Nelson offered to pay the man's debts.

It was because Nelson insisted on sending his ships regularly to Gibraltar for fresh provisions that he was down to 27 ships on the morning of October 20 when the *Victory* received the signal that the Combined Fleet, 33 heavily gunned French and Spanish ships of the line, were at last coming out to fight. Had the two ships at Gibraltar and the four ships heading toward the Mediterranean been with him off Trafalgar, his fleet would have equaled the enemy's. This, however, was no part of his consideration as he gave the order, "General Chase."

Through the day the light breezes freshened and became gusty, and clouds scudded under the sun. The night was squally, but the British frigates kept contact, shadowing the Combined Fleet and signaling back to Nelson. The enemy was heading south under double-reefed topsails, toward the Strait of Gibraltar and away from the rocky headland of Cape Trafalgar, south of Cadiz. Therefore, the two fleets were on a converging course. Throughout the night the Combined Fleet showed lights to help maintain a semblance of order, and the darkened British frigates sailed so close to them that one of the officers aboard the *Defence* remembered afterward, "We seemed at times in the jaws of a mighty host ready to swallow us up." By early the next morning the frigates could also distinguish the lights and signal flares of Nelson's fleet, and Midshipman Hercules Robinson of the *Euryalus* was later to boast, "When we had brought the two fleets fairly together, we took our place between the two lines of lights as a cab might in Regent Street."

Vice Admiral Villeneuve was having trouble keeping his fleet in order. His captains were supposed to form three columns, but most of them had not sailed together before and their formation was ragged. All were out of practice, in any case, because of their seven weeks' incarceration in harbor. And their crews were none of the best. Many took too long to reef topsails, which made them lag even farther out of formation. The men were mostly landlubbers, and many were already seasick. Some fell from the yards, plunging onto the decks or into the sea.

Villeneuve calculated that the blustery south-southeast wind would take him clear of Cape Trafalgar but that he would have to stand down past the Strait before his fleet could come about and lay a line for Gibraltar to enter the Mediterranean. During the late afternoon Villeneuve had a stroke of luck when the wind went into the west—this allowed the ships to come about and head directly for the Strait. However, the wind shift took some of his vessels aback, and they had a difficult time coming about. His formation became more and more disordered. He could only keep on his new course and hope that he would be able to reassemble his scattered fleet with the assistance of daylight.

From his quarter-deck, at 7 p.m., Captain Lucas in the *Redoutable* spotted the signal lights of a column of ships, but could not make out the messages. He reported this fact up the line to Villeneuve in the *Bucentaure*, but it was slow business; the Combined Fleet had no method for complicated signaling at night and messages had to be relayed by speaking trumpet from vessel to vessel. At approximately the same time, the captain of the *Achille* noticed the strange lights and concluded that they were the enemy ships. He called to Rear Admiral Magon aboard the

Algésiras, and Magon, in turn, sailed close to the *Principe de Asturias* to call the news over to Admiral Gravina, who hailed a frigate and dispatched it to advise Villeneuve.

In all this confusion it was 8:30 p.m. before Villeneuve at last received a report clearly stating that the enemy had been sighted. He continued groping through the night, his fleet in disorder. And with dawn he signaled "Form Line of Battle." The French and Spanish ships floundered about, many of them nearly colliding as they tried to maneuver into one line. Off in the distance, Villeneuve studied the orderly ranks of British sails closing in on him. Villeneuve spoke later of how chilling was the sight of Nelson's "irresistible advance." He could see at first glance, as he described it, that Nelson "seemed to be heading *en masse* for my rear squadron, with the double object, apparently, of engaging in greatly superior force and of cutting the Combined Fleet off from Cadiz. I therefore signaled for the fleet to wear all together, and form line of battle in the reverse order."

Each ship was to turn away from the wind instead of trying to come about into it. The maneuver would bring the Combined Fleet on a reciprocal course, headed back toward Cadiz. Its van would now be its rear. Villeneuve would at least have a last chance to retreat to Cadiz if necessary, though he was determined to fight.

The wind had died and a heavy swell was coming in from the west. In trying to wear around, most of the ships drifted even further out of formation. Admiral Gravina, who was supposed to keep his squadron in a position near the center, instead fell in at the rear. Before long, there was little semblance of a line, only a crescent-shaped row of ships, double in some places. As the captains struggled to maneuver their ships into position, Commodore Don Cosme de Churruca of the *San Juan Nepomuceno* looked at the scattered fleet and shook his head, saying to his second-in-command, "The fleet is doomed. The French admiral does not know his business."

On board the *Neptune* one midshipman was struck by the majesty of the scene. "It was a beautiful sight," he recalled, "their broadsides turned towards us, showing their iron teeth." He noticed that there was no pattern to the colors of the ships' hulls; in Nelson's fleet, for easier recognition in battle, the sides of every ship were painted with alternate rows of black and yellow, with black gunports on the yellow bands, presenting what was popularly referred to as "Nelson's checkerboard." The *Neptune*'s midshipman, like a great many of the Britons, was particularly impressed by the magnificent, towering *Santisima Trinidad*. "Her appearance was imposing, her head splendidly ornamented with a colossal group of figures, painted white, representing the Holy Trinity from which she took her name."

Everyone aboard the British ships tried to get a look at the tremendous sight to the east. Many climbed to the upper decks, while the gun crews and powder monkeys peered through their gunports. Aboard the *Royal Sovereign*, Vice Admiral Collingwood was up and dressing when Smith, his servant, came into his cabin. Collingwood's six-foot-two-inch figure stooped under the low beams as he shaved by the light of a gun-

port. Smith looked out the port and saw the long, ragged line of the enemy, "but I could not help looking with greater interest at the admiral," he remembered, "who during all this time was shaving himself with a composure that quite astonished me." Collingwood finished his toilet, went on deck and noticed a lieutenant wearing boots. "You had better put on silk stockings, as I have done," he cautioned the lieutenant; "they would be so much more manageable for the surgeon if one should get shot in the leg."

The sight of the enemy stimulated reactions of awe and anxiety but mostly of eagerness and braggadocio. Some of the men started cheering. In his tiny cabin off the wardroom of the *Bellerophon,* Lieutenant Cumby, the man who the day before had first spotted the *Mars's* warning signal, was shaken awake by the ship's master, Edward Overton. "Cumby, my boy, turn out; here they are all ready for you, three and thirty sail of the line!" Cumby recorded: "You may readily conclude that I did not remain long in a recumbent position." Below, on the gun decks of the *Bellerophon,* known to her sailors as the "Billy Ruff'n," the crews were chalking "Victory or Death" on the guns.

On board the *Ajax* a lieutenant proceeded to his station on one of the gun decks and later said that he "was much struck by the preparations made by the blue-jackets, the majority of whom were stripped to the waist; a handkerchief was tightly bound round their ears, to deaden the noise of the cannon, many men being deaf for days after an action. The men were variously occupied—some were sharpening their cutlasses, others polishing their guns, as though an inspection were about to take place instead of a mortal combat, whilst three or four, as if in mere bravado, were dancing a hornpipe."

Captain Charles Mansfield of the *Minotaur* summoned his men on deck and exhorted them: "I trust that this day will prove the most glorious our country ever saw. I shall say nothing to you of courage. Our country never produced a coward." Captain Charles Tyler of the *Tonnant* offered somewhat more practical inspiration: "My lads, this will be a glorious day for us and the groundwork for a speedy return to our homes." He then ordered bread, cheese and beer for all hands at the guns. "I was one of them," Able Seaman John Cash recalled, "and, believe me, we ate and drank, and were as cheerful as ever we had been over a pot of beer."

A more important focus than the enemy for all eyes was the *Victory's* masthead. At 5:45 a.m. the *Victory* had signaled for the fleet to form the two columns Nelson intended for the battle. At 7 a.m., as the enemy wore around, the *Victory* had signaled the corresponding course change: "Bear Up and Steer Course East Northeast." Then: "Prepare for Battle." After the months of watching and waiting, the British fleet cleared for action. Nelson climbed to the *Victory's* poop, studied the eastern horizon with his telescope and gave the order to clear his cabins and roll in the guns. The men should be especially careful with his portrait of Lady Hamilton, he cautioned them; "take care of my guardian angel." He then went below, and while the sailors swept past him folding up and removing everything else, he sat at his desk and wrote the will in which he left Emma as "a legacy to my King and Country" *(page 145).*

Lieutenant John Pasco, the *Victory*'s signal officer, came to the admiral's cabin with a report. He found Nelson on his knees in front of his desk—the chairs in his cabin having been removed by the men. Nelson was writing in his private diary: "May the Great God, whom I worship, grant to my Country, and for the benefit of Europe in general, a great and glorious victory."

"I waited until he rose," Pasco remembered, "and communicated what I had to report."

Now that the *Victory* was cleared for action, Nelson toured the ship. At each gun deck the men jumped to attention as he appeared. To one of the crews, Nelson said, "My noble lads, this will be a glorious day for England, who ever lives to see it."

Occasionally he stopped to speak to a gunner. He touched one powder monkey on the shoulder and suggested that he take off his shirt because a spark might possibly ignite it. As Nelson climbed back to the quarterdeck the crew spontaneously broke out in a cheer. Visibly affected, Nelson turned and stood looking down at them before he walked aft to the poop deck to take up his telescope once again.

The enemy fleet was now much closer. A gentle, fading breeze was bringing the two lines of British men-of-war straight down on the still-straggling enemy. The Combined Fleet remained in a rough crescent shape, bowed toward the land. The three rows of iron cannon muzzles, which were stretching for nearly five miles across the ocean, gave promise of a savage battle to come. The wall of enemy ships and the two straight lines of British ships, all sails set and pendants and signal flags flying, looked almost like a painting of a grand naval parade in review, the only movement being the slow roll of the ships over the Atlantic swells. Midshipman Robinson never forgot the sight: "the noble fleet with royals and studding sails on both sides, bands playing, officers in full dress, and the ships covered with ensigns"—60 magnificent ships of the line, all of them bent on mutual destruction.

While Nelson studied the enemy fleet, his aides conversed in low voices. His two secretaries, both named Scott (the chaplain was known as Dr. Scott, the other secretary as Mr. Scott), and Dr. Beatty, the ship's surgeon, noted that Nelson was not wearing his sword for the first time any of them could remember. What concerned Beatty was the sight of the decorations sewed on Nelson's coat. He pointed out to Dr. Scott that they made a perfect target, and proposed asking Nelson to cover them. Scott replied, "Take care, Doctor, what you are about; I would not be the man to mention such a matter to him."

Before Beatty could bring up the subject, Nelson turned to the group of officers and said, "I'll now amuse the fleet with a signal: 'Nelson Confides that Every Man Will Do His Duty.' " One of the officers politely suggested changing "Nelson" to "England." Nelson agreed, and walked over to Lieutenant Pasco. "Mr. Pasco," he said, "I want to say to the fleet, 'England Confides that Every Man Will Do His Duty.' You must be quick, for I have one more to add, which is for close action." Pasco knew that No. 16, "Engage the Enemy More Closely," was Nelson's favorite.

Lieutenant Pasco also suggested an amendment. "If your lordship will permit me to substitute 'Expects' for 'Confides,' the signal will be sooner

Memento for a lonely mistress

Moments before he went into the fateful Battle of Trafalgar, Nelson sat at his desk aboard the *Victory* and penned a codicil to his last will and testament. "I leave Emma Lady Hamilton," he wrote, "therefore a legacy to my King and Country, that they will give her an ample provision to maintain her rank in life. I also leave to the beneficence of my Country my adopted daughter, Horatia Nelson Thompson; and I desire she will use in future the name of Nelson only. These are the only favours I ask of my King and Country at this moment when I am going to fight their battle. May God bless my King and Country and all those who I hold dear. My relations it is needless to mention; they will of course be amply provided for."

Nelson's trust in the kindness and charity of his King and country was only partially returned. His legal family was handsomely provided for. Both the widowed Lady Nelson and Nelson's brother, William, were awarded lifetime pensions. But Emma Hamilton and Horatia were never accorded so much as a word of public recognition nor a penny from the Royal Treasury. Horatia died at 81, never knowing for a fact whether Nelson had been her father. Emma, the giddy party-giver, clotheshorse, gambler and gadabout, continued her profligate ways until the annuities that had been left her by Nelson and Sir William were exhausted. Attended only by the devoted Horatia, she died in Calais, France, in 1815, an alcoholic.

Some years later among her few possessions was discovered a gold locket *(below, actual size)*. Its pictorial side is engraved with a sarcophagus that bears initialed medallions signifying Nelson and his ducal title, Brontë. The other side shows Nelson's handwritten codicil—but with some subtle alterations. The references to Horatia and to Nelson's other relatives are missing. Nelson's phrase "those who I hold dear" has been changed to "those I love most dear," as if to suggest that in his final moments Nelson had given thought only to his lover and their daughter to the exclusion of others.

The origins of the locket remain a mystery—but a good guess is that the lonely and neglected Emma had it made as a present to herself—a consolation prize to remind her of the deathbed wish that her lover's wildly adoring nation disdained to honor.

A quaint gold locket—enameled in color, encrusted with seed pearls and engraved with Nelsonian sentiments—was discovered among Lady Hamilton's souvenirs after her death.

completed, because the word 'Expects' is in the signal book, and 'Confides' must be spelt.''

"That will do, Pasco; make it directly.''

All eyes watched the *Victory*'s signal flags run up their halyards and burst in the breeze with the revised message.

Watching from the quarter-deck of the *Royal Sovereign*, the matter-of-fact Admiral Collingwood muttered, "What *is* Nelson signaling about? We all know what we have to do.'' And when the message was repeated to one of the gun crews belowdecks, a gunner asked, "Do your duty? Of course we'll do our duty. I've always done mine, haven't you?'' But through the fleet the cheers could be heard from ship to ship. It was the sort of exhortation to be expected only from Nelson. And when it was immediately followed by Nelson's famous No. 16, "Engage the Enemy More Closely,'' the cheers went up again.

The sound of cheering could also be heard across the water by the officers and men of the Combined Fleet. On most of the Spanish ships the men were being called on deck for prayers. Captain Lucas went through the *Redoutable* accompanied by drums and fifes. He inspected his grenade throwers, each of whom carried a shoulder bag with grenades and a tin tube containing a match to light them; they had been trained to toss two grenades at a time. His sharpshooters presented their muskets. They were sent to their stations in the rigging. "Everywhere,'' Lucas wrote later, "I found my brave fellows burning with impatience to begin.''

Aboard the French ships could be heard the call to clear for action: "Branle-bas-de-combat!'' and the distinctive ruffle of drums sounding the "Générale.'' Aboard the *Santisima Trinidad*, a new hand recalled, someone ordered: "The sand—bring the sand.'' The neophyte sailor watched the bags brought up and emptied on the decks, and revealed his ignorance by asking "a lad who stood next to me, what this was for. 'For the blood,' he said.''

Aboard the *San Juan Nepomuceno*, Commodore Churruca alternately looked through his telescope at the *Bucentaure*'s masthead and shook his head. He turned to watch the two lines of British warships advancing relentlessly on the fleet, looked back at the flagship and said to his second-in-command, "Our van will be cut away from the main body and our rear will be overwhelmed. Half the line will be compelled to remain inactive. The French admiral does not—will not—grasp it. He has only to act boldly, only to order the van ships to wear around once again and double back on the rear squadron. That will place the enemy between two fires.'' Churruca snapped shut his telescope and stalked off, muttering "Perdidos! Perdidos! Perdidos!''—we are lost, lost, lost!

Shortly he called all hands for prayers. "Father,'' he said to the *San Juan*'s chaplain, "perform your sacred office. Absolve the souls of these brave fellows, who know not what fate this battle may have for them.'' After the amens, Churruca addressed his crew: "My sons, in the name of the God of Battles, I promise eternal happiness to all those who today fall doing their duty. On the other hand, if I see any man shirking, I will have him shot on the spot.'' The drums and fifes sounded as the men trotted back to their quarters.

A secret weapon in the numbers

When Nelson hoisted the immortal flag signal that launched the Battle of Trafalgar—"England Expects that Every Man Will Do His Duty" (right)—he was using a technological innovation that had only recently been perfected and that gave the British a great advantage. His means of communication was the Naval flag code devised by Sir Home Popham, a Royal Navy captain whose revolutionary book, *Telegraphic Signals, or Marine Vocabulary,* had been published only five years before.

Various means of transmitting messages between ships had been in Naval use for many years, of course. However, these early systems were crude and were limited to random alarums and commands such as "Enemy in Sight," "Chase" and "Engage the Enemy." What Popham did, in effect, was to give the Royal Navy the power of speech afloat.

The old captain began with a series of 10 distinctively colored and designed flags to which he assigned the numbers 0 through 9. He then applied these flag-symbolized numbers to the alphabet—letting the flag for No. 1 equal A, 2 equal B, 13 equal M and so forth to Z. This made it technically possible by means of flags to spell any word in the English language.

However, it was obvious that a message of any complication would require a blizzard of flags and would take an impossibly long time to transmit and decipher, particularly in the heat of battle. So Popham devised a marine vocabulary, or flag language, by raising flags in groups of two and three up to No. 999 and assigning commonly used words to each number. Thus, for example, the two colored flags Nos. 3 and 0, signifying No. 30, meant "Absence," while No. 41 meant "Admiral" and No. 500 "Mistake."

Popham's two systems—the spelling and the vocabulary—were used in combination. To transmit the captain's

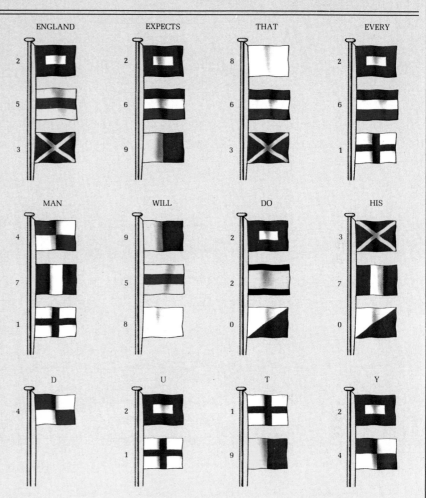

Using formal Naval code, Nelson heartened his fleet with a personal message.

message, a signal officer consulted his dictionary of *Telegraphic Signals* and then ordered that the appropriate flags be hoisted on the halyards. Whenever a word was needed that did not already have a number assigned to it—as in the case of "Duty" in Nelson's signal—the all-purpose letters of the alphabet came to the rescue, and the signalman simply spelled the word out.

To that basic explanation, only a few more details need be added. The second flag in Nelson's word "Do," for which Popham's code numer is 220, differs from the preceding flag in order to avoid the possibility of optical illusion; identical flags flying one above the other—and viewed at long

range through a jiggling, hand-held telescope—seemed to blend into one another. To prevent mistakes, special flags that signified "Ditto" were used when two consecutive identical numbers were indicated.

The reason that Y—the next-to-last letter in the alphabet—is No. 24 and not No. 25 is that the economical Popham made the number 9 do double duty for the letter I and its little-used neighbor J, thus reducing to 25 the code numbers for the alphabet and giving himself another number for his vocabulary. Finally, the reason that U is 21 and not 20 is that in its 18th Century sequence, the alphabet placed U after V instead of before it.

Aboard the *Fougueux*, at 12:10 p.m., Captain Louis Baudoin, watching the *Royal Sovereign* bearing down on him, gave the order to fire the first guns of the Battle of Trafalgar. The *Fougueux*'s master-at-arms later observed that "according to our bad habit in the French Navy," they "fired away over a hundred rounds from our big guns at long range before the English ship had practically snapped a gun lock."

The *Royal Sovereign* had benefited from a recent improvement in ship building: the copper bottom. In the late 18th Century it had been found that a layer of copper plates on a ship's hull retarded marine growth and greatly improved speed. The *Royal Sovereign* was one of the first ships to have been fitted with these plates and she left the rest of her squadron a quarter of a mile astern. Also, as she swept down on the erratically firing *Fougueux*, Collingwood ordered everyone to flatten himself on the deck for safety and to hold any return fire until he so commanded.

Watching from the *Victory*'s poop, Nelson said, "See how that noble fellow Collingwood takes his ship into action!" At the same time, on the *Royal Sovereign*'s quarter-deck, Collingwood was saying to his flag captain, "Rotherham, what would Nelson give to be here!"

While Nelson confers with two of his officers, crewmen hoist the flags that will signal the famous message—"England Expects that Every Man Will Do His Duty"—just before the start of the Battle of Trafalgar on October 21, 1805. The line of massed French and Spanish ships, recalled one young seaman after the battle, "cheered the hearts of every British tar like lions anxious to be at it."

So swift was the movement of the *Royal Sovereign* that she was under attack for only 10 minutes before Collingwood discovered the opening he was looking for—between the *Fougueux* and the Spanish three-decker *Santa Ana*. He sent the *Royal Sovereign* slicing between the two ships and delivered his first devastating broadside onto the 112-gun Spaniard. Aboard the frigate *Euryalus* Midshipman Robinson watched Collingwood "opening the battle with the magnificent *Santa Ana*, cutting the tacks and sheets and halliards of his studdingsails as he reached her, and letting them drop in the water (grieving, I have no doubt, at the loss of so much beautiful canvas), and discharging his double-shotted broadside into her stern."

The *Royal Sovereign*'s first broadside demolished the *Santa Ana*'s ornate stern and put 400 men, who made up almost one half of her crew, out of action. So well drilled were Collingwood's gun crews that within one minute they had also fired into the *Fougueux*. The *Fougueux*'s master-at-arms reported that the *Royal Sovereign* "gave us a broadside from five and fifty guns and carronades, hurtling forth a stream of cannonballs, big and small, and musket shot. I thought the *Fougueux* was shattered to pieces—pulverized. Fire broke out and we tried our best, in spite of the hail of shot, to put the fire out, and with hatchets to cut adrift the mass of wrecked tophamper from the fallen masts and yards and cordage." Somehow or other the gun crews on the *Fougueux* managed to recover from the shock and started firing back at the *Royal Sovereign*. "A well-maintained fire," the *Fougueux*'s master-at-arms commented, "showed the Englishmen that we too had guns and could use them."

The *Santa Ana* also responded in kind. Realizing that his attacker would bear up on his leeward side after breaking the line, Vice Admiral Don Ignatius de Alava concentrated his gun crews on that side. As the two ships came together, the *Santa Ana*'s broadside made the *Royal Sovereign* heel out of the water. From then on it was gun crew versus gun crew—at a range of scarcely 400 yards—and before long the superior speed and stamina of the Britons started to pay off. Collingwood watched the action imperturbably from his poop deck. Midshipman Robinson noted: "I see before me dear old Cuddie (as we called Collingwood) walking the break of the poop, with his little triangular gold-laced cocked hat, tights, silk stockings, and buckles, musing over the progress of the fight and munching an apple."

Noticing that one of his studding sails trailing in the water could still be saved, Collingwood called to his lieutenant, "Come and help me take that in. We shall want it again some other day." Together, as the bullets and cannon balls flew all around them, the two men hauled in the sail, folded it and stowed it away.

On the *Victory*'s poop, Nelson turned his attention from Collingwood to his own approach. At his request everyone was studying the enemy line to identify the flagship of the Combined Fleet. As they watched, there was a puff of smoke and a flash of fire from one of the ships, followed by the thunder of a gun. A cannon ball splashed into the water ahead of the *Victory*. A few minutes went by before the enemy fired again. This cannon ball fell alongside the *Victory*. Then another fell beyond. The enemy had the range. At this point, Hardy belatedly

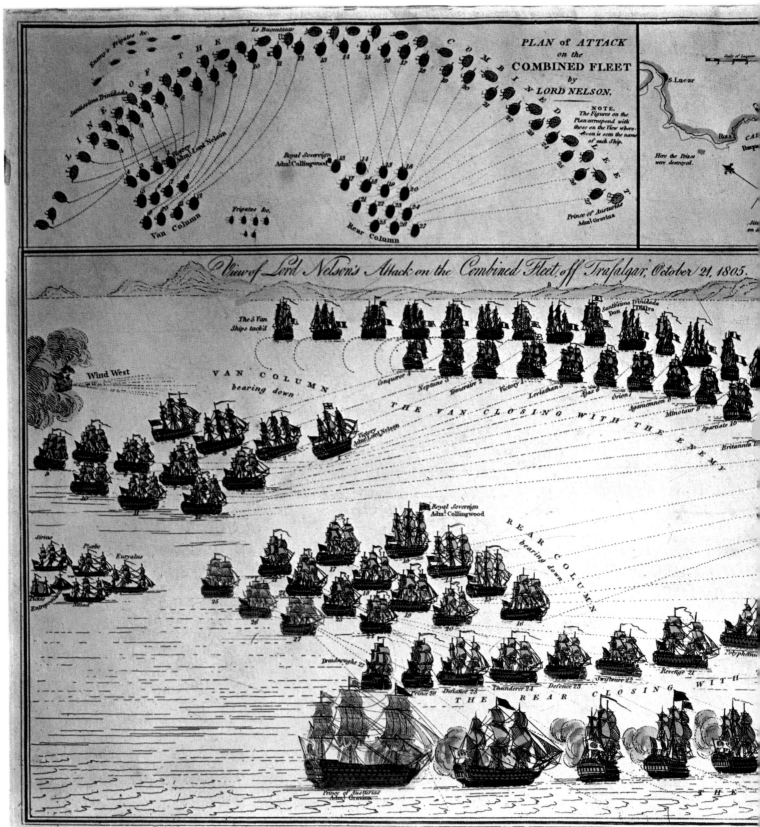

PLAN of ATTACK on the COMBINED FLEET by LORD NELSON.

View of Lord Nelson's Attack on the Combined Fleet, off Trafalgar, October 21, 1805.

Published, Nov. 30, 1805, by JOHN FAIRBURN, 146, Minories; and sold by CHAMPANTE & WHITROW, Jewry-Street, and H. T. HO[...]

brought up the question of the decorations that were sewed over Nelson's chest. Preoccupied with the enemy's fire, Nelson told Hardy that "it was now too late to be shifting a coat."

For 40 minutes, while the *Victory* made her approach and held her fire in order to conserve ammunition, the flagship was bombarded by the enemy. A cannon ball cut a hole in the main-topgallant sail; others cut more holes, and the *Victory*'s pace was slowed. The Combined Fleet's fire was erratic, as Nelson had guessed it would be, and the seas rolling under the vessels made the fire even more inaccurate. However, a lucky shot knocked down the *Victory*'s mizzen-topmast, and other balls shredded her studding sails. While the *Victory* slowly narrowed the gap, another cannon ball crashed into her wheel. Forty men were sent below-decks to steer the ship by her tiller, answering commands shouted down from the quarter-deck.

Mr. Scott was talking to Captain Hardy when a cannon ball smashed into him. Marines tossed the mangled body overboard. Nelson turned and asked, "Is that poor Scott who is gone?" But he knew there was no time now for burial at sea, nor time to mourn a devoted aide. A round of grapeshot mowed down a contingent of marines. Nelson ordered the rest to take cover but kept walking the deck himself. A cannon ball ripped through four folded hammocks in the nettings and shattered a part of the quarter-deck, sending up a shower of splinters. One of them tore the buckle off Hardy's shoe. Nelson smiled and said, "This is too warm work, Hardy, to last long."

Her sails were full of holes, her hull was rolling with the swells, but the *Victory* came straight on, aiming at the center of the enemy line. At this point Nelson could see the signals indicating the flagship *Bucentaure*. But he did not make for her yet. First he had another tactic in mind. Ranging along the ragged enemy line, the *Victory* slowly moved toward the lead ships. It was almost as if Nelson intended an old-style line-ahead engagement. Only after a few minutes did he order the *Victory* to turn and go for the center of the line.

This, more than any other part of his plan *(diagram, page 78)*, was the "Nelson touch." As if he already knew that Villeneuve expected him to concentrate on the center of the Combined Fleet, Nelson made this elaborate feint toward the van before turning as planned and cutting off the enemy's center. Watching the maneuver from the *Orion*, Captain Edward Codrington said, "How beautifully the admiral is carrying his design into effect!"

The *Victory* plunged between the *Bucentaure* and the ship astern of her, Captain Lucas's *Redoutable*. Only then did Nelson give the order to fire. The *Victory*'s carronades and double-shotted guns all boomed at the

Punching out like two mailed fists, Nelson's squadron prepares to crash through the French and Spanish formation in this engraving published in London five weeks after the epic victory. Nelson had predicted that his unorthodox tactic "will bring forward a pell-mell battle, and that is what I want."

same time. One carronade, which was filled with one 68-pound ball and a keg of 500 musket balls, fired directly through a stern window of the *Bucentaure* and caused terrible havoc. The smoke, dust and debris set the *Victory*'s own gun crews coughing, and a cloud of dust showered down over Nelson and Hardy. As soon as the *Victory* was past the *Bucentaure*, Hardy ordered the helm to port. The *Victory* turned for another broadside, and in the process fouled her studding-sail iron on the fore-topsail of the *Redoutable*.

Nelson's feint toward the head of the enemy line may have been the most important tactic in the battle. Admiral Villeneuve was not so stupid as his Spanish colleague Churruca assumed. Villeneuve had planned to order his van to return and surround the British attackers, just as Churruca had proposed. But once again Villeneuve delayed. This time he could have been correct. If Nelson planned to take on the van as well as the center, the British might be able to destroy the French-Spanish leading ships while they were clumsily trying to come about in the near calm. That is precisely what Nelson made Villeneuve think he was going to do. By the time he did turn and go through the line, firing as he went, Villeneuve's signal was too late.

Commander of the Combined Fleet's van was Rear Admiral Dumanoir Le Pelley of the *Formidable*. Dumanoir kept his seven ships sailing straight ahead at first, because it looked as if Nelson would engage them. But when Villeneuve frantically signaled for Dumanoir to return, the latter did not respond for more than an hour, which proved to be a fatal period. Dumanoir later claimed that he could not distinguish the signal in the smoke of battle. He certainly could see that the center and rear of the Combined Fleet were being attacked by the entire British fleet. However, orders were orders, and Dumanoir said that he did not have any way of knowing whether or not Villeneuve intended to keep his van in reserve. Dumanoir only knew that his last orders had been to continue sailing straight ahead.

Villeneuve meanwhile was busy enough clearing away the wreckage from the *Victory*'s first broadside. Guns had been knocked askew; shattered timbers masked some of the gunports. Yet now the *Bucentaure* was receiving some welcome help. The *Redoutable*, next astern, was a 74, which was the smallest French ship of the line, and her captain, Jean Jacques Lucas, was at four feet nine inches the smallest captain in the Combined Fleet. He was also known to be one of the most courageous. When the *Victory* came crashing through the line, Lucas immediately engaged the great 104-gun British flagship.

Lucas's seamen tried to throw their grappling irons over the *Victory*'s rail but it rose too high above that of the *Redoutable*. For the sharpshooters in the Frenchman's tops, however, the difference in size was an advantage; it shortened the range between the *Redoutable*'s mizzen platform and the *Victory*'s upper decks to only 50 feet.

The view from the *Redoutable*'s platform was obscured by crisscrossed rigging and splintered yardarms. Smoke drifted in clouds, alternately hiding and revealing the decks below. Both ships rolled under the swells and rocked with the recoil of their broadsides. In the thunder of the guns nothing else could be heard, and often through the fog of smoke nothing could be seen but the flashes, large and small, of the big guns and the marines' muskets.

It was now that the *Redoutable*'s marksmen repaid Captain Lucas for his days of drill, covering the *Victory*'s deck with a rain of fire that drove nearly everyone to shelter. Only a few figures were left on the quarter-deck. One pair visible to the French sharpshooters was remarkable: a tall, hulking man beside a small, wiry one. They were pacing the larboard rail, and as they turned, it could be seen that the small man had one sleeve pinned to his chest. Every French sailor knew who the little one-armed man was. And his chest was covered with medals, which made an excellent target.

In the candlelight of the *Victory*'s cockpit on the orlop deck the litters were stacked in rows as the wounded men groaned and cursed while they waited for the surgeon. Dr. Beatty had just finished examining one of his closest friends and found that he was dead. There was a commotion near the entrance to the cockpit as two seamen stumbled down the ladder carrying a slight body. Even though there was a kerchief over the chest to conceal the medals, everybody realized who it was. "Mr. Beatty," one of the wounded men called, "Lord Nelson is here; Mr. Beatty, the admiral is wounded."

Beatty and the purser, Mr. Burke, took Nelson from the seamen and carried him to one of the midshipmen's berths, tripping and almost dropping him on the way. Nelson was not able to see in the dark room, and asked who was holding him. After being told, Nelson said, "Ah, Mr. Beatty, you can do nothing for me. I have but a short time to live; my back is shot through."

Beatty called for Dr. Scott, Nelson's surviving secretary, who had been giving lemonade to the wounded. Scott came over, looked at the bloodied jacket and, recalling his discussion about Nelson's medals, said: "Alas, Beatty, how prophetic you were." They gently undressed Nelson. In the moving circle of light from the swinging lantern overhead, Beatty tried to probe for the bullet, but it had gone too deep. There was no exit wound in the back, so the bullet evidently had lodged in Nelson's spine. Beatty asked him what his sensations were. Nelson replied that he felt a gush of blood every time he took a breath, and a severe pain in his backbone. He could not feel anything at all in the lower part of his body. "I felt it break my back," he said.

Captain Hardy came clumping down, bowed over in the low-beamed orlop deck. Beatty whispered that Nelson's wound was almost certainly fatal. Hardy hurried back to the quarter-deck, where he was now in command. Collingwood would succeed Nelson, but so long as the admiral was alive, the captain of his flagship spoke for him.

Hardy had plenty to do. So intent was his concentration that only later did he realize that he had left teeth marks on the pencil case he held in his mouth while writing orders for his signal officers. He had scarcely returned to the quarter-deck when he heard above the uproar a bugle sound on the *Redoutable*, followed by the French boarding cry: "À l'abordage!" The deck of the French ship was too far below the *Victory*'s for

The battle dissected: vignettes of death and destruction

Though many fine artists turned their talents to the Battle of Trafalgar, none succeeded in re-creating that major turning point in history more remarkably than the contemporary British painter Clarkson Stanfield. Honored as one of the foremost marine painters of his day, Stanfield captured all the drama of Trafalgar, all the fire and thunder, on a vast canvas that measured nearly 11 by 18 feet. What is more, he painted his masterwork with such fidelity (as is attested by the panorama below and the details opposite and on the following page) that even the most critical veteran of the engagement could only offer his plaudits.

Stanfield received his commission from London's United Service Club, many of whose members had fought at Trafalgar and wanted a commemorative picture to grace their clubhouse. It took the artist three years to finish his panorama. He chose not simply to depict a moment but to highlight events at the peak of battle. Throughout, he sought the advice of Trafalgar veterans, among them Sir Thomas Hardy, captain of the *Victory*, and Sir Edward Codrington of the *Orion*.

Stanfield himself appeared well satisfied with the result—save for one detail. A few years after it was hung, he asked permission to "lighten the picture" by adding another stretch of sky. The faintly visible band of discoloration across the top of the canvas is the seam along this addition.

Often considered the greatest painting ever done of a battle at sea, Clarkson Stanfield's magnificent reconstruction of the Battle of Trafalgar fairly rumbles with the desperation of the French and Spanish Combined Fleet about two hours after the British, led by Nelson in the Victory, had slashed through the ragged enemy line. The key attached to the frame of the work—enlarged here for clarity— gives the names of the principal ships.

Vice Admiral Cuthbert Collingwood's Royal Sovereign, at far left, lies alongside the dismasted Spanish flagship, the Santa Ana, which has struck her colors. A boatload of British crewmen, presumably a boarding party, has come under her bow. In the foreground, another British party hauls in survivors clinging to a snarl of debris. At right, the Mars and the Temeraire are sandwiching the French Fougueux and pummeling her with salvos.

The Temeraire is caught by the French Redoutable's mizzenmast, which has toppled across the quarter-deck; British crewmen are swarming along the mast to cut it loose. In the foreground, a launch probably bearing Captain Blackwood, commander of the British rear, approaches the Victory to report. At this point Nelson has been fatally wounded and lies amidships on the Victory's orlop deck. Stanfield has marked the spot on the hull with a floating cross of mast and spar.

The stern of the French Bucentaure shows the ordeal of Admiral Villeneuve's flagship. The Victory had raked her with a broadside as she cut through the enemy line; then, in quick order, the Neptune, the Leviathan and the Conqueror had added their deadly greeting. Here, while the Britannia (left background) comes down on her from windward, one of the Bucentaure's officers stands above her toppled mizzenmast and drooping tricolor and hails an allied ship for help.

Two British launches bob beside the gigantic Spanish Santisima Trinidad, while a party clambers on board, believing from the looks of the flag drooping over her gunports that she has struck her colors. The Spaniards politely ushered the Britons back to their boats and refused to surrender for several hours. Behind her, the British Neptune emerges after battering the Santisima Trinidad, and is engaged by the French Intrepide, which is firing her stern guns. To the left, French crewmen cling to the Bucentaure's shattered mainmast as they await rescue.

the boarders to climb over the *Victory*'s rail. However, the *Redoutable*'s main yardarm had swung down across the rail and could be used as a bridge, and pistol- and saber-wielding Frenchmen swarmed onto it. The *Victory*'s marines concentrated their fire on the yardarm and managed to drive the boarders back.

The two ships rubbed sides so closely that the *Victory*'s guns could not be thrust through the ports; Lucas had ordered the ports on the *Redoutable* closed to prevent the *Victory*'s men from boarding. A member of each *Victory* gun crew stood by with a fire bucket and hurled water through the port after the guns were fired in order to douse the flames aboard the *Redoutable* that were caused by the powder blasts before they could spread to the *Victory*. From the middle deck, Marine Lieutenant Rotely of the *Victory* recalled, "there was fire from above, fire from below, besides the fire from the deck I was upon, the guns recoiling with violence, reports louder than thunder, the decks heaving and the sides straining. I fancied myself in the infernal regions, where every man appeared a devil. Lips might move, but orders and hearing were out of the question; everything was done by signs."

Indeed, for a few euphoric moments the *Redoutable*'s Captain Lucas thought that the flagship of the British fleet might be taken by his small-arms fire, which would be a historic triumph if it could be accomplished. "More than two hundred grenades were thrown on the *Victory*," he recorded, "with the utmost success; her decks were strewn with dead and wounded." Notwithstanding the slaughter at the *Redoutable*'s yardarm bridge, Lucas's sharpshooters and grenade throwers seemed to be clearing the way for a boarding party—when another British man-of-war came to the rescue of the *Victory*.

While everyone on board the *Redoutable* was concentrating on the *Victory*, the British three-decker *Temeraire* ranged up on the unprotected side of the *Redoutable* and let go with all three rows of her guns—74 guns in one catastrophic storm of shot. "It is impossible to describe the carnage produced by the murderous broadside of this ship," Captain Lucas recalled. "More than two hundred of our brave men were killed or wounded by it."

And as the *Temeraire* came to the *Victory*'s aid, the French ship *Fougueux*, battered by the *Royal Sovereign* at the battle's beginning but still fighting, came down on the *Temeraire*. Now four ships were locked side by side, the *Victory*, *Redoutable*, *Temeraire* and *Fougueux*, each firing on another, while the *Victory* continued firing on the *Bucentaure* and *Santisima Trinidad* on her larboard side.

On the *Victory*'s nearly deserted quarter-deck 19-year-old Midshipman John Pollard attempted to revenge his fallen admiral by spraying the tops of the *Redoutable* with musket fire. Holding his fire until a Frenchman poked his head up from a canvas strip on the mizzen platform, Pollard rapidly picked off three of the four men he could see. Unnerved by Pollard's accurate fire, the last French sharpshooter waited for him to begin reloading and then made a dash down the rigging. Pollard got the Frenchman as he reached the lower shrouds, and sent him crashing onto the *Redoutable*'s deck. Pollard had revenged the mor-

Surrounded by the ever-faithful Captain
Hardy (standing), Surgeon Beatty
(feeling his pulse) and Chaplain Scott
(rubbing his chest), the fatally wounded
Nelson lies on a litter in this contemporary
oil. A. W. Devis, the artist, boarded
the Victory upon her return to Portsmouth
and made preliminary sketches for
the painting from eyewitness accounts.

tally wounded Nelson by killing the man who had shot him, but he would never know which man it had been.

The two central battles had formed just as Nelson had planned. Within an hour and a half after the *Victory* had gone through the line, the battle of the center was all but won. To the south the rear ships of the Combined Fleet were still fighting, but the outcome was only a matter of time. Within an hour Collingwood's squadron would capture or destroy 12 of the 16 ships he had attacked with his 15 British men-of-war. Meanwhile Admiral Dumanoir in the *Formidable* was still proceeding north, away from the battle, with his seven ships of the van.

At last Dumanoir decided to enter the battle, either because he had finally made out Villeneuve's signal—it had now been repeated by other ships—or because he realized that the alternative was court-martial and probable death. But Dumanoir was too late. It was nearly two hours after the battle had commenced, and his attempt to rejoin his fleet became a comedy of errors. Two of his ships, the *Mont-Blanc* and the *Intrepide*, collided, which caused the *Mont-Blanc*'s foresail to split and the *Intrepide*'s jib boom to rip off. Two Spanish ships drifted off to the east. It took Dumanoir more than another hour to move his remaining five ships, before cat's-paw breezes, back to the battle area. By that time the British had won the battle, and the British men-of-war were more than ready to take on what was left of the French van. When he saw this, Dumanoir bore off to the west. As the French ships glided past, the *Victory* fired a parting broadside at them.

Listening to the concussion of his ship's guns, Nelson cried out, "Oh, *Victory, Victory,* how you distract my poor brain!" Dr. Scott was massaging his chest. Burke tried to get him to drink some of the lemonade. At 4 p.m. Hardy stooped over him. They had won a great victory, he reported. He could count 14 or 15 surrendered enemy ships. "That is well," Nelson replied, "but I bargained for 20." Shortly afterward he said, "Don't throw me overboard."

"Oh, no, certainly not," Hardy answered.

"Then you know what to do. And take care of poor Lady Hamilton," Nelson mumbled. "Kiss me, Hardy."

Hardy knelt and kissed Nelson's cheek. "Now I am satisfied," Nelson whispered. "Thank God, I have done my duty."

Hardy knelt and kissed his commander's forehead.

"Who is that?"

"It is Hardy."

"God bless you, Hardy."

At that point Hardy withdrew. Nelson's breathing became labored and his voice grew faint. Scott heard him murmur: "Doctor, I have not been a *great* sinner." He mentioned Lady Hamilton again and his daughter Horatia, instructing Scott: "And never forget Horatia." Scott heard him whisper once more, "Thank God I have done my duty." His breathing ceased. Nelson was dead.

Other British quarter-decks were stained with the blood of British captains. At nearly the same moment that Nelson was hit, Captain John Cooke of the *Bellerophon*, who had called this first battle under Nelson "the dearest wish of my life," was struck by a cannon ball. He had just killed a French officer on the *Aigle*'s quarter-deck and was reloading his pistol when he was hit. His lieutenant went to take him below to the surgeon. "Let me lie a minute," said Cooke, and died.

When the *Mars* came between the French ships *Fougueux* and *Pluton*, their combined broadsides destroyed most of the British vessel's rigging and decapitated Captain George Duff. His lieutenants covered the body with the Union Jack until the battle was over. ("My dear mamma," Duff's son, Norwich, who was a midshipman on the *Mars*, wrote home the next day, "you cannot possibly imagine how unwilling I am to begin this melancholy letter. . . .")

Aboard the *Royal Sovereign*, Collingwood had had a couple of bad moments. As he stood on his quarter-deck, a splinter had gashed his leg; if he had been wearing boots, they would have protected him. What he thought to be a thump in the back turned out to be the air blast from a near-miss cannon ball. His worst moment, in fact, came when an officer from the *Victory* arrived to report that Nelson had been wounded. "I asked the officer if his wound was dangerous," Collingwood remembered later. "He hesitated, then said he hoped it was not; but I saw the fate of my friend in his eye."

Captain Hargood, on the quarter-deck of the *Belleisle,* her masts shattered and her fallen sails covering some of the gunports, was struck by a huge splinter. It knocked Hargood down, bruising his side from neck to hip. But he remained calm. He ordered oars to be used through the lower gunports to maneuver the ship, and the *Belleisle*'s colors were flown from a pike nailed to the stump of the mainmast. Hargood, back on his feet, joined John Owen, captain of the marines, in watching the progress of the battle as they shared a bunch of grapes.

Inspired by their commanders' example, many British officers and sailors were impelled to take brave, if not foolhardy, action. "To tell the truth of it," one British sailor said, "when the game begun, I wished myself at Warnborough with my plough again; but when they had given us one duster, and I find myself snug and tight, I bid fear kiss my bottom and set to in good earnest." A seaman named Fitzgerald, from the *Tonnant,* climbed aboard the *Algésiras,* scrambled up the rigging to the topmast, cut away the French flag, wrapped it around his waist and made it back to the lower shrouds before a musket shot dropped him into the sea between the ships. Christopher Beaty, a yeoman of signals and one of the eight men on the *Bellerophon*'s quarter-deck not killed or wounded, watched his ship's ensign shot away for the third time, grabbed a Union Jack, ran up the rigging and tied it to the shrouds. In apparent admiration the enemy sharpshooters held fire until Beaty jumped back on deck.

The same spirit affected the wounded. A seaman aboard the *Conqueror,* his leg shattered, lay on deck calmly playing marbles with stray grapeshot while waiting to be carried below. The sockets for the ships' capstan bars had been filled with crude first-aid kits; many of the walking wounded found their way to the capstans, bound their wounds, stuck the rest of the bandage back into the socket and returned to their battle stations. One gravely wounded seaman sang "Rule Britannia" throughout his amputation. An amputee aboard the *Tonnant* cheered so lustily at the news of another French surrender that he broke his ligatures and bled to death.

The British seamen showed scarcely more bravery than did the French and Spanish. However convinced of ultimate defeat, many men and officers of the Combined Fleet fought with defiant determination. The trigger-tempered Admiral Magon, who had flung his wig at his commander's flagship off Finisterre, found his *Algésiras* entangled by her bowsprit in the rigging of the British *Tonnant;* in this position the *Tonnant* could rake the deck of the *Algésiras,* and quickly did. Magon immediately called for boarders. He was starting to lead them onto the *Tonnant*'s decks when one bullet whipped off his hat and his new wig and another went through his right arm. He refused to go below to the surgeon and instead continued directing the boarding party. Another bullet hit him in the shoulder. He was still urging on his boarders when a cannon ball cut him nearly in half. His boarders were mowed down, and all three of the *Algésiras*'s masts went over the side—"carrying with them," in the words of a British officer, "all their sharpshooters to look sharper in the next world."

Commodore Churruca of the *San Juan Nepomuceno* found himself under fire from six British ships. Churruca went below to direct the fire of his guns, succeeding in dismasting one of his attackers, and was returning to the deck when a cannon ball nearly severed his right leg. Rising on his elbow, he called above the noise, "It is nothing. Go on firing." As it became apparent that he would bleed to death, Churruca agreed to be taken below, but he ordered his ensign nailed to the mast. In the surgeon's cockpit, Churruca called for his nephew and told him to say goodbye to the young wife the 44-year-old commodore had married just before leaving Cadiz. Within minutes he was dead. As the news spread, the heart went out of his men. A third of the *San Juan*'s crew had been killed or wounded, all the masts had gone, and the rudder was smashed. The *San Juan*'s flag was pulled down.

Captain Louis Antoine Cyprian Infernet deserved the name of his ship, the *Intrépide*. He was nearly the only captain from the van to get into battle, and saw almost half of his crew killed or wounded. Although all of the *Intrépide*'s masts were shot away and there was eight feet of water in the hold, Infernet stubbornly fought on, slashing the air about him with his curved saber and shouting that he would decapitate anyone who called for surrender. While the shot and shell sang around them, the *Intrépide*'s colonel of infantry kept ducking behind Infernet, until the captain laughed and yelled at him, "Ah, Colonel, do you think I am sheathed in metal, then?" At last the *Intrépide* was battered to a hulk. Infernet's officers had to sneak up under the swinging saber and hold their captain down while the colors were lowered.

The fiercest fighter of the Combined Fleet was little Jean Jacques Lucas of the *Redoutable*. Lucas fought on despite the cross fire of the *Victory* and the *Temeraire*, both of whose gunners, aiming low to avoid hitting each other, were shooting holes through the *Redoutable*'s hull below the water line. By midafternoon the *Redoutable* had lost her mainmast and mizzenmast and was straddled by the wreckage of the *Temeraire*'s top yards. Where the *Redoutable*'s poop had been was a gaping hole; her helm, rudder and sternpost were smashed and her stern was afire. Most of her guns had been destroyed. Five sixths of the crew was out of action, and so riddled were the sides of the ship that the wounded who were lying in the orlop deck were exposed to enemy fire. The *Redoutable*'s pumps were crippled and the water was fast gaining in the hold. Captain Lucas seemed to be the *Redoutable*'s only survivor as he finally was forced to stike her colors. A floating wreck, the *Redoutable* was taken in tow by the *Swiftsure*.

The cruelest fate was reserved for Admiral Villeneuve of the *Bucentaure*. The *Victory*'s opening broadside had reduced the French flagship's interior to wreckage. Through the hole in the line that the *Victory* had opened astern of the *Bucentaure* had come four ships of the *Victo-*

ry's line, the *Temeraire*, *Neptune*, *Leviathan* and *Conqueror*, raking the *Bucentaure* one by one. In the maelstrom that followed, the *Bucentaure*'s guns were put out of action and her decks were heaped with dead and dying gunners. On her gun decks one raking broadside sent cannon balls bouncing along the beams, beheading many of the men; later broadsides, ripping open the gunports, mashed the bodies to pulp. Loose guns crashed back and forth in the rolling sea, churning through the human wreckage. In the *Bucentaure*'s cockpit the surgeon and his mates were overwhelmed by 450 wounded, more than half her crew. On her quarter-deck nearly every officer and man around Villeneuve was hit, until he was virtually alone.

Villeneuve had planned for such a catastrophe: his barge had been ready to take him to another ship. He said to an officer, "The *Bucentaure* has played her part. Mine is not yet over." He called for his barge, but it had been shot full of holes and smashed by falling spars.

Villeneuve then signaled the nearby *Santisima Trinidad* to send a boat for him. There was no answer. He resigned himself to his fate, disconsolately walking the bloody deck and complaining to his flag captain that "amid the slaughter all around there seemed not to be one bullet for him." Finally, with his ship a total wreck, "isolated in the midst of the enemy and unable to move," as Villeneuve was to report later, "I had to yield to my destiny." He looked away as the *Bucentaure*'s captain lowered her colors.

Sir Israel Pellew, captain of the *Conqueror*, saw the *Bucentaure*'s flag go down and sent over James Atcherley, who was captain of his marines, to accept the surrender of the flagship. At the sight of Captain Atcherley's red coat rising over the *Bucentaure*'s rail, four French officers stepped forward to present their swords. One of them was Villeneuve, blackened by smoke but still smartly attired in a long, high-collared uniform coat, green corduroy pantaloons and sharp-toed half boots. At first the admiral thought the captain who had defeated him was the famous Sir Edward Pellew, who as commander of a frigate had once destroyed a 74-gun French ship of the line. Atcherley set him straight: "It is his brother, sir."

"His brother!" cried Villeneuve. "What! Are there two of them?"

Another surrender ceremony turned out to be premature. The giant *Santisima Trinidad*, with her four decks of 130 guns, was a formidable fighter but an easy target, and half a dozen British ships ganged up on her. When her colors were shot away and her guns had fallen silent, Captain Henry Digby of the *Africa* sent over an officer to accept her surrender. The British officer found that Rear Admiral Don Hidalgo Cisneros had been wounded, along with his two top officers. But another Spanish officer politely informed the British emissary that the *Santi-*

Towed by the Neptune, the Victory—with most of her masts shot away—limps to Gibraltar in an 1853 painting. After makeshift repairs, she started the month-long sail to England with Nelson's body on board—preserved in a cask of brandy.

sima Trinidad had not yet given up the fight. The British officer was courteously escorted back to his boat, and the *Santisima*'s gunners withheld their fire until he was safely back on board the *Africa*. The *Santisima Trinidad* resumed fighting. When the Spanish finally did give up, the scene aboard the big warship was described by one member of her crew as "simply infernal. She could not move. The English shot had torn our sails to tatters. It was as if huge invisible talons had been dragging at them. Fragments of spars, splinters of wood, thick hempen cables cut up as corn is cut by the sickle, fallen blocks, shreds of canvas, bits of iron, and hundreds of other things that had been wrenched away by the enemy's fire were piled along the deck. Blood ran in streams about the deck, and in spite of the sand the rolling of the ship carried it hither and thither until it made strange patterns on the planks."

The battle was all but over. Aboard the Spanish flagship, the *Principe de Asturias,* Admiral Gravina had watched the *Bucentaure* and the mighty *Santisima Trinidad* strike their colors. The *Principe*'s mainmast and mizzenmast were riddled and threatening to topple over. Gravina's left arm had been shattered. Realizing that his only hope for survival was to escape, Gravina signaled the frigate *Thémis* to take him in tow, and he instructed all the other ships that could still sail to follow him in making a run for Cadiz harbor. With 11 ragged ships of the line trailing in his wake, Gravina headed for the Spanish coast.

Astern of the fleeing Spaniards, the French ship of the line *Achille* provided a spectacular climax to the battle. By midafternoon 400 members of the *Achille*'s crew, including all of her senior officers, had been killed or wounded, but a junior lieutenant, Ensign de Vaisseau Couchard, kept her remaining gun crews firing. Then an arms chest in the foretop exploded and the sails went up in flames, igniting other sail and spars. The *Achille*'s crewmen tried to chop down the foremast and dump the blazing mass over the side, but the British ship *Prince* fired at the mast and cut it in two. The flaming top-hamper crashed onto the deck of the *Achille* and the fire raced through the ship. Her sailors dived over the side. The British attackers ceased firing and sent their boats to rescue the swimmers. By late afternoon they had saved more than 200—and then the *Achille* blew up. An officer aboard the *Defence* described the sight as "the most awful and grand that can be conceived." The explosion hurled a column of fire and smoke into the air, "representing for a few seconds a prodigious tree in flames, speckled with many dark spots, which the pieces of timber and bodies of men occasioned while they were suspended in the clouds."

Among the *Achille*'s survivors rescued by the British were a pig, which the victors feasted on at their next supper, and a naked young woman, who was taken aboard the *Revenge* and given clothing by the sailors. She identified herself as Jeanette and explained to them that she had followed her husband to sea and had been handing up cartridges to the powder monkeys when the spreading fire had finally driven her into the water. She had not been the only woman aboard the *Achille*; another was saved by the *Britannia*'s crew.

Perhaps the most remarkable survivor of the battle was a dog aboard the *Conqueror*. While clearing for action, the *Conqueror*'s crew had, accidentally or intentionally, thrown the dog out a gunport. It landed on a ridge under the shrouds and clung there throughout the battle, while cannon balls riddled the hull and musket fire peppered the shrouds. After the battle the dog was hauled back through the gunport, unscathed but in an understandable state of shock.

They were among the fortunate survivors. Collingwood assessed the British loss at 1,609 either killed or wounded. The Spanish loss was 1,022 dead and 1,383 wounded. The French made no official count, but the best estimate was that more than 3,000 Frenchmen had died and more than 1,100 were wounded. The total number captured, both Spanish and French, amounted to about 8,000.

The aftermath of Trafalgar proved even crueler than the battle itself. Among Nelson's last instructions as his life ebbed away was "Anchor, Hardy, anchor." Evidently, despite Nelson's pain, or perhaps before he had been shot, his dependable barometer, the stump of his right arm, had warned him that a storm was approaching. Also, the oily swells that rolled under the battling fleets indicated that a hurricane was brewing out on the Atlantic. The victors and the vanquished had only a few hours left in which to repair the worst damage to their ships and dress their wounds before the storm struck.

Collingwood, now in command of the British fleet, did not anchor. Nor is it a certainty that all the anchors in the Royal Navy could have saved the fleet in the storm that swept down on the survivors on the night of October 21, 1805.

It lasted for the better part of a week and in that desperate time there were no victors and no vanquished—simply men struggling to survive. Damaged rigging crashed over the side. Mastless, riddled hulks were driven toward the rocky Spanish coast. The few ships that were still able to bend a sail tried to take the others in tow. English sailors who had eagerly anticipated the prize money they had so dearly won had to watch their captured prizes wallow away downwind to destruction. But it was worst for the wounded as they rolled on their litters while the ships plunged and heeled in the gale-driven seas. Wounds reopened and men bled to death. Aboard the *Tonnant*, 16 men had survived amputations; 14 of them died during the storm.

The battered and holed *Redoutable*, still under tow by the *Swiftsure*, gradually settled into the water. The *Swiftsure*'s crew saved as many wounded as they could, risking their own lives in small boats in the raging seas. But many of the 474 left aboard were still alive when on the day after the battle the *Redoutable* went down.

The *Santisima Trinidad*, once the pride of Spain, was now dismasted and a giant rolling hulk. She refused to sink for almost three days, while crewmen from the British *Ajax* and *Revenge* tossed her dead overboard and lowered what wounded they could into the lurching boats. The big four-decker had carried a crew of 1,115. Fewer than half were saved. On the 24th, in hurricane-force winds, the towing hawsers broke twice and she had to be left to sink. A British boat was pushing away with the last seaman to be rescued when someone heard a mewing sound; the boat returned to find a cat poking its head from the muzzle of a gun. As the

The five fighting ships commanded by Nelson in his decade of triumph from 1795 to 1805 are shown in this painting by Nicholas Pocock done two years after the hero's death. From left to right, the artist has assembled the nimble, 64-gun *Agamemnon*, in which Nelson scored his first victory over the French in 1795; the 74-gun *Captain*, in which Nelson fought at Cape St. Vincent in 1797, capturing two Spanish ships; the *Vanguard* and *Elephant*, also 74s, which flew Nelson's admiral's flag in his victories at the Nile in 1798 and Copenhagen in 1801; and the 104-gun *Victory*, which carried Nelson to immortality at Trafalgar in 1805.

Santisima Trinidad's great hull finally began to subside in a whirlpool of foam, one Spaniard recalled, "up through the hatchways came a hideous shriek. It came from the wretches on the lower deck, who already felt the water rising to drown them."

Some of the fleeing Spaniards, led by Admiral Gravina in the *Principe de Asturias,* made it safely into Cadiz harbor. Gravina escaped death in battle only to be killed by his doctors, who delayed amputating his arm until gangrene set in and it was too late. Gravina is quoted as saying, "I die happy; I am going, I hope and trust, to join Nelson, the greatest hero that the world perhaps has produced."

Admiral Villeneuve's mastless *Bucentaure* washed up on the beach near the harbor entrance she had so grandly left four days earlier. Her British prize crew was rescued by the Spaniards, who in the custom of the day treated them with courtesy. Other Britons who were driven ashore were surprised at the hospitality and the admiring reception they received. One Englishman driven ashore aboard a Spanish prize was rescued by Spanish peasants who gave him figs and wine. When he found he could not walk, a Spaniard brought up a bullock cart, gently lifted him into it and patted him on the shoulder, saying "Bono Engleesh!" before taking him home to treat his leg.

Napoleon's replacement for the defeated Villeneuve, Admiral Rosily, arrived at Cadiz on October 25, in time to report the loss of the battle and to oversee the rescue operations. Burying parties were sent along the coast. The 10-mile stretch of beach north of the headland of Cape Trafalgar was covered for days with wreckage and bodies tumbling in the surf and washing in and out with the tide.

When at last the storm subsided, Collingwood sent a flag of truce into Cadiz with an offer to exchange his prisoners for the captured prizes and their British crews. The town's mayor, the Marquis de la Solana, not only agreed but sent out a cask of wine and a supply of melons, grapes, figs and pomegranates. Collingwood responded with the best the *Royal Sovereign* could offer: a cheddar cheese and a cask of porter.

While the wounded were nursed and the prisoners exchanged, the British fleet's fastest schooner, the *Pickle,* raced for England with the news. For nine days the *Pickle* beat through the gales, and at 1 a.m. on November 6 her captain greeted William Marsden, First Secretary of the Admiralty, who was just going to bed. "Sir," he said, "we have gained a great victory, but we have lost Lord Nelson."

Not until December 22 did the jury-rigged *Victory* reach Portsmouth. She had had to be towed to Gibraltar for repairs. Aboard the flagship was the body of Lord Nelson, preserved in a large cask of brandy and guarded day and night by a sentry; one of the sentries nearly deserted his post when in the middle of the third night there was an exhalation of gas from the body and the lid rose from the cask.

The magnitude of the victory off Trafalgar was matched only by the spectacle of Nelson's funeral *(pages 170-177).* Londoners of all ages and classes mourned him as if they realized that his strategic and tactical genius would make England secure at sea for a century. Admiral Villeneuve, still a prisoner of war, was permitted to witness his conqueror's

A patch box—a small container for cosmetics—bears a portrait of Nelson enameled on porcelain. Such mementos of national mourning were fashionable at the time of the admiral's funeral.

This pottery jug molded with the hero's image was mass-produced in 1810, possibly to commemorate the five-year anniversary of the Battle of Trafalgar.

funeral. He was exchanged in early April, 1806, took a boat across the Channel and sent a message to his old friend Denis Decrés: he was in France and would now face the Emperor; he would await instructions at the Hotel de la Patrie in Rennes. Decrés could not bring himself to mention to Napoleon the name of the man he knew the Emperor blamed for the loss of his great fleet. Alone in Rennes, Villeneuve waited without word from Decrés until April 21. Next morning he was found stabbed to death in his locked room, along with a suicide note to his wife. "How fortunate," he wrote, "that I have no child to be loaded with the weight of my name as its awful inheritance."

Napoleon's only announcement of the battle was to report that "some ships had been lost in a gale following an imprudent engagement." But he held a formal ceremony in which Lucas and Infernet, the shortest and tallest French captains, were honored for their bravery after returning home in a prisoner exchange. "Had all my officers behaved as you did," said Napoleon to the man whose sharpshooter had killed Nelson, "the battle would have been a very different story." And it was Napoleon—stealing Nelson's line—who four months after the Battle of Trafalgar ordered that on every French man-of-war there should be painted prominently the slogan: "La France Compte que Chacun Fera Son Devoir" ("France Expects that Each One Will Do His Duty").

Many years before the Battle of Trafalgar, Nelson had written to his father: "I got my rank by a shot killing a post-captain, and I most sincerely hope I shall, when I go, go out of the world the same way; then we all go in the line of our profession—a parson praying and a captain fighting." One of Nelson's most fitting epitaphs was unwittingly penned by a woman who never knew him. In a letter from her home in Ireland, Lady Castlereagh wrote a friend: "Had I been his wife or mother, I would rather have wept him dead than see him languish on a less splendid day. In such a death there is no sting, and in such a grave everlasting victory."

There were other sailing-fleet battles after Trafalgar, but none so remembered or revered. The day of the majestic, synchronized fleet engagement was dying. Only seven years after Trafalgar, the naval War of 1812 was fought almost entirely by frigate against frigate instead of by the big ships of the line. And 17 years after Trafalgar, the *Comet*, a wooden paddle-wheel steam warship of 80 horsepower, was commissioned in the Royal Navy. The Age of Fighting Sail had ended. Horatio Nelson had died just in time.

The splendid spectacle

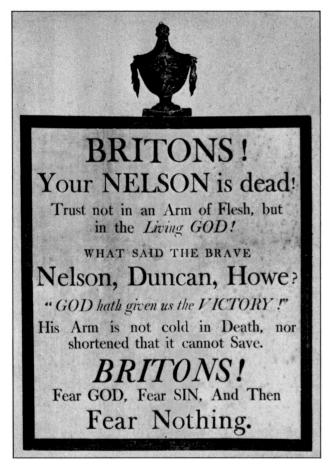

BRITONS!
Your NELSON is dead!
Trust not in an Arm of Flesh, but
in the *Living* GOD!

WHAT SAID THE BRAVE
Nelson, Duncan, Howe?
"*GOD hath given us the VICTORY!*"
His Arm is not cold in Death, nor
shortened that it cannot Save.

BRITONS!
Fear GOD, Fear SIN, And Then
Fear Nothing.

*Reflecting the grief of England, somber
notices of Nelson's death cast him in
heroic company. "The only signs of a great
victory," observed a Londoner, "are
endless posters saying alas, poor Nelson."*

Nelson's death stunned England. "It was as if a great calamity had befallen the land," wrote a foreign observer. In Windsor Castle, George III, who had looked with disfavor on Nelson's affair with Emma Hamilton, wept unashamedly. Worthy tradespeople and Cockney prostitutes alike drank to the passing of "Our Nel." And all through the fleet, men who had served with him were "useless for duty for days," reported an officer. "Chaps that fought like the devil sit down and cry like a wench."

Preserved in a cask of brandy, Nelson's body reached Shearness on December 21 and was transferred to a lead coffin, which was then placed inside a wooden coffin carved from spars of the French flagship *Orient*, defeated in the Battle of the Nile. On Christmas Eve a Navy yacht ferried the coffin up the Thames to Greenwich, where Nelson lay in state from January 5 to 7 while 15,000 mourners filed by. On January 8 tearful throngs lined the Thames as Nelson was moved in a procession of barges six miles to the Admiralty.

The next morning the College of Arms proceeded with the funeral. In frosty clear air, thousands upon thousands jammed Hyde Park and St. Paul's Cathedral. The cortege began with a troop of Light Dragoons, hooves muffled by sand spread overnight by workmen. Then came four infantry regiments—10,000 men in all—many in scarlet coats and black shakos, accompanied by pipes and trumpets playing the "Dead March" from Handel's *Saul*. Behind walked 48 weather-beaten crewmen from the *Victory*, carrying two tattered Union Jacks and Nelson's shot-rent St. George's ensign. Next came peers and nobles of the realm and the Prince of Wales, followed by Nelson's ornate funeral car—"the most elegant and superb ever seen in Europe." The crowds were silent but for murmurs of "Hats Off" and "God Bless" as the funeral car came into view.

So lengthy was the procession that the first horsemen reached St. Paul's before the last carriage left the Admiralty, a mile and a half away. Inside the torchlit cathedral, choirs sang "I Am the Resurrection and the Life" and other hymns. The service lasted four hours and was climaxed when Nelson's crew, about to lay their flags on the coffin, paused to tear pieces from the great ensign to stuff next to their hearts.

"Thus terminated," said the *Naval Chronicle*, "one of the most impressive and most splendid solemnities that ever took place in this Country, or perhaps in Europe."

*Nelson's funeral car, at the top and in
the next-to-last row of this souvenir "order
of procession," resembles the Victory
with winged Fame at her prow, an ensign at
half-staff over a high-windowed poop
and a canopy with six sable plumes.*

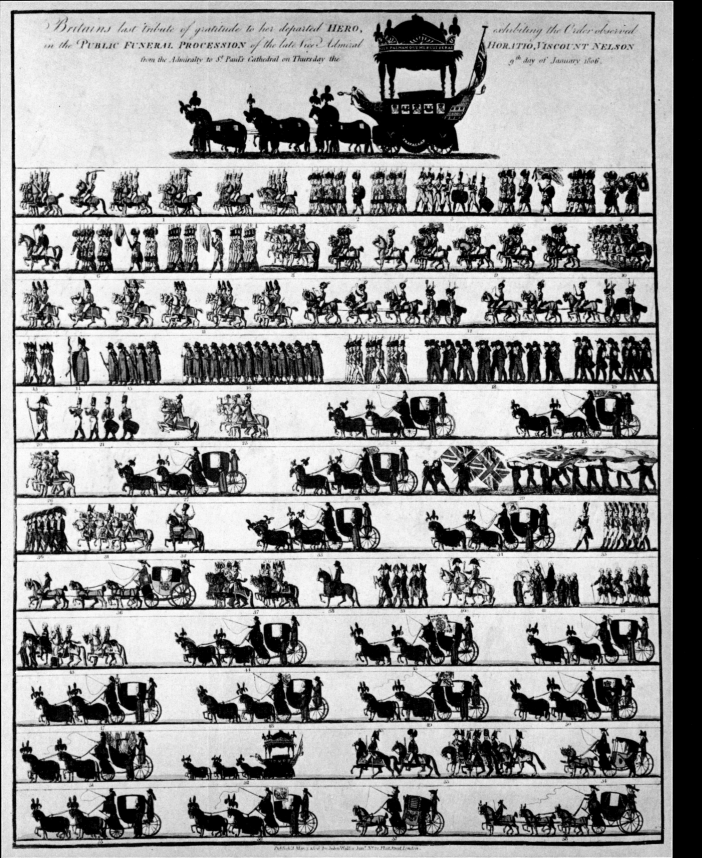

Britains last tribute of gratitude to her departed HERO, exhibiting the Order observed in the PUBLIC FUNERAL PROCESSION of the late Vice Admiral HORATIO, VISCOUNT NELSON from the Admiralty to St. Paul's Cathedral on Thursday the 9th day of January 1806.

Great personages of the realm watch from tiers of seats beneath the mighty dome of St. Paul's at the climax of Nelson's interment. A special chandelier of 130 gas lamps illuminates the proceedings as the Garter King at Arms proclaims Nelson's titles. The great

marble sarcophagus into which the coffin was placed—originally ordered by Cardinal Wolsey in the reign of Henry VIII—was then lowered into the crypt below. The services were over by 6 p.m. however, the mourners lingered late into the night.

Bibliography

Archibald, E. H. H., *The Wooden Fighting Ship in the Royal Navy.* Arco, 1968.

Baynham, Henry, *From the Lower Deck.* Barre Publishers, 1970.

Bennett, Geoffrey:
The Battle of Trafalgar. The Naval Institute Press, 1977.
Nelson the Commander. Batsford, 1972.

Bradford, Ernle, *Nelson: The Essential Hero.* Harcourt Brace Jovanovich, 1977.

Browne, Douglas G., *The Floating Bulwark.* Cassell, 1963.

Bryant, Arthur:
Years of Endurance. Collins, 1944.
Years of Victory. Collins, 1942.

Bugler, Arthur, *H.M.S. Victory: Building, Restoration, and Repair.* Her Majesty's Stationery Office, 1966.

Chapelle, Howard I., *The History of American Sailing Ships.* Bonanza Books, 1935.

Clerk, John, *An Essay on Naval Tactics.* Adam Black, Edinburg, 1807.

Clowes, William Laird, *The Royal Navy,* Vol. III. Sampson Low, Marston and Company, 1899.

Coggins, Jack, *Ships and Seamen of the American Revolution.* Stackpole Books, 1969.

Cronin, Vincent, *Napoleon Bonaparte.* William Morrow, 1972.

Fenwick, Kenneth, *H.M.S. Victory.* Cassell, 1959.

Fitchett, W. H., *Nelson and His Captains.* Smith, Elder, 1902.

Fothergill, Brian, *Sir William Hamilton: Envoy Extraordinary.* Harcourt, Brace & World, 1969.

Fraser, Edward:
The Enemy at Trafalgar. E. P. Dutton, 1906.
The Sailors Whom Nelson Led. Methuen, 1913.

Friendly, Alfred, *Beaufort of the Admiralty: The Life of Sir Francis Beaufort, 1774-1857.* Random House, 1977.

Garbett, Captain H.R.N., *Naval Gunnery: A Description and History of the Fighting Equipment of a Man-of-war.* George Bell and Sons, 1897.

George, Dorothy M., *London Life in the Eighteenth Century.* Capricorn Books, 1965.

Gerin, Winifred, *Horatia Nelson.* Clarendon Press, 1970.

Gill, Conrad, *The Naval Mutinies of 1797.* Manchester University Press, 1913.

Grenfell, Russell, *Horatio Nelson.* Faber, 1968.

Guérard, Albert, *Napoleon I.* Alfred A. Knopf, 1973.

Gutteridge, H. C., ed., *Nelson and the Neapolitan Jacobins.* Navy Records Society, 1903.

Hattersley, Roy, *Nelson.* Saturday Review Press, 1974.

Herold, Christopher, *Bonaparte in Egypt.* Harper & Row, 1962.

Howard, John Eldred, *Letters and Documents of Napoleon.* Oxford University Press, 1961.

Howell, John, ed., *The Life and Adventures of John Nicol, Mariner.* William Blackwood, 1822.

H.M.S. Victory, Official Guide and Short History. 1975.

Hough, Richard, *A History of Fighting Ships.* Octopus Books, 1975.

Howarth, David:
Trafalgar: The Nelson Touch. Atheneum, 1969.
Sovereign of the Seas: The Story of Britain and the Sea. Atheneum, 1974.

Jenkins, E. H., *A History of the French Navy.* Naval Institute Press, 1973.

Kemp, Peter K.:
ed., *History of the Royal Navy.* Putnam's, 1969.
The Oxford Companion to Ships and the Sea. Oxford University Press, 1976.

Kennedy, Ludovic, *Nelson's Captains.* Norton, 1951.

Kennedy, Paul M., *The Rise and Fall of British Naval Mastery.* Scribners, 1976.

Larrabee, Harold A., *Decision at the Chesapeake.* Clarkson N. Potter, 1964.

Laughton, John Knox, *Nelson and His Companions in Arms.* George Allen, 1896.

Legg, Stuart, *Trafalgar.* John Day, 1966.

Lewis, Michael:
The Navy of Britain. George Allen and Unwin, 1948.
A Social History of the Navy 1793-1815. George Allen and Unwin, 1960.

Lloyd, Christopher:
Atlas of Maritime History. Arco Publishing, 1975.
The British Seaman, 1200-1860. Fairleigh Dickinson University Press, 1964.
The Nation and the Navy. Greenwood Press, 1954.
Nelson and Sea Power. English Universities Press, 1973.
The Nile Campaign. Barnes and Noble Books, 1973.

Lloyd, Christopher, and Jack Coulter, *Medicine and the Navy,* Vol. III. Livingston, 1961.

Longridge, C. N., *The Anatomy of Nelson's Ships.* Model and Allied Publications, 1955.

Macintyre, Donald, *Admiral Rodney.* W. W. Norton, 1963.

Mackesy, Piers, *The War for America, 1775-1783.* Longmans, 1964.

Mahan, Alfred Thayer:
The Influence of Sea Power Upon the French Revolution and Empire, 1793-1812. Sampson Low, 1892.
The Influence of Sea Power Upon History. Little, Brown, 1918.
The Life of Nelson. Little, Brown, 1899.
Mahan on Naval Warfare. Little, Brown, 1941.

Manwaring, G. E., and Bonamy Dobrée, *The Floating Republic.* Geoffrey Bles, 1935.

Marchand, Leslie A., *Byron.* Alfred A. Knopf, 1957.

Marcus, C. J., *The Age of Nelson.* Viking, 1971.

Markham, Felix, *Napoleon.* New American Library, 1963.

Masefield, John, *Sea Life in Nelson's Time.* Sphere Books, 1972.

Miller, Nathan, *Sea of Glory*. David McKay, 1974.

Mollo, John, *Uniforms of the Royal Navy During the Napoleonic Wars*. Hugh Evelyn, 1965.

Morison, Samuel Eliot, *John Paul Jones*. Little, Brown and Company, 1959.

Naish, G. P. B.:
H.M.S. Victory. Pitkin Pictorials Ltd., 1972.
ed., *Nelson's Letters to His Wife*. Routledge and Kegan Paul, 1958.

O'Brian, Patrick, *Men-Of-War*. Collins, 1974.

Oman, Carola, *Nelson*. Doubleday, 1946.

Padfield, Peter, *Guns at Sea*. St. Martin's Press, 1974.

Parkinson, C. Northcote, *Britannia Rules*. Wiedenfeld and Nicolson, 1977.

Parry, J. H., *Trade and Dominion: European Oversea Empires in the Eighteenth Century*. Cardinal, 1974.

Pocock, Thomas, *Nelson and His World*. Viking Press, 1968.

Pope, Dudley:
Decision at Trafalgar. J. B. Lippincott, 1959.
The Great Gamble. Simon and Schuster, 1972.

Potter, E. B., ed., *Sea Power*. Prentice-Hall, 1960.

Pratt, Fletcher:
The Empire and the Sea. Henry Holt, 1946.
Preble's Boys. William Sloane, 1950.

Preston, Antony, David Lyon and John H. Batchelor, *Navies of the American Revolution*. Prentice-Hall, 1975.

Rathbone, Philip, *Paradise Merton*. Private publication, 1973.

Reynolds, Clark G., *Command of the Sea*. Robert Hale, 1976.

Richardson, William, *A Mariner of England, 1780-1817*. John Murray, 1908.

Richmond, H. W., *Statesmen and Sea Power*. Oxford University Press, 1946.

Robertson, Charles Napier, *The British Tar in Fact & Fiction*. Harper, 1909.

Sanderson, Michael, *Sea Battles: A Reference Guide*. David & Charles, 1975.

Southey, Robert, *The Life of Nelson*. G. H. Doran.

Southworth, John van Duyn, *The Age of Sails*. Twayne, 1968.

Spinney, David, *Rodney*. U.S. Naval Institute, 1969.

Thompson, J. M., ed., *Napoleon Self-Revealed*. Houghton Mifflin, 1934.

Warner, Oliver:
The Battle of the Nile. Macmillan, 1960.
Nelson. Follett Publishing, 1975.
Nelson's Battles. Macmillan, 1965.
Victory: The Life of Lord Nelson. Little, Brown, 1958.

Wheeler, H. F. B., and A. M. Broadley, *Napoleon and the Invasion of England*. Bodley Head, 1908.

Acknowledgments

The index for this book was prepared by Sarah Hannum Chase. The editors wish to thank the following artists: Roy Andersen (*pages 34–43*), John Batchelor (*pages 17–19*) and Vic Taylor (*end-paper maps*). The editors also wish to thank: In London: David Lyon, Research Assistant, Draught Room; Pieter van der Merwe, Research Assistant, Historical Section; Joan Moore, Photographic Sales; Elizabeth Wiggans, Research Assistant, Department of Printed Books and Manuscripts, National Maritime Museum. Also in England: George Naish, late Honorary Secretary, Society for Nautical Research; Lieutenant B. Witts, H.M.S. *Excellent*, Portsmouth; Colin S. White, The Royal Naval Museum, Portsmouth. In Paris: Claire Bertinetti, Researcher; Hervé Cras, Director for Documentary Studies; Denise Chaussegroux, Researcher; Ghislaine Larmoyer, Researcher; Mar-jolaine Mathikine, Librarian; Marcel Redouté, Director of the Collections, Musée de la Marine; Colonel Marcel Dugué MacCarthy, Curator; Paul Willing, Curator, Musée de l'Armée. Also in France: Joël Audouy, Chief Curator, Archives de la Marine, Château de Vincennes; Henri de Chantemerle de Villette; Dan Lailler, Curator, Musées de Saint-Malo, Saint-Malo. In Madrid: Jaime Fernandez Gimenez; Ana Vigon Sanchez; Sr. Zumalacarregú, Director, Museo Naval. In Washington, D.C.: Samuel L. Morison, U.S. Naval Department; Howard Hoffman, Museum Specialist, Division of Naval History; Philip K. Lundeberg, Curator, Division of Naval History, Museum of History and Technology, Smithsonian Institution; John Lyall, Chief, Naval Publications Division, Hydrographic Center, Defense Mapping Agency; Dr. Peter Olch, National Library of Medicine. The editors also wish to thank: Teodoro Fittipaldi, Director, Museo Nazionale di San Martino, Naples; Louann Ihde, Ridgefield, Connecticut; Neville Kirk, Professor of History Emeritus, U.S. Naval Academy, Annapolis, Maryland; Myrna Smoot, Los Angeles County Museum of Art, Los Angeles, California; Robert Wark, Curator, The Huntington Art Collection, San Marino, California; The New York Public Library; and Sterling Memorial Library, Yale University. Quotations from *Victory: The Life of Lord Nelson* by Oliver Warner, reprinted with permission from Chatto & Windus Ltd., London. Quotations from *Trafalgar* by David Howarth, reprinted by kind permission of William Collins Sons and Co. Ltd., London. Quotations from *Trafalgar* by Stuart Legg (John Day Co.), copyright Stuart Legg, reprinted with permission of Rupert Hart-Davis.

Picture Credits

Index

Printed in Spain by Novograph, S.A., Madrid. Depósito Legal: M-39711-XXVII